What Your Colleagues Are Saying . . .

"This book takes *5 Practices for Orchestrating Productive Mathematics Discussions* to the next level as readers experience what these practices look like in real mathematics classrooms in Grades 6–8. Readers will engage in analysis of videos and student work as they deepen their understanding of the five practices. The authors specifically address the challenges one might face in implementing the five practices in classrooms by providing recommendations and concrete examples to avoid these challenges."

Cathy Martin
Executive Director, Curriculum and Instruction
Denver Public Schools
Denver, CO

"Smith and Sherin have hit a home run with this book. Research has shown the importance of effective discussion in the mathematics classroom. This book provides the structure and practices to implement discussion as well as classroom scenarios and illustrations to bring those practices to light. It is a must-read for any middle school teacher and those who work with middle school teachers. Student understanding of math will be improved through the implementation of the ideas in this book."

Kevin Dykema
Eighth-Grade Math Teacher
Mattawan Middle School
Mattawan, MI

"Every middle school math teacher needs to understand the practices in this book and know how to use them effectively in the classroom. Use of these practices will empower middle school students to understand mathematics and feel like they can do math!"

Lois A. Williams
Adjunct Professor, Mathematics Education Consultant, Author
Mary Baldwin University
Scottsville, VA

"This is a powerful and readable guide to shifting our middle school mathematics instruction toward maximizing our students' learning. But it's the clarity and familiarity of the challenges we all face when trying to implement these five practices—and the practicality and detail of the guidance provided in each chapter to address these challenges—that set this book apart and make it so useful for professional growth."

Steve Leinwand
Researcher/Change Agent
American Institutes for Research
Washington, DC

"I love the practical applications from the middle school classrooms and I love the suggestions for addressing challenging components of each practice. It helped me to more deeply understand the five practices and gave me great questions to ask myself and reflect upon in my classroom. It's a must read to take your teaching to the next level!"

Jennifer Outzs
National Council of Teachers of Mathematics (NCTM) Board of Directors
Middle School Teacher
Seminole Middle School
Pinellas County, FL

"This book is a comprehensive, ready-to-use, professional development plan inside a book's covers! Its components include student work, classroom video, features addressing challenges teachers face, as well as providing reflective opportunities to pause and consider. This amazing, must-have resource will truly engage middle school mathematics teachers in 'doing' *The 5 Practices*."

Francis (Skip) Fennell
Professor of Education and Graduate and Professional Studies Emeritus
Project Director, Elementary Mathematics Specialists and Teacher Leaders Project
McDaniel College
Past President, Association of Mathematics Teacher Educators (AMTE)
Past President, NCTM

"Bring coherence and focus to your class discussions, empower students and assist them in making mathematical connections of substance—Smith and Sherin clarify, exemplify, and profoundly articulate how teachers can bring the *5 Practices for Orchestrating Productive Mathematics Discussions* to life. Each of the practices is unpacked for clarity, exemplified with classroom video and vignettes and the most significant challenges with implementation are shared and discussed. This is a must read for classroom teachers with immediate impact and steps for improvement provided."

Travis L. Lemon
Middle School Mathematics Teacher
Adjunct Professor, Utah Valley University and University of San Diego
American Folk, UT

"Peg Smith has done it again. Building on her previous work with Mary Kay Stein (2018), Smith and coauthor Miriam Sherin have taken the next step in supporting teachers to engage students in rich mathematics discussions. Filled with examples and insights, both in print and on video, this book allows teachers to 'see it in action,' make sense, and reflect on the challenges, and it provides support and guidance to implement the five practices in their own instruction. Perfect for teachers, teacher leaders, coaches, or others who support teachers in their instructional practices, this book literally connects theory to practice and provides honest and thoughtful reflections and guidance to work towards our ultimate goals—students' mathematics learning and agency."

Cynthia H. Callard
Professor and Executive Director
Center for Professional Development and Education Reform
Warner Graduate School of Education and Human Development
University of Rochester
Rochester, NY

"Middle school teachers looking to implement the five practices in their classrooms will find this book to be a practical guide for planning and executing meaningful and impactful discourse in their mathematics instruction. This book will help all teachers to more deeply understand the practices framework while taking the ideas to the next level to ensure students develop mathematical understanding beyond routine procedures."

Linda M. Gojak
Past President, NCTM, NCSM
Presidential Award for Mathematics and Science Teaching
K-8 Mathematics Specialist

"The authors insightfully anticipate teachers' challenges and have designed a creative tool to support teacher learning. Their book is filled with highly practical reflective questions all tied to the five practices, enabling teachers to think for themselves. The result is a book that empowers middle level teachers to determine the best ways to advance their own professional development to improve students' mathematical lives."

Ruth M. Heaton
Chief Executive Officer
Teachers Development Group
West Linn, OR

"This book is so incredibly practical and grounded in the hands-on implementation of the five practices! It takes the ideas of the earlier book, which focused more on the "what" of each practice, and looks closer at the when, why, and how that is so important for teachers in their planning. In each chapter, I found myself nodding in agreement as the authors described challenges in using the five practices and thoroughly enjoyed the opportunities to reflect on the practices in relation to my own planning and teaching."

Kristin Gray
Director of Elementary Curriculum and Professional Learning
Illustrative Mathematics

"At Illustrative Mathematics we were looking for a framework that would enable us to embed in our curriculum ambitious but achievable goals for teacher practice. The five practices was the perfect fit: a memorable, learnable set of principles that could be used by novice and veteran teachers alike to get their students thinking and sharing their reasoning."

Bill McCallum
President, Illustrative Mathematics
University Distinguished Professor of Mathematics
The University of Arizona

"This book is packed with practical guidance, support, and actual footage of what it looks like to enact ambitious teaching through these practices. If there's a teacher or leader out there wondering how to ensure their classroom embraces ambitious teaching that is empowering and equitable, this is your guide. Read it. Practice it. Make it yours. There just isn't anything else out there pushing us to think and act as strategically in our math classrooms like this does."

Levi J. Patrick
Assistant Executive Director of Curriculum and Instruction
Title IV, Part A Project Director
Oklahoma State Department of Education

The Five Practices in Practice **at a Glance**

Candid quotes from been-there teachers illuminate the topic of each chapter.

> “I’ve learned a lot about myself as a teacher. For example, when you’re trying to move a student forward toward the goal and they’re struggling, how do you get them there without giving them the answer? Focusing on the assessing and advancing questions, figuring out what they know, and then letting them think and kind of grapple with the idea—that has really been the biggest shift in my mind.”
>
> —MICHELLE MUSUMECI, EIGHTH-GRADE TEACHER

Pause and Consider moments invite teachers to reflect on and make connections to their own practice.

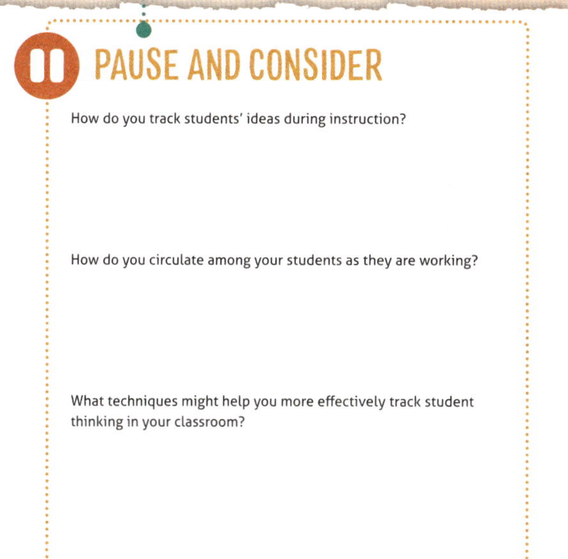

PAUSE AND CONSIDER

How do you track students' ideas during instruction?

How do you circulate among your students as they are working?

What techniques might help you more effectively track student thinking in your classroom?

TEACHING TAKEAWAY

You can often gauge the effectiveness of advancing questions by noticing whether students immediately begin to explore it!

explore, or reconsider ideas about the task. Mrs. Mossot

> *I'm hoping that after I pose the question, they have to about it, or do a little bit of work, or have a little confe other students they're working with where I can go in, the other groups are doing, and then come back to th*

This ability for students to pursue an advancing quest as you pose advancing questions, you will want to gaug reaction. Do they begin working? Can you see them t something over? Do they ask each other questions? Mrs. S that when "they kind of stop and think, there's kids th the wheels turning in their head and they might go an That's when I know that they were ready for that [advan

Of course, what is most essential is that your advancing c students to move forward in their thinking. After you question, you will want to give students time to wo want to check back in with the group to see how they Ms. Musumeci explained that in her experience,

Teaching Takeaways provide on-your-feet support for teachers, so they can jump into implementing the strategies discussed.

Video showcase panels highlight the rich film footage available for each topic and include related questions for consideration.

Analyzing the Work of Teaching 4.7

Following Up With Students—Part Two

Video Clip 4.7

Mrs. Mossotti visits Nietzsche, Ejub, and AJ on two separate occasions while they are working on the State Fair task.

As you watch Video Clip 4.7, consider the following questions:

1. What does Mrs. Mossotti learn about her students' understanding during her first visit to the group?
2. What question does the teacher leave students to pursue?
3. When the teacher checks in with the group later (her second visit), what progress have students made? What does she leave them to work on?

Videos may also be accessed at **resources.corwin.com/5practices-middleschool**

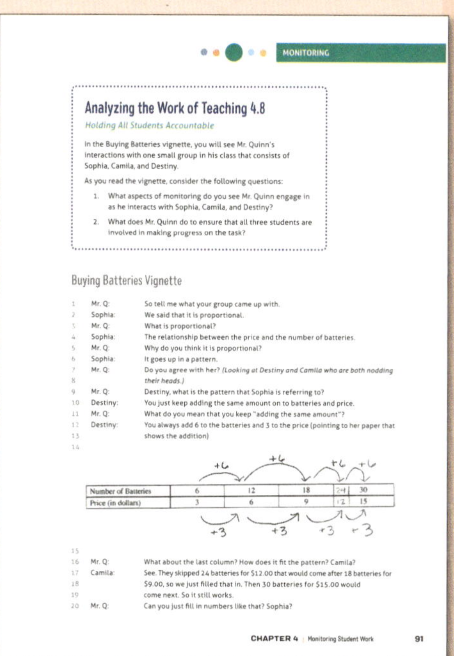

MONITORING

Analyzing the Work of Teaching 4.8

Holding All Students Accountable

In the Buying Batteries vignette, you will see Mr. Quinn's interactions with one small group in his class that consists of Sophia, Camila, and Destiny.

As you read the vignette, consider the following questions:

1. What aspects of monitoring do you see Mr. Quinn engage in as he interacts with Sophia, Camila, and Destiny?
2. What does Mr. Quinn do to ensure that all three students are involved in making progress on the task?

Buying Batteries Vignette

Mr. Q: So tell me what your group came up with.
Sophia: We said that it is proportional.
Mr. Q: What is proportional?
Sophia: The relationship between the price and the number of batteries.
Mr. Q: Why do you think it is proportional?
Sophia: It goes up in a pattern.
Mr. Q: Do you agree with her? *(Looking at Destiny and Camila who are both nodding their heads.)*
Mr. Q: Destiny, what is the pattern that Sophia is referring to?
Destiny: You just keep adding the same amount on to batteries and price.
Mr. Q: What do you mean that you keep "adding the same amount"?
Destiny: You always add 6 to the batteries and 3 to the price (pointing to her paper that shows the addition)

Number of Batteries	6	12	18	24	30
Price (in dollars)	3	6	9	12	15

Mr. Q: What about the last column? How does it fit the pattern? Camila?
Camila: See. They skipped 24 batteries for $12.00 that would come after 18 batteries for $9.00, so we just filled that in. Then 30 batteries for $15.00 would come next. So it still works.
Mr. Q: Can you just fill in numbers like that? Sophia?

CHAPTER 4 | Monitoring Student Work 91

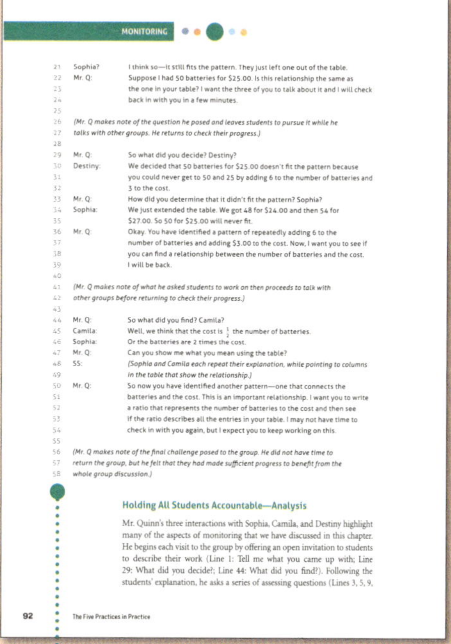

MONITORING

Sophia? I think so—it still fits the pattern. They just left one out of the table.
Mr. Q: Suppose I had 50 batteries for $25.00. Is this relationship the same as the one in your table? I want the three of you to talk about it and I will check back in with you in a few minutes.

(Mr. Q makes note of the question he posed and leaves students to pursue it while he talks with other groups. He returns to check their progress.)

Mr. Q: So what did you decide? Destiny?
Destiny: We decided that 50 batteries for $25.00 doesn't fit the pattern because you could never get to 50 and 25 by adding 6 to the number of batteries and 3 to the cost.
Mr. Q: How did you determine that it didn't fit the pattern? Sophia?
Sophia: We just extended the table. We got 48 for $24.00 and then 54 for $27.00. So 50 for $25.00 will never fit.
Mr. Q: Okay. You have identified a pattern of repeatedly adding 6 to the number of batteries and adding $3.00 to the cost. Now, I want you to see if you can find a relationship between the number of batteries and the cost. I will be back.

(Mr. Q makes note of what he asked students to work on then proceeds to talk with other groups before returning to check their progress.)

Mr. Q: So what did you find? Camila?
Camila: Well, we think that the cost is $\frac{1}{2}$ the number of batteries.
Sophia: Or the batteries are 2 times the cost.
Mr. Q: Can you show me what you mean using the table?
SS: *(Sophia and Camila each repeat their explanation, while pointing to columns in the table that show the relationship.)*
Mr. Q: So now you have identified another pattern—one that connects the batteries and the cost. This is an important relationship. I want you to write a ratio that represents the number of batteries to the cost and then see if the ratio describes all the entries in your table. I may not have time to check in with you again, but I expect you to keep working on this.

(Mr. Q makes note of the final challenge posed to the group. He did not have time to return the group, but he felt that they had made sufficient progress to benefit from the whole group discussion.)

Holding All Students Accountable—Analysis

Mr. Quinn's three interactions with Sophia, Camila, and Destiny highlight many of the aspects of monitoring that we have discussed in this chapter. He begins each visit to the group by offering an open invitation to students to describe their work (Line 1: Tell me what you came up with; Line 29: What did you decide?; Line 44: What did you find?). Following the students' explanation, he asks a series of assessing questions (Lines 3, 5, 9,

92 The Five Practices in Practice

Illustrative vignettes and examples demonstrate real-world applications of the concepts discussed in each chapter.

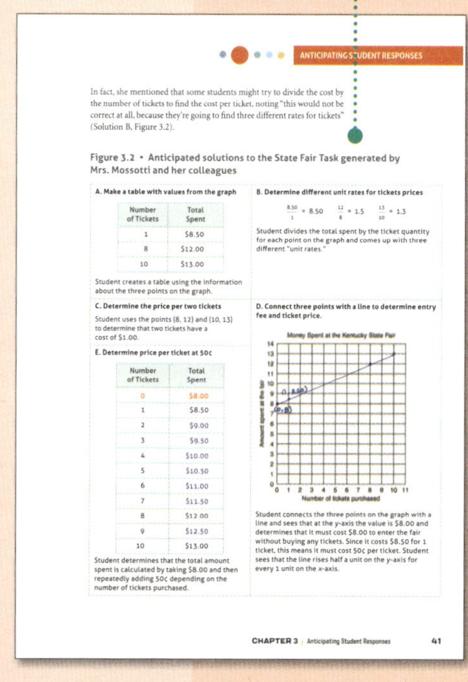

ANTICIPATING STUDENT RESPONSES

In fact, she mentioned that some students might try to divide the cost by the number of tickets to find the cost per ticket, noting "this would not be correct at all, because they're going to find three different rates for tickets" (Solution B, Figure 3.2).

Figure 3.2 • Anticipated solutions to the State Fair Task generated by Mrs. Mossotti and her colleagues

A. Make a table with values from the graph

Number of Tickets	Total Spent
1	$8.50
8	$12.00
10	$13.00

Student creates a table using the information about the three points on the graph.

B. Determine different unit rates for tickets prices

$\frac{8.50}{1} = 8.50$ $\frac{12}{8} = 1.5$ $\frac{13}{10} = 1.3$

Student divides the total spent by the ticket quantity for each point on the graph and comes up with three different "unit rates."

C. Determine the price per two tickets

Student uses the points (8, 12) and (10, 13) to determine that two tickets have a cost of $1.00.

D. Connect three points with a line to determine entry fee and ticket price.

Student connects the three points on the graph with a line and sees that at the *y*-axis the value is $8.00 and determines that it must cost $8.00 to enter the fair without buying any tickets. Since it costs $8.50 for 1 ticket, this means it must cost 50¢ per ticket. Student sees that the line rises half a unit on the *y*-axis for every 1 unit on the *x*-axis.

E. Determine price per ticket at 50¢

Number of Tickets	Total Spent
0	$8.00
1	$8.50
2	$9.00
3	$9.50
4	$10.00
5	$10.50
6	$11.00
7	$11.50
8	$12.00
9	$12.50
10	$13.00

Student determines that the total amount spent is calculated by taking $8.00 and then repeatedly adding 50¢ depending on the number of tickets purchased.

CHAPTER 3 | Anticipating Student Responses 41

An in-depth **Linking the Five Practices to Your Own Instruction** feature helps teachers move even deeper into implementation, providing detailed support and additional reflective opportunities.

MONITORING

It is now time to teach the lesson you planned in Chapters 2 and 3! (Or if you prefer, select another lesson. Just make sure that you have engaged in Practice 0 and have anticipated student responses and questions before you begin.) We encourage you to video record the lesson so that you can reflect back on what occurred during the lesson.

1. Before teaching the lesson, consider how you are going to make sure you visit every group and remember the questions you leave groups to pursue. Also, consider whether there are any specific instructions you want to give students regarding your expectations for how you expect them to work in their groups.
2. As you teach the lesson, use your monitoring chart to keep track of the strategies students are using. Be sure you are checking in with every group and returning to groups to see if they are making good progress.
3. Following the lesson, use these questions to guide reflection on your monitoring:
    - Did you interact with each group in the class? If not, what could you do differently to ensure that you have a chance to check in with all of your students? Did you return to groups when you said you would to check on their progress?
    - To what extent did students use the strategies you had anticipated? What was unexpected?
    - To what extent were the assessing questions you anticipated in planning useful in your interactions with students? Did they help you make students' thinking clear and public?
    - To what extent were the advancing questions you anticipated in planning useful in your interactions with students? Did they help students make progress on the task?
    - To what extent were you able to involve all members of a group in the conversation? What might you do differently in the future to hear the voices of more students?
4. What did you learn about students' understanding of mathematics as a result of teaching the lesson?
5. What lessons have you learned about monitoring that will help you in planning and enacting the next lesson you teach?

96 The Five Practices in Practice

Figure 2.6 • The Pizza Party task

Pizza Party

You ordered pizza for your birthday party. When the party was over you still had $4\frac{5}{6}$ pizzas left over. Your mother decided to freeze the remaining pizza. She put $\frac{2}{3}$ of a pizza (one serving) in each freezer bag.

1. How many servings would your mother be able to freeze?
2. How much more pizza does your mother need to make another serving?

Draw a picture, build a model, construct a number line, or make a table to explain your solution.

Source: Task adapted from Nolan, Dixon, Roy & Andreasen, 2016.
Image Source: bonetta/iStock.com

During the discussion with her colleagues regarding her goals and task, Mrs. Saroney indicated that this would be the first time that students

Clearly designed tasks promote mathematical reasoning and problem solving.

Figure 4.2 • Challenges associated with monitoring

CHALLENGE	DESCRIPTION
Trying to understand what students are thinking	Students do not always articulate their thinking clearly. It can be quite demanding for teachers, in the moment, to figure out what a student means or is trying to say. This requires teachers to listen carefully to what students are saying and to ask questions that help them better explain what they are thinking.
Keeping track of group progress—which groups you visited and what you left them to work on	As teachers are running from group to group, providing support, they need to be able to keep track of what each group is doing and what they left students to work on. Also, it is important for a teacher to return to a group to determine whether the advancing question given to them helped them make progress.
Involving all members of a group	All individuals in the group need to be challenged to answer assessing and advancing questions. For individuals to benefit from the thinking of their peers, they need to be held accountable for listening to and adding on, repeating and summarizing what others are saying.

Challenge and Description charts distill and demystify some of the common issues teachers encounter when teaching the concepts at hand.

What It Takes/Key Questions charts break down the critical components of the practice and explain what it takes to succeed and the questions you need to ask yourself to stay on track.

students' thinking forward (advancing questions). Figure 4.1 highlights the key components of this practice.

Figure 4.1 • Key questions that support the practice of monitoring students' responses

WHAT IT TAKES	KEY QUESTIONS
Tracking student thinking	How will you keep track of students' responses during the lesson?
	How will you ensure that you check in with all students during the lesson?
Assessing student thinking	Are your assessing questions meeting students where they are?
	Are your assessing questions making student thinking visible?
Advancing student thinking	Are your advancing questions driven by your lesson goals?
	Are students able to pursue advancing questions on their own?
	Are your advancing questions helping students to progress?

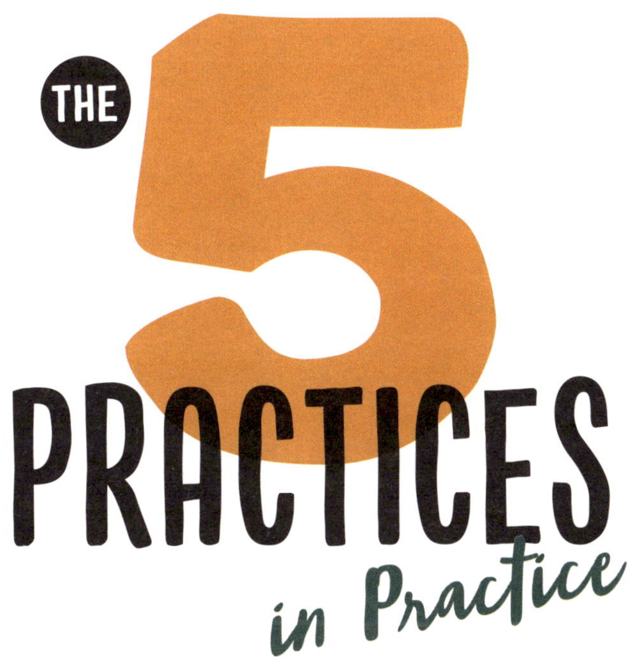
THE
5
PRACTICES
in Practice

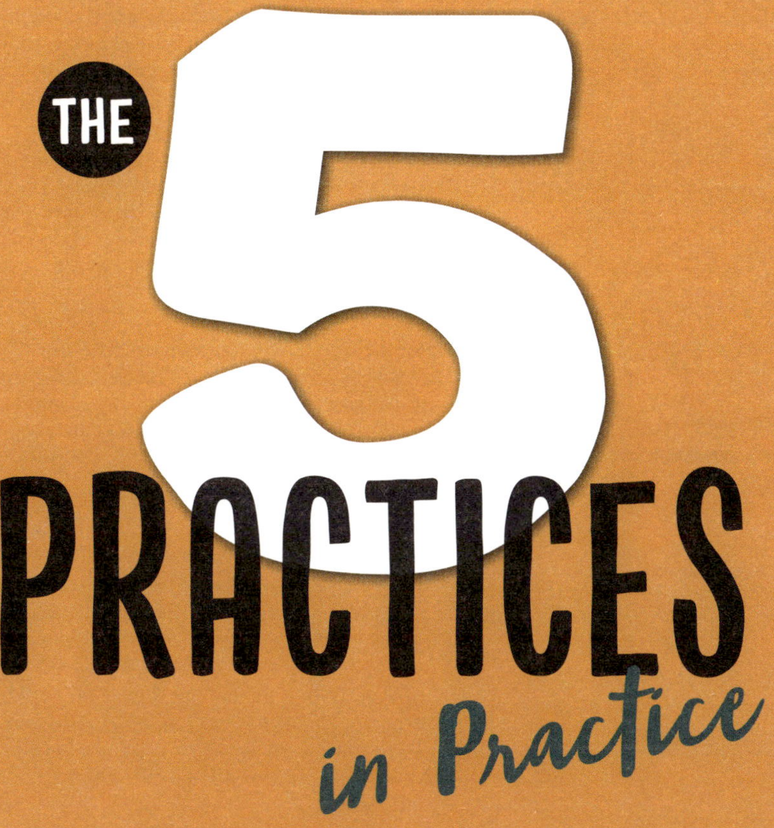

Successfully Orchestrating Mathematics Discussions in

Your Middle School Classroom

Margaret (Peg) Smith
Miriam Gamoran Sherin

Foreword by
Dan Meyer

A JOINT PUBLICATION

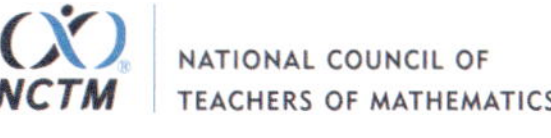

For information:

Corwin
A SAGE Company
2455 Teller Road
Thousand Oaks, California 91320
(800) 233–9936
www.corwin.com

SAGE Publications Ltd.
1 Oliver's Yard
55 City Road
London, EC1Y 1SP
United Kingdom

SAGE Publications India Pvt. Ltd.
B 1/I 1 Mohan Cooperative Industrial Area
Mathura Road, New Delhi 110 044
India

SAGE Publications Asia-Pacific Pte. Ltd.
18 Cross Street #10-10/11/12
China Square Central
Singapore 048423

Executive Editor, Mathematics: Erin Null
Associate Editor: Julie Nemer
Senior Editorial Assistant: Jessica Vidal
Production Editor: Tori Mirsadjadi
Copy Editor: Ashley Horne
Typesetter: Integra
Proofreader: Lawrence W. Baker
Indexer: Jeanne R. Busemeyer
Cover and Interior Designer: Gail Buschman
Marketing Manager: Margaret O'Connor

Library of Congress Cataloging-in-Publication Data

Names: Smith, Margaret Schwan, author. | Sherin, Miriam Gamoran, author. | Meyer, Dan (Mathematics teacher), author of foreword.
Title: The five practices in practice : successfully orchestrating mathematics discussions in your middle school classroom / Margaret Smith and Miriam Sherin; foreword by Dan Meyer.
Description: Thousand Oaks, California : Corwin, [2019] | Includes bibliographical references and index.
Identifiers: LCCN 2018048159 | ISBN 9781544321189 (pbk. : alk. paper)
Subjects: LCSH: Mathematics—Study and teaching (Middle school) | Mathematics—Study and teaching (Primary) | Middle school education.
Classification: LCC QA135.6 .S56518 2019 | DDC 372.7—dc23
LC record available at https://lccn.loc.gov/2018048159

Printed in the United States of America.

This book is printed on acid-free paper.

SFI label applies to text stock

19 20 21 22 23 10 9 8 7 6 5 4 3 2 1

Contents

CHAPTER 5 Selecting and Sequencing Student Solutions

CHAPTER 6 Connecting Student Solutions

CHAPTER 7 Looking Back and Looking Ahead

Visit the companion website at
resources.corwin.com/5practices-middleschool
for downloadable resources.

List of Video Clips

Note From the Publisher: *The authors have provided video and web content throughout the book that is available to you through QR (quick response) codes. To read a QR code, you must have a smartphone or tablet with a camera. We recommend that you download a QR code reader app that is made specifically for your phone or tablet brand.*

Videos may also be accessed at ***resources.corwin.com/5practices-middleschool***

Foreword

Why did you become a math teacher?

Perhaps you loved math. Perhaps you were good at math; good, at least, at the thing you called math then. Friends and family would come to you for help with their homework or studying, and you prided yourself not just on explaining the *how* of math's operations but also the *why* and the *when*, helping others see the purpose and application behind the math.

Helping other people understand and love the math *you* understood and loved—perhaps that sounded like a good way to spend a few decades.

Or perhaps you loved kids. Perhaps even at a young age you were an effective caregiver, and you knew how to care for more than just another person's tangible needs. You listened, and you made people feel *listened to*. You had an eye for a person's value and power. You understood where people were in their lives, and you understood how the right kind of question or observation could propel them to where they were going to *be*.

Spending a few decades helping people feel heard, helping them unleash and use their tremendous capacity—perhaps you thought that was a worthwhile way to spend what you thought would be the hours between 7AM and 4PM every day.

Or perhaps you loved both math and kids. It's possible of course that neither of the two previous exemplar teachers will speak fully to the path that brought you to math teaching, although one of them speaks fully to mine. Yet, in my work with math teachers, I find they often draw their professional energy from one source or the other, from math's ideas or its people.

It took me several frustrated years of math teaching—and years of work with other teachers—to realize that each of those energy sources is vital. Neither source is renewable without the other.

If you draw your energy from mathematics, your students can become abstractions and interchangeable. You can convince yourself it's possible to influence *what they know* without care for *who they are*, that it's possible to treat their *knowledge* as deficient and in need of fixing without risking negative consequences for their *identity*. But students know better. Most of them know what it feels like when the adult in the room positions himself or herself as all-knowing and the students in the room as all-unknowing. A teacher's love and understanding of mathematics won't help when students have decided their teacher cares less about them than about numbers and variables, bar models and graphs, precise definitions, and deductive arguments.

If you draw your energy only from students, then the day's mathematics can become interchangeable with any other day's. Some days, it may feel like an act of care to skip students past mathematics they find frustrating or to skip mathematics altogether. But the math you skip one day is foundational for the math another day or another year. Students will have to pay down their frustration later, only then with compound interest. Your love and care for students cannot protect them from the frustration that is often fundamental to learning.

I could tell you that the only solution to this problem of practice is to develop a love of students *and* a love of mathematics. I could relate any number of maxims and slogans that testify to that truth. I could perhaps convince some of you to believe me.

But the maxim I hold most closely right now is that we act ourselves into belief more often than we believe our way into action. So I encourage you more than anything right now to adopt a series of productive *actions* that can reshape your *beliefs*.

Here are five such actions: anticipate, monitor, select, sequence, and connect.

Those actions, initially proposed by Smith and Stein in 2011, and ably illustrated here with classroom videos, teacher testimony, and student work samples, can convert a teacher's love for math into a love for students and vice versa, to act her way into a belief that math and students both matter.

For teachers who are motivated by a love of students, those five practices invite the teacher to learn more mathematics. The more math teachers know, the easier it is for them to find value in the ways their students think. Their mathematical knowledge enables them to monitor that thinking less for *correctness* and more for *interest*. Would presenting this student's thinking provoke an *interesting* conversation with the class, whether the circled answer is correct or not? A teacher's mathematical knowledge enables her to connect one student's interesting idea to another's. Her math knowledge helps her connect student thinking together and illustrate for the students the enormous value in their ideas.

For the teachers like me who are motivated by a love of mathematics, teachers who want students to love mathematics as well, those five practices give them a rationale for understanding their students as people. Students are not a blank screen onto which teachers can project and trace out their own knowledge. Meaning is *made* by the student. It isn't *transferred* by the teacher. The more teachers love and want to protect interesting mathematical ideas, the more they should want to know the meaning students are making of those ideas. Those five practices have helped me connect student ideas to canonical mathematical ideas, helping students see the value of both.

Neither a love of students nor a love of mathematics can sustain the work of math education on its own. We work with *math students*, a composite of their mathematical ideas and their identities as people. The five practices for orchestrating productive mathematical discussions, and these ideas for putting those practices into practice, offer the actions that can develop and sustain the belief that both math and students matter.

You might think your path into teaching emanated from a love of mathematics or from a love of students. But it's the same path. It's a wider path than you might have thought, one that offers passage to more people and more ideas than you originally thought possible. This book will help you and your students learn to walk it.

—Dan Meyer
Chief Academic Officer, Desmos

Preface

In 2001, a group of researchers at the University of Pittsburgh launched the ASTEROID (A Study of Teacher Education: Research on Instructional Design) project. The project investigated what mathematics teachers learned from participation in practice-based teacher education courses—courses that used cognitively demanding mathematical tasks, narrative cases, and student work as a focus of critique, inquiry, and investigation (Smith, 2001). Mary Kay Stein and I, Peg, were co-principal investigators of the project, and I was the course instructor.

The first course, taught in the summer of 2002, focused on proportional reasoning. The goals of the course were both to enhance teachers' own ability to reason proportionally and enhance their capacity to teach proportional reasoning. The students in the course were 14 elementary and three secondary teachers, some of whom had just completed their Master of Arts in Teaching degree and others who were working on their Master of Education degrees. In order to investigate what teachers learned and how our instruction supported or inhibited learning, we videotaped each class session. We also gave teachers pre-/post-tests, interviewed them, and kept notebooks of all work produced in the course.

As the research team watched videos of teacher-students solving cognitively challenging (aka high-level) tasks, they noticed a certain pattern in the way I, as the instructor, facilitated work around and discussions of the tasks. I had solved the problems in multiple ways prior to the class, often seeking input from graduate students on alternative approaches. The researchers saw how I interacted with students as they worked and how I made notes of what specific students were doing. They saw how I identified students to present their solutions, how I ordered the solutions in particular ways, and how I helped my students make connections between different strategies, ensuring the mathematical ideas were central. While I was aware of what I was doing, I did not give much thought to why I was doing it, and I did not codify my actions.

The research team noticed the regularity of my teaching pattern and the impact it appeared to have on the quality of the discussions around high-level tasks. They recognized the parallel between a teacher educator teaching teachers and K–12 teachers teaching children. They were excited by the potential this model had to support the work of K–12 classroom teachers. We all knew we were on to something powerful. We gave labels to each of the identified actions so that others could learn them and voila!—the five practices—anticipating, monitoring, selecting, sequencing, and connecting—were born!

From that moment forward—in collaboration with others—I have written about the five practices in journal articles, and my coauthor, Mary Kay Stein and I published the book that anchors this new series, which you may know as *5 Practices for Orchestrating Productive Mathematics Discussions* (2011). The book sold over 100,000 copies before we published the second edition in 2018.

What accounts for the surprising success of the five practices? Over the last three decades, there has been a growing consensus that traditional forms of mathematics teaching were not sufficiently preparing students for success in school and beyond. The release of the *Common Core State Standards for Mathematics* (National Governors Association Center for Best Practices & Council of Chief State School Officers, 2010) brought new demands for more ambitious teaching and an increased focus on the importance of engaging students in mathematical discussion. Such discussion gives students the opportunity to share ideas and clarify understandings, develop convincing arguments regarding why and how things work, develop a language for expressing mathematical ideas, and learn to see things from other people's perspective.

So one answer to the question is that the five practices provide a five-step model of what teachers can do before and during instruction that gives them some control in facilitating discussions—an aspect of instruction that has proven to be especially challenging. The five practices are *doable* and something teachers could continue to get better at doing over time.

Despite the uptake of the five practices by teachers and teacher educators, teachers continue to find aspects of the practices challenging. Questions such as "Where do I find good tasks?," "How do I find time to adequately plan?," "What do I do if students all think about a problem the same way?," and "How do I wrap up the conversation at the end of a lesson without taking over?" abound.

In addition, teachers and teacher educators repeatedly ask me, "Do you have any video of teachers doing the five practices?" The need for authentic examples of what these practices look like in real classrooms was clear.

The Five Practices in Practice: Successfully Orchestrating Mathematics Discussions in Your Middle School Classroom (Smith & Sherin, 2019) is the first book in a series that addresses many of the questions that teachers have raised with me over the years, and it provides what teachers and teacher educators have been clamoring for—classroom video of teachers engaged in orchestrating productive discussions. (Books that focus on elementary and high school will follow.)

This book goes beyond the first and second editions of the original *5 Practices* by providing a detailed unpacking of the practices and by identifying specific challenges teachers face related to each practice. The book includes numerous examples drawn from middle school classrooms to illustrate aspects of the five practices and the associated challenges.

A central component of these examples is video excerpts from middle school classrooms that provide vivid images of real teachers using the five practices in their efforts to orchestrate productive discussions.

We hope this book will be a valuable resource for teachers!

—Peg Smith

Acknowledgments

Since the publication of *5 Practices for Orchestrating Productive Mathematics Discussions* (Smith & Stein, 2011), we have worked with and heard from hundreds of teachers who have reported on their successes and struggles in implementing the five practices in their classrooms. We have taken their feedback to heart. This book is our attempt to provide additional guidance on enacting the five practices in middle school classrooms.

While the writing herein is the product of our collaboration, this book would not have been possible without the work, support, and commitment of a number of individuals. Specifically, we acknowledge the contributions of the following:

- Erin Null, Executive Editor for Corwin Mathematics, who encouraged us to write this book and provided thoughtful suggestions and insightful feedback at every step of the process.
- The producers at SAGE (Donna Du and Julie Slattery) and the video crew (Davis Lester, Steve Scarantino, and Matt Langley), whose expertise is evident in the compelling video clips, which are at the heart of this book.
- The Syracuse City School District, who embraced this project from its inception and provided enthusiastic support throughout the planning, filming, and writing process. In particular,
    - The teachers in the Syracuse City School District—Jennifer Mossotti (HW Smith Pre-K–8), Michelle Musumeci (Huntington Pre-K–8), and Michelle Saroney (Salem-Hyde Elementary)—who agreed to make their teaching public so that others could learn from their struggles and triumphs.
    - The principals in the Syracuse City School District—Theresa Haley (HW Smith Pre-K–8), Joanne Harlow (Huntington Pre-K–8), and Patricia Floyd-Echols (Salem-Hyde Elementary)—who enthusiastically welcomed us into their schools and accommodated our filming schedule.
    - District Leaders—Jaime Alicea (Superintendent of Schools), Linda Mulvey (Chief Academic Officer), Nathan Franz (Assistant Superintendent for Teaching and Learning), and Melanie Cifonelli (Director of Mathematics)—who were instrumental in making the filming for this book possible.

Finally, we would like to thank our colleagues, Victoria Bill and Michael Steele, and four anonymous reviewers, for their feedback on a draft version of this book. Their insights and suggestions were greatly appreciated and enhanced this final product.

Publisher's Acknowledgments

Corwin gratefully acknowledges the contributions of the following reviewers:

Cathy Battles
Educational Consultant
University of Missouri—Kansas City Regional Professional Development Center
Kansas City, MO

Natalie Crist
Supervisor of Elementary Mathematics
Baltimore County Public Schools
Baltimore, MD

Kevin Dykema
Eighth-Grade Math Teacher
Mattawan Middle School
Mattawan, MI

Cathy Martin
Executive Director, Curriculum and Instruction
Denver Public Schools
Denver, CO

Jennifer Novak
Education Associate, Mathematics
Delaware Department of Education
Elkridge, MD

Lois A. Williams
Adjunct Professor, Mathematics Education Consultant, Author
Mary Baldwin University
Scottsville, VA

Cathy Yenca
Middle School Mathematics Teacher
Eanes Independent School District
Austin, TX

About the Authors

Margaret (Peg) Smith is a Professor Emerita at the University of Pittsburgh. Over the past two decades, she has been developing research-based materials for use in the professional development of mathematics teachers. She has authored or coauthored over 90 books, edited books or monographs, book chapters, and peer-reviewed articles including the best seller *5 Practices for Orchestrating Productive Mathematics Discussions* (coauthored with Mary Kay Stein). She was a member of the writing team for *Principles to Actions: Ensuring Mathematical Success for All* and she is a coauthor of two recent books (*Taking Action: Implementing Effective Mathematics Teaching Practices in Grades 6–8 and 9–12)*, which provide further explication of the teaching practices first described in *Principles to Actions*. She was a member of the Board of Directors of the Association of Mathematics Teacher Educators (2001–2003; 2003–2005), of the National Council of Teachers of Mathematics (2006–2009), and of Teachers Development Group (2009–2017).

Miriam Gamoran Sherin is Associate Provost for Undergraduate Education and the Alice Gabrielle Twight Professor of Learning Sciences at Northwestern University. Her research interests include mathematics teaching and learning, teacher cognition, and the role of video in supporting teacher learning. Sherin investigates the nature and dynamics of teacher noticing, and in particular, the ways in which teachers identify and interpret student thinking during instruction. *Mathematics Teacher Noticing: Seeing Through Teachers' Eyes*, edited by Sherin, V. Jacobs and R. Philipp, received the AERA Division K 2013 Excellence in Research in Teaching and Teacher Education award. In 2016, Sherin and her colleagues were awarded the National Council of Teachers of Mathematics, Linking Research and Practice Outstanding Publication Award.

“I’ve always been good at engaging students, but the five practices have taken it to a whole other level. Kids actually discuss math among themselves. They have opportunities to talk about a problem, talk about the way they solved it, and bounce ideas off each other.”

—MICHELLE SARONEY, SIXTH-GRADE TEACHER

CHAPTER 1

Introduction

At the heart of efforts to help middle school students learn mathematics is the idea of *ambitious teaching*. It's referred to as *ambitious* because of the substantial student learning goals that it encompasses—that all students have opportunities "to understand and use knowledge … [to] solve authentic problems" (Lampert & Graziani, 2009, p. 492). The Common Core State Standards (CCSS) for Mathematics (National Governors Association Center for Best Practices & Council of Chief State School Officers, 2010) provide a powerful vision of these goals through their description of grade-level, domain-specific content standards and the cross-cutting Standards for Mathematical Practice.

We believe that the phrase *ambitious teaching* is also appropriate because teaching in ways that align with these goals is a formidable task! To help you and other teachers understand what this looks like, *Principles to Actions: Ensuring Mathematics Success for All* (National Council of Teachers of Mathematics, 2014) describes a set of eight teaching practices that serve as a foundation for ambitious teaching (Figure 1.1). These practices are based on what we know from research about how to effectively support students' learning of mathematics.

Ambitious teaching also requires attention to equity. Mathematics has long been considered a gatekeeper, limiting opportunities for some

Figure 1.1 • Eight effective mathematics teaching practices

Establish mathematics goals to focus learning. Effective teaching of mathematics establishes clear goals for the mathematics that students are learning, situates goals within learning progressions, and uses the goals to guide instructional decisions.
Implement tasks that promote reasoning and problem solving. Effective teaching of mathematics engages students in solving and discussing tasks that promote mathematical reasoning and problem solving and allow multiple entry points and varied solution strategies.
Use and connect mathematical representations. Effective teaching of mathematics engages students in making connections among mathematical representations to deepen understanding of mathematics concepts and procedures and as tools for problem solving.
Facilitate meaningful mathematical discourse. Effective teaching of mathematics facilitates discourse among students to build shared understanding of mathematical ideas by analyzing and comparing student approaches and arguments.
Pose purposeful questions. Effective teaching of mathematics uses purposeful questions to assess and advance students' reasoning and sense making about important mathematical ideas and relationships.
Build procedural fluency from conceptual understanding. Effective teaching of mathematics builds fluency with procedures on a foundation of conceptual understanding so that students, over time, become skillful in using procedures flexibly as they solve contextual and mathematical problems.
Support productive struggle in learning mathematics. Effective teaching of mathematics consistently provides students, individually and collectively, with opportunities and supports to engage in productive struggle as they grapple with mathematical ideas and relationships.
Elicit and use evidence of student thinking. Effective teaching of mathematics uses evidence of student thinking to assess progress toward mathematical understanding and to adjust instruction continually in ways that support and extend learning.

Source: National Council of Teachers of Mathematics. *Principles to Actions: Ensuring Mathematical Success for All*. Reston, VA: National Council of Teachers of Mathematics, 2014. Reprinted with permission.

students while promoting opportunities for others (Martin, Gholson, & Leonard, 2010). The middle school years in particular often play a significant role in determining students' future mathematics course-taking options (Balfanz & Byrnes, 2006). Ambitious teaching requires you to challenge these long standing practices and provide access and opportunity for every student so that they can develop strong positive identities as learners of mathematics (Aguirre, Mayfield-Ingram, & Martin, 2013).

At the center of ambitious teaching is a focus on classroom discourse. As you facilitate meaningful discussions with students, you will typically engage in several of the effective mathematics teaching practices, including asking purposeful questions, eliciting and using evidence of student thinking, connecting to various mathematical representations, and supporting productive struggle among students as they learn mathematics (Figure 1.1). In addition, allowing students to share their thinking with the class can help to position all students as valuable resources for learning and promote an equitable learning environment.

In these ways, organizing discussions around students' ideas becomes critical for successfully enacting ambitious instruction.

What does it take then to organize and implement effective discussions? In this book, we present guidelines for using the five practices described by Smith and Stein (2018) in their book *5 Practices for Orchestrating Productive Mathematics Discussions*.

The Five Practices in Practice: An Overview

The five practices are a set of related instructional routines that can help you design and implement lessons that address important mathematical content in ways that build on students' thinking (Figure 1.2). Warning: There is actually a Practice 0, which serves as a foundation for the remaining practices—yup, this means there are six practices in total, but for historical reasons, we will still call the set "the five practices." (In case you are wondering how this could have happened, here is the scoop: After some early articles about the five practices were published, a mathematics coach with whom Peg was working suggested to her that a practice was missing—that before

Figure 1.2 • The five practices in practice

<table>
<tr><td colspan="2" rowspan="2">Practices that take place while planning for instruction</td><td>Practice 0: Setting goals and selecting tasks (Chapter 2) Specifying learning goals and choosing a high-level task that aligns with those goals</td></tr>
<tr><td>Practice 1: Anticipating student responses (Chapter 3) Exploring how you expect students to solve the task and preparing questions to ask them about their thinking</td></tr>
<tr><td rowspan="4">Practices that take place during instruction but are considered while planning</td><td>Students work individually or in small groups</td><td>Practice 2: Monitoring student work (Chapter 4) Looking closely as students work on the task and asking questions to assess their understanding and move their thinking forward</td></tr>
<tr><td rowspan="2">As you move from small group work to whole class discussion</td><td>Practice 3. Selecting student solutions (Chapter 5) Choosing solutions for students to share that highlight key mathematical ideas that will help you achieve lesson goals</td></tr>
<tr><td>Practice 4: Sequencing student solutions (Chapter 5) Determining the order in which to share solutions to create a coherent storyline for the lesson</td></tr>
<tr><td>Whole class discussion</td><td>Practice 5: Connecting student solutions (Chapter 6) Identifying connections among student solutions and to the goals of the lesson that you want to bring out during discussion</td></tr>
</table>

teachers could engage with the five practices, they needed to set goals and select a task. Though this idea was already implied in the five practices, the coach persuaded Peg to make it explicit, and hence Practice 0 was born!)

Teachers often think that ambitious teaching requires you to make all your instructional decisions during instruction based on what students say and do in class. The five practices, however, help you think through all aspects of the lesson *in advance* of teaching, thus limiting the number of in-the-moment decisions you have to make during a lesson. Careful planning prior to a lesson reduces what you need to think about during instruction, allowing you time to listen more actively, question more thoughtfully, and respond more acutely.

The first two practices, *setting goals and selecting tasks*, lay the groundwork for the remaining five practices. It is essential to be clear on what you want students to learn and to choose a cognitively demanding task that aligns with those goals. Once you have the task in mind, you can move to *anticipating student responses*. Here, the purpose is to think about how students might solve the problem, what challenges they might face, and how you will respond to their thinking. One benefit to doing so is that you can develop—before class—targeted questions you might want to ask students about these different approaches.

Although the next four practices take place during instruction, you will also want to think them through carefully during planning. *Monitoring student work* involves giving students time—usually in groups—to work on the task, while you circulate among them. As you look closely at how students are progressing, you can use the questions you developed earlier to assess what students understand and to try to move their thinking forward. As you prepare to transition students into a whole-class discussion, you will engage in *selecting student solutions*—deciding which solutions you want to have shared in the discussion and who should present those solutions—as well as *sequencing student solutions*—deciding how you want to order the presentation of the solutions. Selecting and sequencing require close attention to the mathematical ideas that are highlighted in different solutions and to helping all students have access to the ideas shared in the discussion. As you plan the lesson you will consider what you want to be on the lookout for as you monitor students' work, what solutions will help you surface the mathematical ideas you are targeting, and what order of solutions will provide access to all students.

The final practice, *connecting student solutions*, takes place as the discussion unfolds in your classroom. The purpose is to make explicit the connections between students' solutions and the mathematical goals of the lesson. Drawing out these connections for students is essential to ensure that students take away from the discussion what you intended. This too is something you can consider as you plan the lesson!

Together, the five practices can help you prepare for and carry out meaningful discussions with your students, discussions that revolve around the thinking of your students. And that is the essence of ambitious instruction!

Purpose and Content

The purpose of this book is to deepen your understanding of the five practices as described by Smith and Stein (2018). Toward that end, Chapters 2 to 6 comprise two parts: unpacking the practice (Part One) and challenges teachers face in enacting the practice (Part Two). In Part One, we describe in some detail what is involved in engaging in the practice, provide questions that you should ask yourself as you undertake the practice, and use an example from a middle school classroom to illustrate the components of the practice. In Part Two, we highlight aspects of the practice that have proven to be challenging for teachers, suggest ways you can address the challenge, and provide examples of how teachers are overcoming the challenge.

Throughout these chapters, we encourage you to actively engage with the content. Towards this end, we have create three types of opportunities for engagement: *Pause and Consider* questions (reflection), *Analyzing the Work of Teaching* activities (analysis), and *Linking the Five Practices to Your Own Instruction* assignments (implementation). The Pause and Consider questions give you the opportunity to think about an issue, in some cases drawing on your own classroom experience, prior to reading more about it. The Analyzing the Work of Teaching activities engage you in analyzing aspects of teachers' planning for and enacting of grade-level lessons. The Linking the Five Practices to Your Own Instruction assignments provide you with the opportunity to put the ideas discussed in the chapter to work in your own classroom.

Throughout the book we have included a range of different types of examples drawn from middle school classroom to illustrate aspects of the five practices and the associated challenges. The video excerpts and related classroom artifacts—featuring the three teachers who are introduced later in the chapter—provide vivid images of real teachers using the five practices in their efforts to orchestrate productive discussions. The narrative examples that appear in the book are based on our experiences working with middle school teachers through professional development initiatives and teacher education courses. These examples are intended to provide insights into specific challenges teachers face when engaging in the five practices and are not exact representations of a specific teacher's practice. Each of these teachers has been given a pseudonym (e.g., Neil Tanner, Elaine Richard, Nancy Haines, and Devon Washington featured in Chapter 2). The video and narrative examples are not intended as exemplars to be copied but rather as opportunities for analysis, discussion, and new learning.

If you are coming to the five practices for the first time, you might find it helpful to start with *5 Practices for Orchestrating Productive Mathematics*

Discussions by Peg Smith and Mary Kay Stein (2018). Smith and Stein's book offers a wonderful, easy-to-read introduction to and overview of the five practices. The book you are reading now takes a much deeper dive into the five practices, asking you to stop and think, watch videos of the practices in action, and consider what is challenging about each practice. While you can certainly start here, the overview of the five practices provided by Smith and Stein (2018) may help you get the big picture before taking a deeper dive!

This book will be a valuable resource for looking closely at what it takes to be successful with the five practices. For each practice, we offer key questions, which identify the essential components of the practice. We suspect these questions will enhance your understanding of the practices and perhaps provide new information about the goals and expectations for each practice. This book also describes challenges associated with each practice that teachers we have worked with have encountered, as well as specific suggestions for successfully addressing these challenges. If you have already been using the five practices, we suspect that some of these challenges may be familiar to you and that these discussions will be particularly useful.

Classroom Video Context

In identifying teachers to feature on video, we felt that it was important to select a school district that would feel authentic to readers—one that faced challenges of diversity, poverty, and student performance but was working hard to improve mathematics teaching and learning. We selected Syracuse, New York, for several reasons—the district met our authenticity criteria. Peg had been working in the district for several years, and the district was willing to be featured in this book.

Syracuse City School District (SCSD) is an urban district located in Syracuse, New York. SCSD has a diverse student population K–12 (as shown in Figure 1.3) with 87 percent of students qualifying for free or reduced lunch and 17 percent of students classified as English Language Learners. The nearly 22,000 students attend 17 elementary schools, 11 middle and K–8 schools, and five high schools.

Figure 1.3 • Race/ethnicity of the SCSD students

American Indian/Alaska Native	1%
Black	49%
Hispanic	14%
Asian/Pacific Islander	8%
White	22%
Multiracial	6%

Source: Syracuse City School District, 2018

As stated on its website (http://www.syracusecityschools.com), SCSD is "Striving to become the most improved urban school district in America!" The vision for mathematics learning in the district is that "All students in the Syracuse City School District will graduate as *powerful thinkers* who are *mathematically proficient* and *persevere in solving problems in innovative ways*."

Toward this end, SCSD has been providing ongoing professional development opportunities to teachers to improve instruction and, ultimately, student learning outcomes.

A District Engages in the Five Practices

Video Clip 1.1
In Video Clip 1.1, Melanie Cifonelli, director of mathematics, explains the district's step-by-step journey to improve mathematics instruction over the past three years.

To read a QR code, you must have a smartphone or tablet with a camera. We recommend that you download a QR code reader app that is made specifically for your phone or tablet brand.

Videos may also be accessed at **resources.corwin.com/5practices-middleschool**

A key feature of the professional development efforts in SCSD is a focus on the five practices. Melanie Cifonelli describes how the five practices support the vision for mathematics in SCSD.

These practices really help to highlight and help to build these skills within students. I've seen a mindset shift in many of our students when I walk into classrooms that use the five practices on a regular basis. I see students who are not afraid to stand up in front of the class and share their thinking. I see students who are not afraid to question each other, and I see students who are excited to share their thinking and who are okay with being incorrect or maybe having some faulty thinking.

And they're okay with changing their thinking in front of a group of people. This is a major shift in mathematics and it's something that we really want to see in all of our students, that problem solving means we don't really necessarily know the answer, we don't necessarily know how to get there, but it takes questioning, it takes trying, it takes failing to move us forward.

Meet the Teachers

The video recordings and related classroom artifacts are drawn from the work of three Grades 6–8 teachers in SCSD—Jennifer Mossotti, Michelle Musumeci, and Michelle Saroney. The lesson taught by Jennifer Mossotti will be used in Part One of Chapters 2 to 6 to unpack the focal practice. By focusing on the same teacher across chapters, you will have a coherent picture of instruction in her classroom and a better understanding of how the practices provide synergy. The lessons taught by Michelle Musumeci and Michelle Saroney will be used in Part Two of Chapters 2 to 6 to provide illustrations of how specific challenges can be addressed.

Jennifer Mossotti has been working in SCSD since she started teaching 12 years ago. She is certified to teach mathematics in Grades 7–12 as well as students with disabilities in Grades 7–12. She is currently teaching mathematics at HW Smith Pre-K–8 School, where she has been for the past two years. She became a teacher because she always loved school and working with children.

Jennifer feels many of her students think that past (bad) experiences in the mathematics classroom are indicative of future results. She wants to turn this thinking around by helping them first develop an understanding of the concepts underlying procedures they will be learning so that they are not simply mindlessly following a series of steps. She explains, "When students have the mindset that there is a reason for the steps that they are doing, it's much easier for them to think about what comes next or what mistakes may have been made. And when they start to understand the 'method to the madness,' their confidence grows exponentially."

Using the five practices has helped Jennifer plan lessons and orchestrate discussions that provide each and every student with the opportunity to learn mathematics with understanding. Jennifer explains:

> *Some students present challenging behavior, some are harder workers than others, some have language barriers, some have issues at home that are beyond my comprehension, and some are on grade level, and many are not. But at the end of the day, the work of the five practices will bring the largest opportunities for all students to show progress from their current level and will outweigh typical stand-and-deliver instruction.*

Michelle Musumeci has a bachelor's degree in mathematics and began her professional career as an actuary at Blue Cross and Blue Shield (BCBS). Although she had a great job at BCBS, she did not feel that she was making a difference in anyone's life. She missed working with kids (she had worked in a summer counseling program right after graduation) and decided to pursue a teaching career. She enrolled in a masters of arts in teaching program and became certified to teach mathematics in Grades 5–9 and 7–12.

Michelle currently teaches mathematics at Huntington pre-K–8, a position she has held for 13 years. She now realizes, even on the toughest days, that teaching was what she was meant to do. Michelle wants her students to feel like they can do mathematics no matter what their previous experience was. She believes *all* students can learn in her classroom, not just about math, but also about being part of a community, about teamwork, about positivity, and about perseverance.

Michelle feels that the five practices gave her a framework for organizing her thoughts about how she was going to run a lesson. According to Michelle, "The framework makes lesson planning less abstract, and it really helps me anticipate what's going to happen. Instead of just trying to make decisions in the moment, it encourages me to think ahead. It pushes me to really get at the goal and move students toward that goal so they can get the most out of their thinking."

Michelle Saroney has been teaching in SCSD for 15 of her 16 years in the profession. In her first career as a therapeutic recreation specialist, she taught people with addictions or disabilities how to enjoy life no matter what their circumstances. Through this work, she discovered a passion for teaching and enrolled in a program that offered a master's degree in education with an elementary teaching certification.

Michelle is currently a sixth-grade mathematics teacher at Salem Hyde Elementary School where she has been working for the past nine years. She wants her students to have a passion for learning mathematics. She explains: "It makes me so sad when on the first day of school, students talk about how they hate math or they don't understand why they have to learn it because they are 'never going to use it.'" At the beginning of each school year, she tells her students that her goal is to make mathematics real to them and prove to them how we use mathematics every day and not just in school. She strives to make her classroom a problem-solving, safe place where students are collaborating with others to solve hands-on or real-world mathematical problems.

Michelle indicated that using the five practices has improved her teaching. She explains:

> *I've always put a lot of time into planning, and I feel like I've always been really good at engaging students, but since I've been using the five practices in my planning, it has just taken it to a whole other level. I'm planning out the strategies … planning my questioning around those strategies. … It makes me more prepared to teach my students, to guide them to those goals, whatever the goals are for the lesson.*

These three teachers are making their teaching practice public so that others can learn from their efforts. Hiebert, Gallimore, and Stigler (2003) argue that we must respect teachers "brave enough to open their classroom doors" (p. 56). To honor their courage, as you read about and view excerpts from their classrooms, we encourage you to avoid critiquing what you see or discussing what the teacher "should have done." Instead, our goal is to use the access we have been given as an opportunity for learning—for serious reflection and analysis—in an effort to improve our own teaching in ways that open up new opportunities for our students to learn.

Using This Book

You will likely get the most out of this book if you are committed to ambitious teaching that provides students with increased opportunities to engage in productive discussions in mathematics classrooms. Through engaging with the ideas in the book, you will learn much about how to increase students' engagement in and learning from classroom discussions.

This book can be used in several different ways. You might read through the book on your own, stopping to engage with the questions, activities, and assignments as suggested. Alternatively, and perhaps more powerfully, you can work through the book with colleagues in professional learning communities, department meetings, or when time permits. The book would also be a good choice for a book study with a group of peers interested in improving the quality of their classroom discussions. You might also encounter this book in college or university education courses for practicing or preservice teachers or in professional development workshops during the summer or school year. We will explore more ideas about ways to make the five practices central to your instruction in Chapter 7.

Norms for Video Viewing

The video excerpts that accompany this book are intended to provide authentic middle school examples on which to base discussions of the five practices. To take full advantage of these examples, we encourage you to consider the following three norms for video viewing. These norms are based on recent research that documents how video can support teacher learning and reflection (Sherin & Dyer, 2017; Sherin & van Es, 2009).

Focus on student sense-making. The majority of the video clips that you will watch in this book focus on students. That is intentional. While the five practices describe actions that you as the teacher will take, this work involves looking closely at what students do and say. The videos thus provide an opportunity for you to do just that outside of the immediate demands of teaching.

As you explore students' actions in the videos, we encourage you to look beyond simply whether a student's idea is correct or incorrect. Instead, examine what it is that the student understands. What is the student's idea? Where does it come from? Why is it sensible, given what the student understands? Focus on what it is that makes sense about the students' thinking.

Be specific about what you notice. Much of the value of video viewing is the sense that you can slow down classroom interactions and have the time to notice what is taking place in a detailed way. In addition, with video you can often focus on just a subset of events and look closely, for example, at what a particular student is saying and to whom, what gestures or drawings the student is making, and more.

As you view the video excerpts, we encourage you to be specific about what you notice. Provide detailed evidence to support your claims about what is happening. Explain what it is you see in the video that leads you to a particular interpretation.

Consider alternative interpretations. As you watch the video, you may find yourself quickly making assumptions about what is taking place and why. As teachers, we must often respond quickly, diagnosing student confusions, responding to student questions, and making changes in the direction of a lesson. Video, however, provides the luxury of time. Use this to your advantage!

Once you have an idea of what you think is taking place in the video, look for alternatives. How else might you understand what is happening? This is particularly important when examining students' ideas. Rather than assume you know the reason behind a students' strategy or statement, look for alternatives. Considering alternate interpretations is important because when we assume we understand what a student means, we often limit ourselves to what we have heard from students previously.

Getting Started!

You are now ready to begin a deep dive into the five practices. In the next five chapters, you will learn more about the practices. We encourage you to keep a journal or notebook in which you can respond to questions that are posed and make note of questions you have. Such a journal can be helpful in conversations with other teachers or in reflecting from time to time about how your thinking is evolving and changing.

“The five practices help me make sure that I know the key points that I’m going to use as the foundation throughout the teaching that occurs from that point forward—so, knowing exactly why I’m doing this task at this point in my sequence of lessons, and exactly what points are like the big rocks and big understandings.”

—JENNIFER MOSSOTTI, EIGHTH-GRADE TEACHER

CHAPTER 2

Setting Goals and Selecting Tasks

Before you can begin to work on the five practices, you must first set a goal for student learning and select a task that aligns with your goal and providing opportunities for students to learn important mathematics content and to engage in essential mathematical practices. Smith and Stein (2018) have described this as *Practice 0*—a necessary step in which teachers must engage as they begin to plan a lesson that will feature a whole class discussion. As they explain:

> *To have a productive mathematical discussion, teachers must first establish a clear and specific goal with respect to the mathematics to be learned and then select a high-level mathematical task. This is not to say that all tasks that are selected and used in the classroom must be high level, but rather that productive discussions that highlight key mathematical ideas are unlikely to occur if the task on which students are working requires limited thinking and reasoning. (Smith & Stein, 2018, p. 27)*

In this chapter, we first unpack what is involved in setting goals and selecting tasks and illustrate what this practice looks like in an authentic middle school classroom. We then explore challenges that teachers face in engaging in this practice and provide an opportunity for you to explore setting a goal and selecting a task in your own teaching practice.

Part One: Unpacking the Practice: Setting Goals and Selecting Tasks

What does it take to engage in this practice? This practice requires first specifying the learning goal for the lesson and then identifying a high-level task that aligns with the learning goal. The key questions, shown in Figure 2.1, are intended to help you focus on important aspects of the practice.

Figure 2.1 • Key questions that support the practice of setting a goal and selecting a task

WHAT IT TAKES	KEY QUESTIONS
Specifying the learning goal	Does the goal focus on what students will learn about mathematics (as opposed to what they will do)?
Identifying a high-level task that aligns with the goal	Does your task provide students with the opportunity to think, reason, and problem solve?
	What resources will you provide students to ensure that all students can access the task?
	What will you take as evidence that students have met the goal through their work on this task?

In the sections that follow, we provide an illustration of this practice drawing on a lesson taught by Jennifer Mossotti in her eighth-grade classroom. As you read the description of what Mrs. Mossotti thinks about and articulates while planning her lesson, consider how her attention to the key questions influence her planning.

Specifying the Learning Goal

Your first step in planning a lesson is specifying the goal(s). Consider Goals A and B for each of the mathematical ideas targeted in Figure 2.2. How are the goals the same and how are they different? Do you think the differences matter?

For each of the mathematical ideas targeted in Figure 2.2, the goal listed in Column A is considered a performance goal. Performance goals indicate what students will be able to do as a result of engaging in the lesson. By contrast, each of the goals listed in Column B is a learning goal. The learning goals explicitly state what students will understand about mathematics as a result of engaging in a particular lesson. The learning goal needs to be stated with sufficient specificity such that it can guide your decision-making during the lesson (e.g., what task to select for students to work on, what questions to ask students as they work

Figure 2.2 • Different goals for learning specific mathematical ideas

TARGETED IDEA	GOAL A	GOAL B
Slope	Students will be able to find the slope of a line given two points.	Students will recognize that slope is the ratio of the vertical change to the horizontal change between *any* two points on the line.
Multiplying binomials	Students will be able to use FOIL (first-outer-inner-last) to find the product of any two binomials.	Students will recognize that the binomials $(x + a)$ and $(x + b)$ are factors, each of which can represent a dimension of a rectangle, and that the product of these factors is an area. The resulting area can be represented algebraically as $x^2 + ax + bx + ab$. This algebraic representation also results from applying the distributive property twice: $(x + a)(x + b) = x(x + b) + a(x + b) = x^2 + bx + ax + ab$.
Proportions	Students will be able to use cross multiplication to find the missing value in problems where the quantities being compared are in a proportional relationship.	Students will recognize that a proportion consists of two ratios that are equivalent to each other (e.g., $\frac{a}{b} = \frac{ax}{bx}$) and that missing values in the proportion can be found by determining the scale factor x that relates the two ratios or by determining the relationship (multiplicative) between a and b and recognizing that ax and bx must have the same relationship.

on the task, which solutions to have presented during the whole class discussion). According to Hiebert and his colleagues (2007):

> *Without explicit learning goals, it is difficult to know what counts as evidence of students' learning, how students' learning can be linked to particular instructional activities, and how to revise instruction to facilitate students' learning more effectively. Formulating clear, explicit learning goals sets the stage for everything else. (p. 51)*

In general, "the better the goals, the better our instructional decisions can be, and the greater the opportunity for improved student learning" (Mills, 2014, p. 2).

According to Hunt and Stein (in press), "too often, we define what mathematics we wish students to come to 'know' as performance, or what students will 'do,' absent the understandings that underlay their behaviors." If we want students to learn mathematics with understanding, we need to specify what exactly it is we expect them to understand about mathematics as a result of engaging in a lesson. Hence, goals you set for a lesson should focus on what is to be learned not solely on performance.

Mrs. Mossotti was beginning a unit on linear functions with her eighth-grade students. Since students' experience with linear functions in

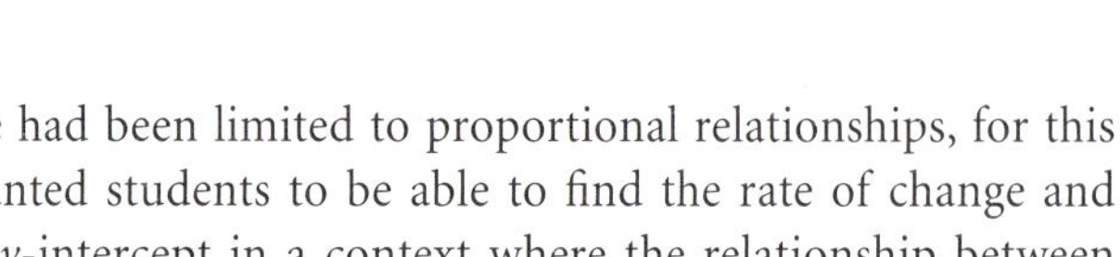

seventh grade had been limited to proportional relationships, for this lesson she wanted students to be able to find the rate of change and interpret the y-intercept in a context where the relationship between variables was not proportional. As a result of the lesson, she wanted her students to understand that:

1. The rate of change can be seen as the ratio of the change in the y-variable compared to the change in the x-variable, as the rate expressed with the words "for each, per, for every" in a verbal description or as the coefficient of x in the equation $y = mx + b$.
2. Some functions do not *start* at zero. That is, the point (0,0) is not a solution for all linear functions.
3. The y-intercept can be understood as the initial value of a linear function in a real-world context.

TEACHING TAKEAWAY

Specificity is one of the keys to setting learning goals and finding appropriately aligned tasks.

This level of specificity at which Mrs. Mossotti articulated the learning goals for the lessons will help her in identifying an appropriate task for her students, and subsequently, it will help her in asking questions that will move students toward the goal and in determining the extent to which students have learned what was intended.

Identifying a High-Level Task That Aligns With the Goal

Your next step in planning a lesson is to select a high-level task that aligns with the learning goal. High-level or cognitively challenging mathematical tasks engage students in reasoning and problem solving and are essential in supporting students' learning mathematics with understanding. By contrast, low-level tasks—tasks that can be solved by applying previously learned rules and procedures—require limited thinking or understanding of the underlying mathematical concepts. According to Boston and Wilhelm (2015, p. 24), "if opportunities for high-level thinking and reasoning are not embedded in instructional tasks, these opportunities rarely materialize during mathematics lessons." In addition, research provides evidence that students who have the opportunity to engage in high-level tasks on a regular basis show greater learning gains than students who engage primarily in low-level tasks during instruction (e.g., Stein & Lane, 1996; Stigler & Hiebert, 2004; and Boaler & Staples, 2008).

Tasks that provide the richest basis for productive discussions have been referred to as *doing-mathematics* tasks. Such tasks are nonalgorithmic—no solution path is suggested or implied by the task and students cannot solve them by the simple application of a known rule. Hence students must explore the task to determine what it is asking them to do and develop and implement a plan drawing on prior knowledge and experience to solve the task (Smith & Stein, 1998).

While the level of cognitive demand is a critical consideration in selecting a task worthy of discussion, there are other characteristics that you should also consider when selecting a task. These characteristics help ensure that students will have the opportunity to engage in the mathematics practices/processes (e.g., make sense of problems and persevere in solving them, reason abstractly and quantitatively, construct viable arguments) that are viewed as essential to developing mathematical proficiency. When sizing up the potential of a task, keep in mind the questions shown in Figure 2.3.

Figure 2.3 • Questions to help you *size* up the potential of a task

- Are there multiple ways to enter the task and to show competence?
- Does the task require students to provide a justification or explanation?
- Does the task provide the opportunity to use and make connections between different representations of a mathematical idea?
- Does the task provide the opportunity to look for patterns, make conjectures, and/or form generalizations?

Selecting tasks that have these additional characteristics does not guarantee that students will engage in the mathematical practices. However, the use of the five practices together with such tasks will help ensure that this will occur. So rather than thinking about separate process goals, such as the Standards for Mathematical Practice advocated for in the Common Core State Standards for Mathematics (2010), we encourage you to consider characteristics of tasks that will provide your students with the opportunities to engage in such processes.

TEACHING TAKEAWAY

Doing-mathematics tasks, rather than procedural exercises, lend themselves to rich and productive mathematical discussion.

For her lesson, Mrs. Mossotti created the State Fair Task, shown in Figure 2.4. She selected the context of the state fair for three reasons. First, the context was relatable to her students since the New York State Fair took place in her students' hometown. Second, the y-intercept had meaning in this context since attendees have to pay a fee to enter the fair and ride tickets are an additional cost that you pay after entry. Third, she thought that there would be different ways to enter and solve the task.

Mrs. Mossotti carefully chose the points that she would include on the graph. As she explained:

> *I purposely chose the values here of one ticket purchased, plus the entry fee, eight tickets and ten tickets. If I had chosen two points of consecutive amounts of tickets purchased, I think it would have been too obvious for them to figure out the ticket price. [So] I chose eight tickets purchased and ten tickets purchased for a difference of two*

tickets, and if they can understand the difference of two tickets will have a different cost, then they can start to work from there. But at the same time, I've also purposely put in the cost for one ticket plus the entry fee. Some of them [may] think that this is a price per ticket. I'll ask questions so that they understand that if this is the price for one ticket, how come eight of them are only just a little bit more?

In order to ensure that students would have access to the task, Mrs. Mossotti planned to provide students with resources on which they could draw in solving the task—but would leave it up to the students to

Figure 2.4 • The State Fair task

The State Fair

You are going to the Kentucky State Fair in August. You are trying to figure out how much you should plan to spend. The graph below shows how much three different people spent after going through the main gate and then buying their ride tickets. Every ride ticket is the same price.

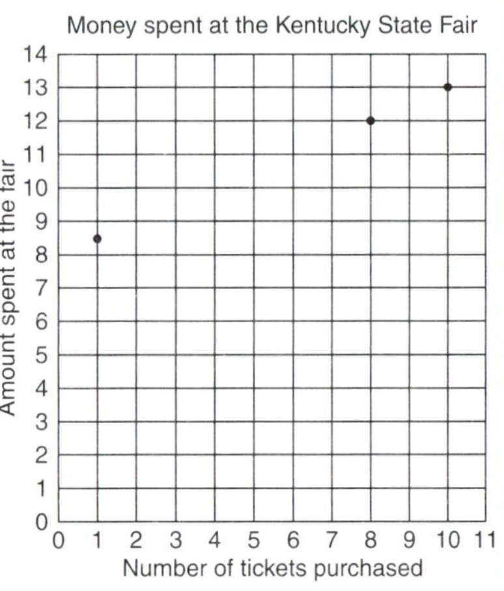

1. After entering the fair, you decide to buy four ride tickets. What will be your total cost for attending the fair? How do you know?
2. Describe how the cost increases as you buy more tickets. Be specific.
3. After entering the fair, you decide you want to go on a lot of rides. What will be the total cost for attending the fair and then purchasing 15 ride tickets?
4. Write a description, in words or numbers and symbols, that can be used to find the total cost after entering the fair and purchasing any number of tickets.
5. How does the ticket price appear in your description or expressions?
6. How does the ticket price appear in the graph?

Extension

1. If you went to the Kentucky State Fair, how many ride tickets could you buy with $25.00?
2. If you could enter the Kentucky State Fair for free, how would the graph look different?

Source: Jennifer Mossotti. Ferris wheel photo by Hannah Morgan on Unsplash.

decide which, if any of them, would be useful. These included: rulers (so students could draw a line connecting the three points), calculators (so students could compute quickly and accurately), patty paper (so students could trace the vertical and horizontal change between two points and move it like a transformation), extra blank paper (so students had plenty of space to try things out), and highlighters (so students could make some aspect of the graph salient). In addition to these material resources, Mrs. Mossotti also decided that she would provide *human* resources by having students work on the task in pairs or trios so that they would have others with whom to confer.

When asked what students would say, do, or produce that would provide evidence of their understandings of the goals in the lesson through their work on this task, Mrs. Mossotti was quite specific. She indicated that students would do and say things such as:

- It costs $1.00 more for two more tickets so it must be 50¢ for each ticket *(determined the rate of change).*
- The cost for 0 tickets is NOT $0.00 *(recognized that the y-intercept is not 0)*
- I can add 50¢ three more times to $8.50 to find the total cost for four tickets *(determined the rate of change).*
- The increase in price from one ticket to eight tickets is $3.50, so if I divide $3.50 by 7, I get 50¢. So that must be the cost per ticket *(determined the rate of change).*
- The cost for every/for each/per/for one ticket is 50¢ *(determined the rate of change).*
- Since the graph does not start at zero, I cannot just divide the total amount spent by the number of tickets to find the price per ticket *(recognized that the* y*-intercept is not 0 so that the relationship is not proportional).*
- No matter how many tickets I decide to buy, I have to pay money to enter the fair before buying the ride tickets *(recognized that the* y*-intercept has meaning in the context).*

Jennifer Mossotti's Attention to Key Questions: Setting Goals and Selecting Tasks

During her initial stage of lesson planning, Mrs. Mossotti paid careful attention to the key questions. First, in setting her goals for the lesson, she clearly articulated what it was she wanted students to learn about mathematics as a result of engaging in the task. The specificity with which she stated her goals made it possible to determine what students understood about these ideas and to formulate questions that would help move her students forward. While she wanted her students to determine the rate of change, she also wanted to make sure that they understand what rate of change is and how it is represented graphically.

Second, she selected a high-level *doing-mathematics* task that aligned with her goals. Students could not solve the state fair task by application of a known rule or procedure; it would require students' perseverance and sense making. She *sized up* the task (see Figure 2.3) to ensure that it had several other important characteristics. Specifically, there were a number of general approaches that students could use to enter the task (e.g., making a table, drawing a line connecting the three points, focusing on the change between two points, tracing the points/line and translating it) and the material and human resources that the teacher planned to provide would support their work. The task used several different representations—it began with both a context and a graph and asked students to write a description using words or numbers and symbols—and it required students to explain, "How do you know?" (Question 1). Finally the task asked students to generalize their findings by describing in words or numbers and symbols how to find the cost of entering the fair and purchasing any number of tickets. Hence through their work on the task, students could learn important mathematics and engage in key practices.

The State Fair task, along with the resources Mrs. Mossotti made available to students, allowed all students to enter the task at some level. Rather than differentiating instruction by providing different students with different tasks, she selected one task and met the needs of different learners by providing a range of resources for students to consider and questions that would challenge learners at different levels. For example, the inclusion of the extension questions provided a challenge for students who were able to quickly make progress on the task, while questions 1–3 provided scaffolding for writing the general description in question 4 for other students.

Finally, Mrs. Mossotti indicated some things that she expected students to say and do that would provide evidence students were making progress on the ideas she wanted them to learn. By considering this evidence in advance of the lesson, she was ready to pay close attention to students' work for indications that they were making progress in their understanding.

Through her careful attention to setting goals and selecting a task, Mrs. Mossotti's planning was off to a productive start and she was ready to engage in the five practices. In the next chapter we will continue to investigate her planning process as she anticipates what she thinks her students will do when presented with the task and how she will respond. We now turn our attention to the challenges that teachers face in setting goals and selecting tasks.

Part Two: Challenges Teachers Face: Setting Goals and Selecting Tasks

As we described in the chapter opening, setting goals and selecting tasks are foundational to orchestrating productive discussions. Setting goals and selecting tasks, however, are not without their challenges. In this section, we focus on four specific challenges associated with this practice, shown in Figure 2.5, that we have identified from our work with teachers.

Figure 2.5 • Challenges associated with setting goals and selecting tasks

CHALLENGE	DESCRIPTION
Identifying learning goals	Goal needs to focus on what students will learn as a result of engaging in the task, not on what students will do. Clarity on goals sets the stage for everything else!
Identifying a doing-mathematics task	While *doing-mathematics* tasks provide the greatest opportunities for student learning, they are not readily available in some textbooks. Teachers may need to adapt an existing task, find a task in another resource, or create a task.
Ensuring alignment between task and goals	Even with learning goals specified, teachers may select a task that does not allow students to make progress on those particular goals.
Launching a task to ensure student access	Teachers need to provide access to the context and the mathematics in the launch but not so much that the mathematical demands are reduced and key ideas are *given away*.

Identifying Learning Goals

Identifying learning goals is a challenging but critical first step in planning any lesson. It is challenging because we often focus on what students are going to be able to do as a result of engaging in a lesson, not on what they are going to learn about mathematics. When Michelle Saroney, one of our three featured teachers, first described her goal for the lesson she planned to teach in her sixth-grade classroom, she stated her goal in terms of the standard she wanted to address: "interpret and compute quotients of fractions and solve word problems involving division of fractions by fractions" (NY6.NS – New York State Next Generation Mathematics Learning Standards, p. 79). When pressed to be more specific about what she wanted students to learn about mathematics, she acknowledged, "The goals are my most difficult part of planning tasks." While Mrs. Saroney was clear regarding what her students would do—solve the pizza party task shown in Figure 2.6—she struggled to articulate what she wanted them to understand about mathematics as a result of engaging in the task. [NOTE: This standard is one of the most misunderstood standards at Grade 6 and often translates into instruction on the traditional algorithm with no visual models. See https://achievethecore.org/aligned/misunderstood-middle-school-mathematics-standards-grade-6/]

Figure 2.6 • The Pizza Party task

Pizza Party

You ordered pizza for your birthday party. When the party was over you still had $4\frac{5}{6}$ pizzas left over. Your mother decided to freeze the remaining pizza. She put $\frac{2}{3}$ of a pizza (one serving) in each freezer bag.

1. How many servings would your mother be able to freeze?
2. How much more pizza does your mother need to make another serving?

Draw a picture, build a model, construct a number line, or make a table to explain your solution.

Source: Task adapted from Nolan, Dixon, Roy & Andreasen, 2016.
Image Source: bonetta/iStock.com

During the discussion with her colleagues regarding her goals and task, Mrs. Saroney indicated that this would be the first time that students would be solving a division problem that involved a mixed number and the first time this year that they would be solving a contextual problem. Through the conversation she tried to clarify in detail what understandings of mathematics students would need to solve the pizza task and as a result determined the following learning goals for the lesson. Specifically, as a result of engaging in the lesson, she wanted her students to understand that:

1. When you scale a fraction up or down, you have not changed the amount it represents ($\frac{2}{3} = \frac{4}{6}$); equivalent fractions represent the same area and name the same position on a number line. *Since the mixed number and the fraction in the task did not have the same denominator, students would need to be able to rewrite* $\frac{2}{3}$ *as* $\frac{4}{6}$ *and know that they were equivalent.*
2. When you are dividing by a fraction, the remainder is expressed as a fraction of the divisor. *The* $\frac{1}{6}$ *of a pizza left over after making 7 servings needs to be interpreted as* $\frac{1}{4}$ *of a serving.*
3. When you find "how many ___ are in____?" you are doing division. That is, in $a \div b$ you are trying to find how many times b is contained in a. *What division actually means whether you are working with fractions or whole numbers.*

Mrs. Saroney also noted that the task had many features that would provide opportunities for her students to engage in the mathematical practices, including asking for an explanation and using and making connections between different representations.

With new clarity regarding what she wanted students to understand, Mrs. Saroney was now ready to anticipate what students would do with the task and prepare questions that would help her illuminate what her students understood about these ideas.

Mrs. Saroney is not alone in her struggle to identify learning goals. Consider, for example, a lesson that Neil Tanner was planning for his eighth-grade students featuring the downloading music task (see Figure 2.7). Mr. Tanner initially indicated that his goal for the lesson was "for students to find the point of intersection of two linear functions." This goal clearly stated what students were going to do but provided no insight into what he wanted his students to understand about systems of equations. Here are a few things Mr. Tanner *could* target explicitly in his lesson:

- The solution to a system of two unique nonparallel linear equations in two variables is represented graphically by the point of intersection of the lines, and it is represented by the ordered pair (x, y) that makes both equations true statements or satisfies the equations simultaneously.
- Two unique nonparallel linear equations switch positions at the point of intersection—the equation with the y-intercept closer to $(0, 0)$ and the larger rate of change will be closer to the x-axis before the point of intersection and the equation with the y-intercept furthest away from $(0, 0)$ and a smaller rate of change will be closer to the x-axis after the point of intersection.
- Systems of linear equations can be solved using tables, graphs, and equations and the different representations can be connected.

Figure 2.7 • Downloading Music task

Downloading Music

You are trying to decide which service you should use to download music. TUNE IN charges \$1.00 for each song you download, plus an \$8.00-per-month membership charge. NOTEABLE charges 50¢ for each song you download, plus a \$12.00-per-month membership charge. How many songs would you have to download in a month before NOTEABLE is a better deal? Explain your reasoning.

Image Source: oleksii arseniuk/iStock.com

Why does this level of specificity matter? It matters because with this level of specificity, Mr. Tanner will be able to determine not only whether or not his students can find the solution to the system, but whether they can explain what the solution means (first bullet), begin to see how systems of equations work in general (second bullet), and see that different representations can be used and connected to each other (third bullet). So when Mr. Tanner actually interacts with his students as they work on the task, with these targets in mind, he can press them to explain what happens at, before, and after the point of intersection and how the rate of change and the y-intercept impact the relative position of the function. In addition, this level of specificity will help Mr. Tanner consider the solutions he would want students to share during the whole class discussion and the questions he wants to ask about them later in the lesson. Hence, the specificity of the goal is going to provide guidance to him during the lesson and help him determine what his students do and do not understand. This information will then help him in planning subsequent lessons. (See Hunt and Stein (in press) for a description of three interconnect phases that teachers can use individually or collaboratively to create and refine goals for student learning.)

Identifying a Doing-Mathematics Task

TEACHING TAKEAWAY

If your textbook does not provide worthwhile enough tasks for discussion, you have options: adapt, seek out, or create your own!

While doing-mathematics tasks provide the optimal vehicle for whole-class discussions, not all curricular materials are replete with such tasks. Traditional textbooks tend to feature more procedural tasks that provide limited opportunities for reasoning and problem solving. While such resources do include *word problems*, they are often solved using procedures that have been previously introduced and modeled and require limited thinking. While standards-based texts (Senk & Thompson, 2003) contain some procedural tasks, they also include high-level tasks that promote reasoning and problem solving. If you are using a resource that does not include high-level tasks, what should you do? In this section we will explore three possible options—modify an existing task, find a task in another resource, or create your own task.

Adapting an Existing Task

Some textbook tasks give students too much information and leave little for students to figure out on their own. Take for example the Patterns task shown in Figure 2.8. In the original task (left side of Figure 2.8), the table is done, equations are provided, and very little thinking is needed. Part 1 requires determining which equation returns the correct value for P when values for t are substituted. Part 2 is a *plug and chug* task that can be solved by substituting 20 in the equation selected in Part 1. While students are asked to graph in Part 3, this is nothing more than a plotting points exercise.

When Elaine Richard saw the Patterns task in her algebra textbook, she decided to modify the task so that her students would have to do more

Figure 2.8 • The original and modified Patterns task

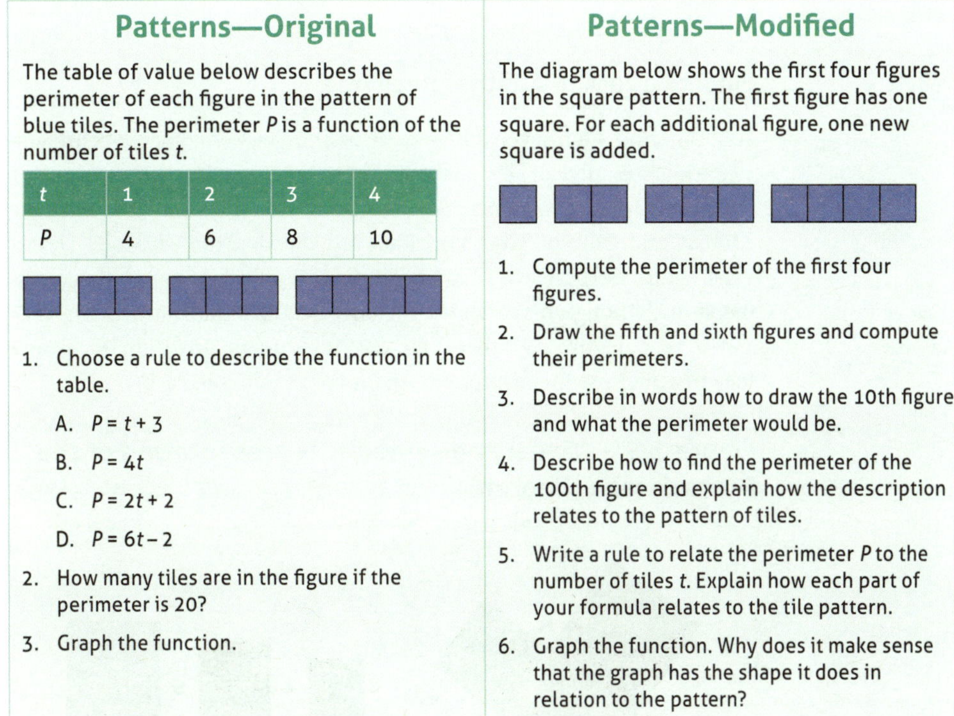

Patterns—Original

The table of value below describes the perimeter of each figure in the pattern of blue tiles. The perimeter P is a function of the number of tiles t.

t	1	2	3	4
P	4	6	8	10

1. Choose a rule to describe the function in the table.
   A. $P = t + 3$
   B. $P = 4t$
   C. $P = 2t + 2$
   D. $P = 6t - 2$
2. How many tiles are in the figure if the perimeter is 20?
3. Graph the function.

Patterns—Modified

The diagram below shows the first four figures in the square pattern. The first figure has one square. For each additional figure, one new square is added.

1. Compute the perimeter of the first four figures.
2. Draw the fifth and sixth figures and compute their perimeters.
3. Describe in words how to draw the 10th figure and what the perimeter would be.
4. Describe how to find the perimeter of the 100th figure and explain how the description relates to the pattern of tiles.
5. Write a rule to relate the perimeter P to the number of tiles t. Explain how each part of your formula relates to the tile pattern.
6. Graph the function. Why does it make sense that the graph has the shape it does in relation to the pattern?

thinking and reasoning. In comparing the original task to the modified task, you will see that Ms. Richard made the following changes:

- The table has been eliminated and instead students must determine the perimeters of the first four trains from the figure.
- Students now need to draw the next two figures and to describe and compute the perimeter of larger figures without drawing and counting.
- Rather than determine which of the given equations produces the table of values, students must write a rule that could be used to find the perimeter of any figure in the pattern and explain how each part of the rule relates to the square pattern.
- In addition to graphing the function, students must explain why the graph of the function is linear.

By making these changes, Ms. Richard has transformed a low-level task into a doing-mathematics task. In addition, her modified task has the additional characteristics we previously discussed—it can be entered and solved in several different ways, it requires students to use and make connections between different representations, it asks students to explain their thinking, and it asks students to generalize. (See Arbaugh, Smith, Boyle, Stylianides, and Steele, 2018; Boyle & Kaiser, 2017; and Smith & Stein, 2018 for more insight on how to modify tasks.)

Finding a Task in Another Resource

You can find high-level doing-mathematics tasks in many print and electronic resources. The challenge is to find a task that meets your mathematical needs, is accessible to your students, and fits with the content and flow of your curriculum. Consider, for example, Devon Washington's experience at the beginning of a unit on the Pythagorean theorem. Although his textbook included pictures that showed why $c^2 = a^2 + b^2$ (e.g., Figure 2.9), there was little for students to figure out before they began to use the formula to find missing values for a, b, and c.

Figure 2.9 • Visual and symbolic representation of the Pythagorean theorem

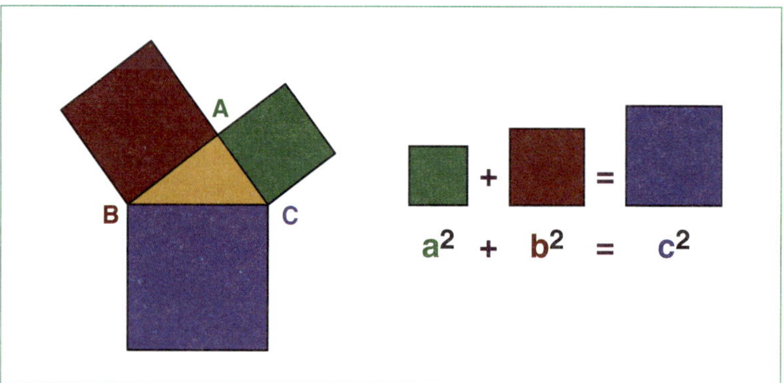

Source: Adapted from Image by Openclipart-Vectors, pixabay.com CC0 Creative Commons https://creativecommons.org/publicdomain/zero/1.0/deed.en

Mr. Washington wanted his students to *discover* the theorem so that they would know not just what it was but where it came from and why it made sense. As a result, he decided to replace the opening activity in his book with one he found online at map.mathshell.org. The lesson, entitled "Discovering the Pythagorean Theorem" (MARS Shell Center Team, 2007–2015), featured a series of activities that provide students the opportunity to find areas of *tilted* squares (see an example in Figure 2.10), to look for patterns by investigating the areas of different squares, to make a conjecture about any *x* by *y* square, and to consider visual proofs of the theorem. (The entire lesson can be found at http://map.mathshell.org/lessons.php?unit=8315&collection=8.)

Figure 2.10 • The first activity in the "Discovering the Pythagorean Theorem" lesson

The dots on the grid are all one unit apart.

The square shown here can be described as a '3 *by* 5' square. The first number in the description *always* represents the horizontal tilt of the square.

1. Find its area.

   Show all your reasoning.

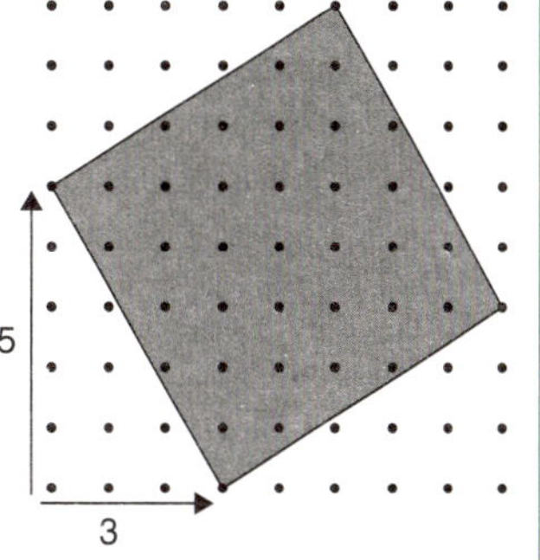

Source: This task is part of a carefully engineered lesson, "Discovering the Pythagorean Theorem" from the Mathematics Assessment Project, which can be downloaded for free from http://map.mathshell.org/lessons.php?unit=8315&collection=8

By replacing the first task in the unit with a doing-mathematics task, Mr. Washington provided his students with the opportunity to develop a conceptual understanding of the Pythagorean theorem. This became a base on which he could then build procedural fluency in using the theorem and subsequently for using the theorem to compute the distance between two points and derive the distance formula. (For an extended discussion on building procedural fluency from a base of conceptual understanding, see Smith, Steele, & Raith, 2017.)

Mr. Washington found a website that had a storehouse of good tasks. But not all websites are of equal value. In Appendix A, we have included a list of web resources that may be helpful to you in finding doing-mathematics tasks. This list is not exhaustive but should be helpful in getting started.

Creating a Task

If you cannot find a task you want to use, you may decide to create one yourself. This was the case for Nancy Haines. Ms. Haines's eighth-grade students were beginning a unit on exponential functions. While the unit in her book actually started with a good task—folding a sheet of paper into equal parts and counting the number of regions formed with each fold—she wanted to start the unit with a task that she thought students would find more engaging. Toward this end, she created the Ice Bucket Challenge task shown in Figure 2.11.

Figure 2.11 • The Ice Bucket Challenge task

Ice Bucket Challenge

Throughout the summer of 2014, having a bucket filled with ice and cold water dumped on someone's head became pretty popular. Everyone across the country was getting involved with this activity! But why were they doing this?

In order to raise awareness for the ALS (Amyotrophic Lateral Sclerosis) Association, people would challenge others to either donate money to the organization within 24 hours, or they would have to dump water on their heads. The creators of the Ice Bucket Challenge believed that if three new people were challenged every time, eventually, billions across the country would donate and know about the ALS Association.

At Stage One of the process, a person challenged three others to take part in the Ice Bucket Challenge. At Stage Two, each of these three people challenged three others. How many people participated at Stage Five? How many people participated at Stage 10? Describe a function that would model the Ice Bucket Challenge process at any stage. Explain how your function models the situation.

PAUSE AND CONSIDER

What characteristics of the Ice Bucket Challenge task make it a good choice for the introductory lesson in a unit on exponential functions?

Because it cannot be solved by using a known rule or procedure, thus requiring students to reason and problem solve, the Ice Bucket Challenge is a doing-mathematics task. The task has other characteristics that make it a good choice for the lesson as previously described:

- It can be entered and solved in several different ways (e.g., draw a picture, make a table, use words to describe what is happening).
- It requires students to use and make connections between different representations (i.e., the context and a written or symbol rule).

- It asks students to explain their thinking.
- It asks students to generalize by describing a function that would model the process at any stage.

While creating tasks is certainly an option, it is a challenging endeavor! If you decide to create a task yourself, we encourage you to ask others to review and solve the task so that you can identify any possible pitfalls before you give it to students. This is exactly what Ms. Haines did with the Ice Bucket Challenge task!

Ensuring Alignment Between Task and Goals

Another challenge teachers often face is making sure that there is alignment between the task and the goal. That is, ensuring that the task they have selected as the basis for instruction provides students with the opportunity to explore the mathematical ideas that are targeted during the lesson.

Suppose, for example, you are teaching a lesson about slope. You decide that you want students to understand that slope is the ratio between a change in one variable relative to a corresponding change in another variable. You select a task that asks students to find the slope of lines given two points (e.g., (1, 6) and (3, 9)) without graphing. This basic *naked numbers* task does not provide students the opportunity to develop any understanding of what slope means. By eliminating graphing as a possible solution path, students are left to apply the formula for calculating slope $\left[\frac{(y_2 - y_1)}{(x_2 - x_1)}\right]$. As a result, students may end up with correct solutions but with limited understanding regarding the meaning of slope. In this situation, you have established a *learning* goal but have paired it with a low-level task that requires only application of a known procedure.

A mismatch between tasks and goals can also occur in a less extreme way. For example, Mr. Tanner initially selected the downloading music task, shown in Figure 2.7, for his lesson on systems of equations we discussed in the last section. Mr. Tanner selected this task because he thought students would relate to the context, and he liked the idea that students would have to explain their reasoning and would have to find the point of intersection to answer the question. Since this was an introductory task, and students had not yet learned how to solve systems algebraically, students would be able to use tables (with or without writing an equation first) and graph by hand.

So what's the mismatch? In the original version of the task, TUNE IN charged 99¢ per song (plus the additional $8.00 per month membership charge). The point of intersection of the system in the downloading

music task (8.163, 16.082) would be nearly impossible to determine with the strategies to which students currently had access. While Mr. Tanner may ultimately want students to deal with *messy* numbers and be able to interpret what such a point means in context, such messiness could be reserved for a time when students have access to algebraic strategies and/or graphing calculators. But for now, if students could not find the point of intersection with some degree of accuracy, they would have difficulty achieving the lesson goals.

In this situation, it was an easy fix. After some discussion, Mr. Tanner changed the per-song charge for TUNE IN from 99¢ to $1.00 as shown in Figure 2.7. This minor change made the task more accessible to students given their current knowledge and experience and made it possible to achieve the learning goals that Mr. Tanner had established.

Ensuring alignment between your goals and task is essential and the foundation on which to begin to engage in the five practices. If you find that your task does not fit your goals, consider the ways in which you can modify the task to provide more opportunities for students to think and reason as we described previously.

Launching a Task to Ensure Student Access

Launching or setting up a task refers to what the teacher does prior to having students begin work on a task. While it is not uncommon to see teachers hand out a task, ask a student volunteer to read the task aloud, and then tell students what they are expected to produce as a result of the work on the task, research suggests that attention to the way in which the task is launched can lead to a more successful discussion at the end of the lesson. Jackson and her colleagues (Jackson, Shahan, Gibbons, & Cobb, 2012) describe the benefits of an effective launch:

> *Students are much more likely to be able to get started solving a complex task, thereby enabling the teacher to attend to students' thinking and plan for a concluding whole-class discussion. This, in turn, increases the chances that all students will be supported to learn significant mathematics as they solve and discuss the task (p. 28).*

So what constitutes an effective launch? In Analyzing the Work of Teaching 2.1, you will explore Mrs. Mossotti's launch of the State Fair task. We invite you to engage in the analysis of a video clip and consider the questions posed before you read our analysis. [NOTE: While the launch of a task occurs during instruction, it is planned for prior to instruction. Rather than describing what Mrs. Mossotti intended to do, we decided to take you into her classroom so that you could see for yourself!]

Analyzing the Work of Teaching 2.1

Launching a Task

Video Clip 2.1
In this activity, you will watch Video Clip 2.1 from Jennifer Mossotti's eighth-grade class.

As you watch the clip consider:

- What did the teacher do to help her students *get ready* to work on the State Fair task?
- What did the teacher learn about her students that indicated they were ready to engage in the task?
- Do you think the time spent in launching the task was time well spent?

Videos may also be accessed at
resources.corwin.com/5practices-middleschool

Launching a Task—Analysis

The first part of Video Clip 2.1 focused on ensuring that students understood the context of the problem. In fact, Mrs. Mossotti learned that all but one of her students (one who was new to the class that very day) had actually attended the fair. Since the Kentucky State Fair featured in the task paralleled the New York State Fair in some ways (e.g. ride tickets are purchased after entering the fair), students' real-world knowledge would not be in conflict with the task they would be working on.

Mrs. Mossotti made the decision to show the video clip of her son Mason on his first ride at the fair in an effort to capture students' attention and motivate them to work on the task. The students in her class know her three children, and she often tells stories about them in class. Prior to the lesson, Mrs. Mossotti described her plan:

> *So, I am launching it with a video of my middle child, who is by far my most difficult child. Sometimes I will refer to some of the students in my class as the Mason of the class that day. The video is*

going to be Mason going on his very first ride at the New York State Fair. He is petrified. Then literally a second into the ride, he was very, very happy.

TEACHING TAKEAWAY

Taking the time to build relationships with students helps them feel more connected and can support their learning.

While it may strike you as unusual that Mrs. Mossotti shared a video clip of her son with the class, sharing aspects of her personal life in class helped her in building relationships with her students. Students are often more motivated to participate and learn when they feel a personal connection to the classroom (Horn, 2017).

In the next part of the launch, Mrs. Mossotti hands students a copy of the first page of the State Fair task, which contains the graph (without the questions that follow). Here she is focused on ensuring that the students could read the graph. By asking students to "write down two things that you notice," Mrs. Mossotti gave all students access to the task (everyone would be able to say something), and their responses would help her determine whether students could identify key features of the graph.

Students' responses revealed that they recognized that the graph showed the number of tickets and the amount of money spent, that the amount spent increased as the number of tickets increased, that the maximum number of tickets shown on the x-axis was 11 and the maximum cost shown on the y-axis was $14.00, and that 10 tickets for $13.00 was one point on the graph. The teacher's role during this time was to record what students said. Although she intervened to ask a clarifying question as needed, she did not comment on the students' contributions.

It is also worth noting that Mrs. Mossotti recorded students' initials next to their contributions. In so doing, she was giving students *credit* and ownership of the idea. By publically acknowledging her students in this way, she was helping them build their mathematical identities and giving them an opportunity to be seen by their peers as competent.

As a result of the launch, Mrs. Mossotti learned that students could relate to the context of the problem and that they were able to read and make sense of the graph, which was central to the task. She did not give out the questions that went with the task initially because she did not want students to get too far ahead or give too much away. Prior to the lesson, Mrs. Mossotti indicated, "I'm not going to give them any mathematical knowledge or background in terms of the math for the task itself." She wanted to make sure that students would have to think and reason their way through the problem.

TEACHING TAKEAWAY

A comprehensive launch ensures all students understand the entirety of the task, so that time is not spent later answering clarifying questions from groups or individuals.

Was the time spent launching the task time well spent? We could argue that it was essential to ensuring that students understood enough about what they were being asked to do to begin their work on the task. Too often, students are given a task and do not understand some aspect of it. When this occurs, the teacher then ends up moving from one group to the next answering questions that could have been cleared up with a more comprehensive launch.

Jackson and her colleagues (2012, p. 26) list "four crucial aspects to keep in mind when setting up complex tasks to support all students' learning":

1. Key Contextual Features of the Task
2. Key Mathematical Ideas of the Task
3. Development of Common Language
4. Maintaining the Cognitive Demand

Mrs. Mossotti launch embodied most of the features described by Jackson and colleagues. She made sure that students understood the context of the State Fair task (1), that they were able to read and make sense of the graph (2), and that the cognitive demand of the task was maintained by not suggesting a pathway to follow or giving away too much information (4). She did not explicitly distinguish between the entry fee and the amount paid for each ticket because this is at the heart of what she wanted students to figure out. Developing a common language (3) is often needed when there is vocabulary used in the task that might not be familiar to some or all of the students. For example, in the Downloading Music task (see Figure 2.7), you would want to make sure that all students understood what *downloading* meant and could describe it in their own words. In the State Fair task, however, this did not appear to be necessary.

Perhaps the most challenging part of launching a task is making sure that you do enough to ensure that students understand the context and what they are being asked to do but not so much that there is nothing left for students to figure out. For example, in the Downloading Music task, you would not want to provide students with a table and tell them to calculate the cost of buying one to 10 songs for each service. This would lower the demand of the task by providing a strategy for students to use and limit their opportunity to figure out what to do and how. In the Pizza Party task (Figure 2.6), you would not want to tell students that it was a division problem because that is something you want them to determine.

Conclusion

In this chapter, we have discussed the importance of setting clear goals for student learning and selecting a task that is aligned with the goal, and we have described what is involved in these practices and the challenges associated with them. Our experience tells us that if you do not take the time to seriously consider Practice 0 as a first step in carefully planning your lesson, the remainder of the practices will be built on a shaky foundation.

Mrs. Mossotti's work in setting a goal and selecting a task provided a concrete example of a teacher who thoughtfully and thoroughly engaged in this practice. Engaging in this practice in a deep and meaningful way does not happen overnight. It takes time and practice. As Mrs. Mossotti said, "Even if it feels like a failure the first time, or even if it feels like it's taking a lot more time than you anticipated, that time is going to be earned back when students have that conceptual understanding. . . ."

Mrs. Saroney and Mr. Tanner's efforts to determine what students would learn during their lesson and to ensure that the goals and tasks align made salient the challenges that teachers can face and overcome when engaging in this practice. In both cases, working with colleagues helped these teachers make progress in Practice 0.

Setting Goals and Selecting Tasks—Summary

Video Clip 2.2
To hear and see more about setting goals and selecting tasks, watch Video Clip 2.2.

Videos may also be accessed at **resources.corwin.com/5practices-middleschool**

In the next chapter, we explore the first of the five practices: *anticipating*. Here, we will return to Mrs. Mossotti's lesson and consider what it takes to engage in this practice and the challenges it presents.

Linking the Five Practices to Your Own Instruction

SETTING GOALS AND SELECTING TASKS

Identify a mathematical idea that you will be teaching sometime in the next few weeks. Working alone or with your colleagues:

1. Determine what it is you want students to learn about mathematics as a result of engaging in the lesson. Be as specific as possible. It is okay to indicate what students will do during the lesson, but do not stop there!
2. Select a high-level cognitively demanding *doing-mathematics* task that is aligned with your goals. Make sure that there are different ways to enter and engage with the task. Identify resources that are likely to help students as they work on the task.
3. Identify what students will say and do that will indicate that they are meeting the goals you have established.
4. Plan a launch that takes into account the four crucial aspects identified by Jackson and her colleagues.

Reflect on your planning so far. How does it differ from how you have previously thought about goals and tasks? In what ways do you think the differences will matter instructionally?

> “I feel like when choosing a task, I wanted there to be a lot of different ways that kids could solve it and to think through the concept at hand.”
>
> —JENNIFER MOSSOTTI, EIGHTH-GRADE TEACHER

CHAPTER 3

Anticipating Student Responses

Now that you have identified a learning goal and have settled on a task that aligns with that goal, it is time to explore the next practice, anticipating students' responses. Anticipating students' responses takes place before instruction, during the planning stage of your lesson. This practice involves taking a close look at the task to identify the different strategies you expect students to use and to think about how you want to respond to those strategies during instruction. Anticipating helps prepare you to recognize and make sense of students' strategies during the lesson and to be able to respond effectively. In other words, by carefully anticipating students' responses *prior* to a lesson, you will be better prepared to respond to students *during* instruction.

Smith and Stein (2018) explain anticipating in the following way:

> *[Anticipating involves making] an effort to actively envision how students might mathematically approach the instructional task or tasks that they will work on and consider[ing] questions that could be asked of the students who used specific strategies. This involves much more than simply evaluating whether a task is at the right level of difficulty or of sufficient interest to students, and it goes beyond considering whether or not they are getting the "right" answer.*

> *Anticipating students' responses involves developing considered expectations about how students might mathematically interpret a problem, the array of strategies—both correct and incorrect—that they might use to tackle it, and how those strategies and interpretations might relate to the mathematical concepts, representations, procedures, and practices that the teacher would like his or her students to learn.* (p. 10)

In this chapter, we first unpack anticipating into its key components and illustrate what this practice looks like in an authentic middle school classroom. We then explore what we have learned is challenging for teachers about this practice and provide an opportunity for you to explore anticipating in your own teaching practice.

Part One: Unpacking the Practice: Anticipating Student Responses

What is involved in anticipating students' responses? This practice involves getting inside the problem (thinking about different ways students might solve the task), planning to respond to students using assessing and advancing questions, and preparing to notice key aspects of students' thinking in the midst of instruction. Figure 3.1 highlights the key components of this practice.

Figure 3.1 • Key questions that support the process of anticipating students' responses

WHAT IT TAKES	KEY QUESTIONS
Getting inside the problem	How do you solve the task?
	How might students approach the task?
	What challenges might students face as they solve the task?
Planning to respond to student thinking	What assessing questions will you ask to draw out student thinking?
	What advancing questions will help you move student thinking forward?
Planning to notice student thinking	What strategies do you want to be on the lookout for as students work on the task?

Getting Inside the Problem

The first step is to get inside the problem! Many teachers find it useful to start by thinking about their own approach. How do you solve the task? You will want to think generally about the approach you use and at a detailed level about steps in your process (which may be different from someone else). Next, consider how students might approach the task. You might investigate the problem using a different representation or think about how manipulatives might shape the way students explore the task. Do some approaches move students more easily toward the learning goals you established? You could also think about whether the task has different entry points. Often when students begin a task by working on different parts of the problem, their solutions look different (Lambert & Stylianou, 2013). Finally, as you explore these various approaches, keep in mind any challenges you think students will face as they solve the task. Are certain parts of the task likely to be difficult for students? Do you expect that students who use certain approaches will face particular kinds of challenges? Where do you think students might get stuck?

In Analyzing the Work of Teaching 3.1, we return to the State Fair task (Figure 2.4) that Mrs. Mossotti selected for her eighth-grade students. In this activity, you will engage in solving and thinking deeply about the task. We will then look at the strategies that Mrs. Mossotti anticipated her students would use in solving the task.

Analyzing the Work of Teaching 3.1

Getting Inside a Problem

Solve the State Fair task in at least two different ways. Then consider:

- What did you need to know to solve the task?
- What do you think might be challenging for students about this task?

Getting Inside a Problem—Analysis

While there are several ways *you* might approach this problem, we will explore two possible methods here—connecting the points and finding the slope. In connecting the three given points, you would note that they all fall on the same line and that the line intersects the y-axis at (0, \$8.00). This could lead you to conclude that it costs \$8.00 to enter the fair. By comparing the two points (0, \$8.00) and (1, \$8.50) you can see that it costs 50¢ per ticket and that the equation for the line containing these four points would be $c = .50t + \$8.00$. You can then use the equation to find the cost of 4 tickets.

Alternatively you could take any two of the three given points and determine the slope of the line that contains these two points by using the slope formula, $m = \frac{(y_2 - y_1)}{(x_2 - x_1)}$. For example, if you use (1, \$8.50) and (8, \$12.00) you would get $\frac{(12 - 8.50)}{(8 - 1)}$, so m would be .50 or 50¢. You could then use the slope-intercept form of a line ($y = mx + b$) and substitute .50 for m and one of the three points for x and y to find b. This would result in the equation $y = .50x + 8$. You can then use the equation to find the cost of 4 tickets.

In order to use the first strategy (connecting the points), you would need to know that if all the points are on a line you can represent the line with the equation $y = mx + b$; that a line can be extended in either direction and the value of the point where the line intersects the y-axis is of the form $(0, y)$; that if the difference in the x-values is 1, then the difference in the y-values is the rate of change; and that m is the rate of change and b is the y-value of the y-intercept in the equation $y = mx + b$. In order to use the second strategy (finding the slope), you would need to know that the points all fall on the same line; the formula for slope; and the slope-intercept form of a line. In both of these solutions, you need to know a fair amount of algebra!

TEACHING TAKEAWAY

Exploring the ways *you* would solve the task is just the first step in anticipating! Leverage colleagues and prior student work to anticipate the various entry points and strategies your students might use.

Middle school students may be challenged by this task because they do not yet have a solid foundation in algebra that would give them access to the same methods we might gravitate to. For example, they may not realize that the y-intercept can be something other than (0, 0) and that it has meaning in this context. They may not recognize that there is a constant rate of change since the points given are not consecutive. They also may not realize that the three given points do not represent all the options for buying tickets.

Through collaboration with colleagues, Mrs. Mossotti identified several possible methods for solving the task (see Figure 3.2) that went beyond how she might have solved the task herself. Based on using a similar task last year, she expected to see some students create a table using the three points from the graph (1, \$8.50), (8, \$12.00), and (10, \$13.00) without knowing what to do next (Solution A, Figure 3.2). Mrs. Mossotti suspected that the idea of the entrance fee could be "an issue for a lot of students." As she explained, "I think when they look at, for example, 8 and 12, they might think that 12 is the cost for 8 tickets without actually reading the y-axis to realize that it's the amount that they've spent total."

In fact, she mentioned that some students might try to divide the cost by the number of tickets to find the cost per ticket, noting "this would not be correct at all, because they're going to find three different rates for tickets" (Solution B, Figure 3.2).

Figure 3.2 • Anticipated solutions to the State Fair Task generated by Mrs. Mossotti and her colleagues

A. Make a table with values from the graph

Number of Tickets	Total Spent
1	$8.50
8	$12.00
10	$13.00

Student creates a table using the information about the three points on the graph.

B. Determine different unit rates for tickets prices

$\frac{8.50}{1} = 8.50$ $\frac{12}{8} = 1.5$ $\frac{13}{10} = 1.3$

Student divides the total spent by the ticket quantity for each point on the graph and comes up with three different "unit rates."

C. Determine the price per two tickets

Student uses the points (8, 12) and (10, 13) to determine that two tickets have a cost of $1.00.

D. Connect three points with a line to determine entry fee and ticket price.

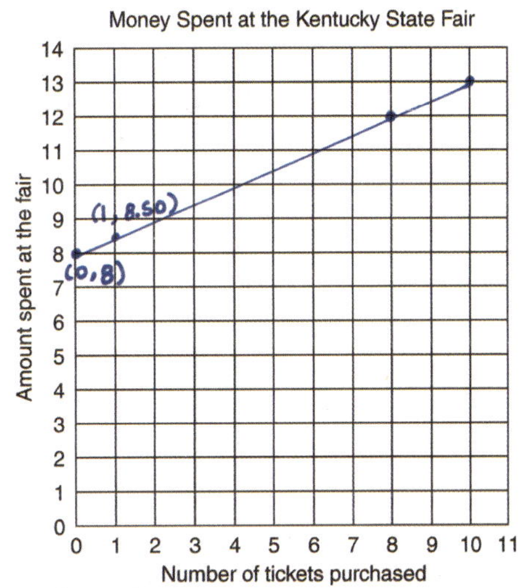

Student connects the three points on the graph with a line and sees that at the y-axis the value is $8.00 and determines that it must cost $8.00 to enter the fair without buying any tickets. Since it costs $8.50 for 1 ticket, this means it must cost 50¢ per ticket. Student sees that the line rises half a unit on the y-axis for every 1 unit on the x-axis.

E. Determine price per ticket at 50¢

Number of Tickets	Total Spent
0	$8.00
1	$8.50
2	$9.00
3	$9.50
4	$10.00
5	$10.50
6	$11.00
7	$11.50
8	$12.00
9	$12.50
10	$13.00

Student determines that the total amount spent is calculated by taking $8.00 and then repeatedly adding 50¢ depending on the number of tickets purchased.

Mrs. Mossotti also described a few other ways that students might determine the price per ticket. In one approach, students would recognize that if 8 tickets cost $12.00 and 10 tickets cost $13.00, two tickets must cost $1.00 (Solution C, Figure 3.2). Mrs. Mossotti also suggested that "some of them are going to use the fact that the graph looks like a line and connect the points and then go from there to start to figure out the price for each ticket." She anticipated that the *y*-intercept at (0, $8.00) would be particularly notable for some students, suggesting to them that the cost of 0 tickets was $8.00, and that 1 ticket was 50¢ (Solution D, Figure 3.2). Mrs. Mossotti predicted that other students might use the information given to determine the total cost for a different number of tickets, noticing the relationship between the three given points (Solution E, Figure 3.2). Throughout this process, Mrs. Mossotti and her colleagues considered in detail the different ways her students might approach the State Fair task and also the reasoning underlying the students' ideas.

Planning to Respond to Student Thinking

With your ideas about potential student solutions in mind, the next step is to think about how you will respond to students. We have found two kinds of questions to be particularly useful in supporting students' work (Figure 3.3). Assessing questions help to draw out students' thinking about a problem and are a valuable way for you to investigate what a student understands or why a student decided to take a particular approach. Rather than infer what a student is doing or thinking from glancing at their work, assessing questions prompt students to explain their reasoning to you. Franke et al. (2009) explain that such questions are important because they help teachers "to more fully understand student thinking and, therefore, to make more informed instructional decisions" (p. 390). Asking students, "Can you tell me what you did?" can often be a good initial assessing question. You can then move to more specific questions that ask students to explain particular parts of their solution strategy and will help you to confirm, for example, whether or not students understand the reasoning behind their approach.

Figure 3.3 • Key characteristics of assessing and advancing questions

ASSESSING QUESTIONS	ADVANCING QUESTIONS
• Are based closely on the work the students have produced • Clarify what the students have done and what the students understand about what they have done • Give the teacher information about what the students understand	• Use what students have produced as a basis for making progress toward the target goal of the lesson • Move students beyond their current thinking by pressing students to extend what they know to a new situation • Press students to think about something they are not currently thinking about

Source: Adapted from Smith & Stein. *5 Practices for Orchestrating Productive Mathematics Discussions – Second Edition.* Reston: VA. National Council of Teachers of Mathematics, 2018. Reprinted with permission.

Advancing questions have a different purpose. They are intended to help to move students' thinking forward toward the lesson goals. But rather than telling students what to do next, advancing questions are designed to build on what students currently understand and encourage them to "think about something they are not currently thinking about" (Smith & Stein, 2018, p. 44). Advancing questions are not designed as hints. Instead, they ask students to consider particular aspects of their solution or strategy in a new way or to consider how their strategy applies more broadly.

TEACHING TAKEAWAY

Assessing questions illuminate what a student knows; advancing questions help students extend their thinking forward toward the lesson goal.

During the anticipating stage, you will want to prepare both assessing and advancing questions that you will be able to use during instruction. One useful strategy is to prepare assessing and advancing questions for each of the student solutions that you anticipate. The assessing questions will help you establish what students know. Sometimes these questions will help confirm what you think a student is doing; other times these questions will help to clarify when the students' intentions are not clear to you. The advancing questions will help students move beyond where they currently are. This could include asking students to examine the limitations in their current approach or generalize their approach to other situations.

PAUSE AND CONSIDER

Select two solution strategies from Figure 3.2 for the State Fair task and write a few assessing questions for each approach. In addition to general questions that ask students to "Tell me what you did?" identify one or two more specific questions. Next, come up with a few advancing questions for each of the two strategies.

	Assessing Questions	Advancing Questions
Solution Strategy		
Solution Strategy		

Mrs. Mossotti created a monitoring chart (see Figure 3.4) where she listed the strategies she had anticipated and then developed assessing and advancing questions for each of the strategies in Figure 3.2 as well as for the case of students who are not able to get started with the task. (Other features of a monitoring chart, shown in Figure 3.4, will be discussed in the next section of this chapter.) For example, for Solution A in which students create a table using the points on the graph but are unsure of the next steps, her assessing questions aim to uncover what students understand about the table. The question, "Does this mean that 1 ticket has a cost of $8.50?" may help Mrs. Mossotti gain information about what the student thinks $8.50 represents. "Does this mean I can only buy 1, 8, or 10 tickets?" will help her assess whether students understand that there are other possible points on the graph (and in the table) beyond the three that were given. If students do understand that other numbers of tickets are possible, then Mrs. Mossotti will be in a good position to ask the advancing question, "What is a way to determine values that are missing from the table?" This question builds directly on the way students have chosen to organize the information in the task, while encouraging them to extend their strategy.

Consider also the assessing and advancing questions for Solution D. Here students have drawn a line through the points on the graph and determined that 0 tickets have a cost of $8.00. Mrs. Mossotti's assessing questions first ask the students about the reasonableness of this approach—she wants to understand both what the students did and what the students understand about the strategy. "Why did you draw a line?" "What does this point (the *y*-intercept) mean?" Mrs. Mossotti also has an advancing question prepared that she can use if appropriate—"How could the total amount spent for any point on the line be calculated?" This question is design specifically to build on students' recognition that the total amount increases by 50¢ for each additional ticket and that at 0 tickets the value is $8.00.

Planning to Notice Student Thinking

So far, we have focused on identifying the strategies you expect students to use in class as well as how you can respond when students use these strategies during class. The practice of anticipating also involves preparing yourself to notice what students are doing in the midst of instruction. Classrooms are often a whirlwind of activity! As the teacher, there is much for you to attend to—Are students on task? Do they have the materials they need? Are students collaborating productively? How much time is left in the period? Sherin and van Es (2009) explain that the ability to notice students' mathematical thinking in the midst of all that is taking place is a key component of teaching expertise today. In particular, teachers need

Figure 3.4 • Assessing and advancing questions developed by Mrs. Mossotti as shown in her monitoring chart

SOLUTION STRATEGY	ASSESSING QUESTIONS	ADVANCING QUESTIONS	WHO & WHAT	ORDER
Students cannot get started.	• Where on the graph do you estimate 4 tickets would be? • Let's role play, here is my wallet, and I am about to enter the state fair ... you tell me what happens and when I will need to pay money	• Is there a way to determine the actual amount spent for 4 tickets besides estimating?		
Solution A. Student creates a table using the information about the three points on the graph. Number of Tickets / Total Spent 1 / $8.50 8 / $12.00 10 / $13.00	• Does this mean you can only buy 1 ticket, 8 tickets, or 10 tickets? • Does this mean that 1 ticket has a cost of $8.50?	• What is a way to determine values that are missing from the table? • How much would 9 tickets cost? How do you know? • What if I do not buy any ride tickets? Would I need to spend any money?		
Solution B. Student divides the total spent by the ticket quantity for each point on the graph and comes up with three different "unit rates." $\frac{8.50}{1} = 8.50$ $\frac{12}{8} = 1.5$ $\frac{13}{10} = 1.3$	• So sometimes tickets have different prices? How do I get to buy the cheap ticket ... something seems funny here? • What do each of these numbers mean? • 8.5 what? For what?	• Why is one ticket so expensive but 12 tickets so cheap, for each ticket? Are they having a special sale that I do not know about? • Is there a way to use the values from each point to find out a single ticket price?		

(Continued)

Figure 3.4 (*Continued*)

SOLUTION STRATEGY	ASSESSING QUESTIONS	ADVANCING QUESTIONS	WHO & WHAT	ORDER
Solution C. Student uses the points (8, 12) and (10, 13) to determine that 2 tickets have a cost of $1.00.	• Do you have to buy tickets in pairs? • What if I only wanted one ticket; why doesn't it show 50¢ on the graph? • What exactly did you pay money for after buying 8 tickets?	• Knowing this, could you determine the cost after buying 5 tickets? 10 tickets? How?		
Solution D. Student connects the three points on the graph with a line and sees that at the *y*-axis the value is $8.00 and determines that it must cost $8.00 to enter the fair without buying any tickets. Since it costs $8.50 for 1 ticket, this means it must cost 50¢ per ticket. Student sees that the line rises half a unit on the *y*-axis for every 1 unit on the *x*-axis.	• Why did you draw a line? • What does this point (the *y*-intercept) mean? • Talk about how the graph is changing. Describe how the cost is changing.	• How could the total amount spent for any point on the line be calculated?		
Solution E. Student determines that the total amount spent is calculated by taking $8.00 and then repeatedly adding 50¢ depending on the number of tickets purchased.	• How did you know that we start with $8.00? Why not start with 12 or any other number? What does starting with $8.00 mean?	• How would your expression be different if the ticket price was 75¢. How would this be reflected on the graph?		
Other				

Source: Adapted from Smith & Stein. *5 Practices for Orchestrating Productive Mathematics Discussions, Second Edition.* Reston: VA. National Council of Teachers of Mathematics, 2018. Reprinted with permission.

to be able to sift through all the *noise* of the activity to identify what is important in what students are doing and saying.

Planning to notice involves preparing yourself to attend to those aspects of the lesson that you expect to be significant, while also being open to new ideas that might arise. Preparing a monitoring chart prior to instruction is a valuable approach for doing this (see Figure 3.4). The monitoring chart is a place where you can organize the strategies you anticipate that students will use along with the corresponding assessing and advancing questions for each strategy. Teachers often find it useful to list *Other* as a final strategy to remind them to be on the lookout for additional approaches that students might use. The monitoring chart also includes a *Who and What* column as a reminder to prepare to notice not just which strategies are being used but also who is using them. (We will discuss how to use the *Who and What* and *Order* columns in Chapters 4 and 5 respectively.) (A blank copy of the monitoring chart can be found in Appendix B.)

TEACHING TAKEAWAY

A monitoring chart helps keeps track of the work you anticipated and the questions you prepared *in advance* of the lesson but also helps you stay focused, intentional, and actively listening *during the lesson*!

In addition to preparing yourself to be aware of how students will approach the task, you may want to also identify key ideas that you think are particularly important to keep track of as the lesson unfolds. For example, as Mrs. Mossotti prepared for instruction, she had in mind a few key aspects of students' thinking that she planned to be on the lookout for. First, as stated earlier, she was concerned that students might not understand the implications of the y-intercept as representing an entry fee. Because she thought this could get in the way of students' progress on the task, she planned to be on the lookout for this issue. Second, she was curious to see if students used both tables and graphs, as she anticipated; thus this was something she was also planning to attend to during the lesson.

Jennifer Mossotti's Attention to Key Questions: Anticipating

As Mrs. Mossotti anticipated what her students would do, how she would respond to them, and what she would be on the lookout for, she kept her focus on the key questions. She approached this work by first *getting inside the problem* and identifying different solution strategies that she thought her students might use. Mrs. Mossotti then created assessing and advancing questions for each of these strategies. Her assessing questions were designed to draw out students' thinking, while the advancing questions were intended as prompts to move students' thinking forward. Finally, Mrs. Mossotti prepared herself to notice students' responses during instruction by developing a monitoring chart shown in Figure 3.4. Her monitoring chart included the key strategies she anticipated students would use, assessing and advancing questions for each, as well as a column labeled *Who and What* where she planned to record what students did in class. Let's now look at some of the key challenges teachers face as they anticipate students' responses.

Part Two: Challenges Teachers Face: Anticipating Student Responses

As we described at the beginning of the chapter, anticipating what students are likely to do in a lesson, how you will respond, and what you will keep track of during the lesson, is foundational to orchestrating productive discussions. Anticipating, however, is not without its challenges. In this section, we focus on three specific challenges associated with anticipating, shown in Figure 3.5, that we have identified from our work with teachers.

Figure 3.5 • Challenges associated with the practice of anticipating

CHALLENGE	DESCRIPTION
Moving beyond the way *you* solve a problem	Teachers often feel limited by their own experience. They know how to solve a task but may not have access to the array of strategies that students are likely to use.
Being prepared to help students who cannot get started on a task	Teachers need to be prepared to provide support to students who do not know how to begin work on the task so that they can make progress without being told exactly what to do and how.
Creating questions that move students toward the mathematical goals	The questions teachers ask need to be driven by the mathematical goals of the lesson. The focus needs to be on ensuring that students *understand* the key mathematical ideas, not just on producing a solution to the task.

Moving Beyond the Way YOU Solved the Problem

You may, at times, feel limited by your own experiences—you know one way to solve a task and cannot imagine other ways to do it. Why do you need more than one solution method? When students are presented with a high-level task, one for which "a predictable, well-rehearsed approach or pathway is not explicitly suggested by the task, task instructions, or a worked-out example" (Smith & Stein, 1998, p. 348), students must determine a course of action based on their prior knowledge and experience. Since their prior knowledge and experiences are different from yours, they are likely to think about the situation in very different ways. By anticipating what students are likely to do *prior* to a lesson, you will be better positioned to support students *during* the lesson.

In exploring this challenge, we begin by examining the eighth-grade lesson planned by Michelle Musumeci. Ms. Musumeci's students had been working with single linear equations and were just starting to focus on systems of equations. As a result of engaging in the lesson, she wanted her students to understand that:

1. there is a point of intersection between two (unique nonparallel) linear equations that represents where the two equations have the same x- and y-values; this point is the solution to the system since it satisfies both equations;
2. the two equations *switch positions* at the point of intersection and that the one that was on *top* before the point of intersection is on the *bottom* after the point of intersection because the equation with the smaller rate of change will ultimately be the equation closer to the x-axis regardless of the value of the y-intercept; and
3. tables, graphs, equations, and context can be connected by identifying the slope and y-intercept in each representational form.

Ms. Musumeci selected the Buying T-Shirts task, shown in Figure 3.6, as the main activity in the lesson because the task aligned with her lesson goals. In addition, students could draw on prior experiences with tables, graphs, and equations to enter and solve the task, and the context was one that students could relate to since about half the students in the class were on the volleyball team and they were, in fact, ordering team shirts.

Figure 3.6 • Buying T-Shirts task used in Ms. Musumeci's lesson

Buying T-Shirts

The volleyball team at Huntington wants to order t-shirts with their team name and logo. They are considering purchasing the shirts from either Crazy Tees or T-Shirts R Us. Review the information from the two companies shown below.

Crazy Tees	T-Shirts R Us
Tee shirts with your team name and logo! Only \$15.00 per shirt.	Tee shirts with your team name and logo! Only \$10.00 per shirt and a one-time charge of \$50.00 for setup.

1. When should you choose Crazy Tees?
2. When should you choose T-Shirts R Us?

Justify your decisions using tables, graph, or equations.

Source: Adapted from 2015 MARS, Shell Center, University of Nottingham.

Ms. Musumeci began the practice of anticipating by solving the task herself. She then conferred with colleagues to come up with different ways students could solve the task based on experience and what they had seen before in similar situations or previous years. Ms. Musumeci commented:

> *I've never done this task itself before, but I've done similar ones in other years. So I think as the planning process went on, as we shared the lesson plan back and forth, and we looked at the monitoring tool and all of that, more things would pop up. Every time I looked at it, another possible solution would come to me based on what somebody else had said. So I think the planning process really helped with that.*

As a result of the back-and-forth between colleagues, they came up with the set of solutions shown in Figure 3.7. While Ms. Musumeci and her colleagues recognized that the point of intersection could be found using the algebraic methods of substitution and elimination (as noted in in Figure 3.7, Solution E), there was no reason to expect that given students' prior knowledge and experience that they would have access to these methods. They knew they needed to consider strategies beyond the one that might have been most accessible to them to ensure that students had other ways of engaging with the task.

In addition to solution strategie, Ms. Musumeci and her colleagues also identified possible errors, misconceptions, and other details with which students might struggle:

- Confuse fixed and variable costs ($50n + 10$ instead of $10n + 50$)
- Add the \$50.00 charge for EACH shirt ($50n + 10n$)
- Graph cost as the independent variable and number of shirts as the dependent variable
- Create an appropriate scale (goes up high enough on the y-axis to see the point of intersection)
- Neglect the set-up fee of \$50.00 for T-Shirts R Us ($10n$)

The key factor in Ms. Musumeci's anticipating is that she did not have to *go it alone*. By working in collaboration with colleagues—who were not teachers in her school—she was able to expand on the set of ideas she was able to come up with on her own. As Ms. Musumeci explained:

> *It helps me a lot just by being able to bounce ideas off other people, because sometimes you know, being a math teacher when the math comes easily to you, you don't always think about what somebody might do if the math doesn't come easily to them. So, I think just talking it out and seeing how even another math teacher or a math coach might think about the task opens your mind to see different ways of looking at it. If you saw one way, and someone else sees another, then you start thinking, "Oh, okay, you know, maybe a student would approach it this way." So I think it helps you just see other perspectives.*

Figure 3.7 • Solutions to the Buying T-Shirts task generated by Ms. Musumeci and her colleagues

A. Table – Incremented by 5

Number of Shirts	$ Crazy Tees	$ T-Shirts R Us
5	75	100
10	150	150
15	225	200
20	300	250
25	375	300

Student concludes that the two companies charge the same amount for 10 shirts. Crazy Tees is going to be cheaper for fewer than 10 shirts and T-Shirts R Us will be cheaper for more than 10 shirts.

B. Table – Incremented by 1

Number of Shirts	$ Crazy Tees	$ T-Shirts R Us
1	15	90
2	30	70
3	45	80
4	60	90
5	75	100
6	90	110
7	105	120
8	120	130
9	135	140
10	150	150

Student makes a table and increments by 1's. He or she might stop at 9 and think that Crazy Tees is always cheaper. If he or she does not go beyond 10, he or she might not be able to tell you what happens at 11.

C. Graph – Slope Triangle

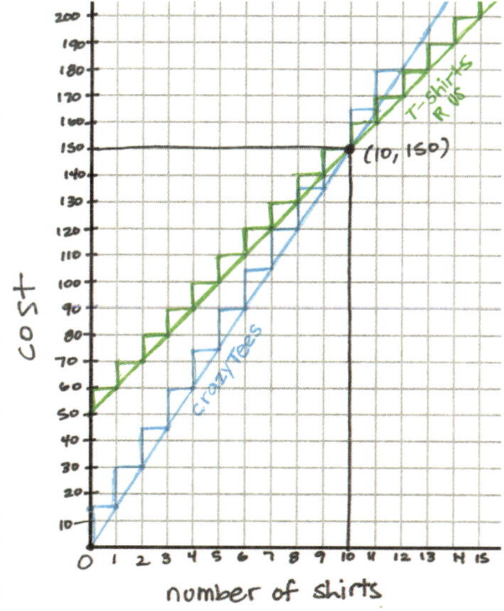

Student makes slope triangles using the *y*-intercept and the rate of change (up 10 and over 1 or up 15 over 1) to determine the point of intersection.

D. Table – Incremented by 10

Number of Shirts	$ Crazy Tees	$ T-Shirts R Us
0	0	50
10	150	150
20	250	250
30	450	350

Student concludes that Crazy Tees is better if you buy fewer than 10 shirts, but T-Shirts R Us is a better buy for 10 or more. (Student might also use another increment that does not give the point of intersection.)

(Continued)

Figure 3.7 (*Continued*)

E. Equation

Cost CT = $15n$

Cost TRU = $10n + 50$

Student first creates two equations then makes a table and/or graph.

(The point of intersection could also be found by using substitution or elimination, but student is not likely to have access to these strategies.)

F. Graph – Table

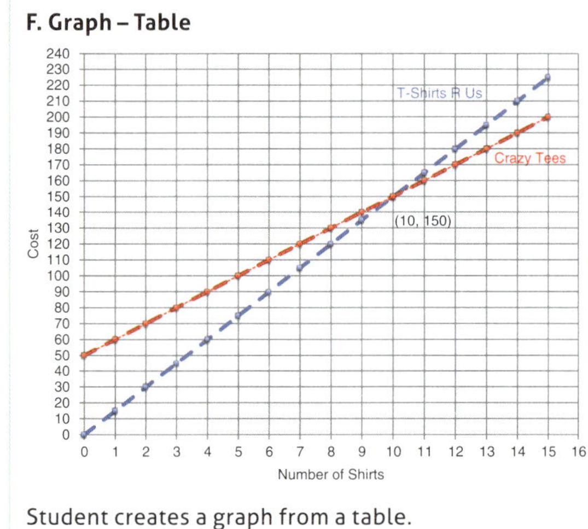

Student creates a graph from a table.

Mrs. Saroney (who we introduced in Chapter 2) echoed the value of collaboration in anticipating student solutions. She indicated that as the only sixth-grade teacher in her building, it could be difficult to find collaborators to help in this process of anticipating. In anticipating solutions for the pizza party task (see Figure 2.6), she had a few colleagues outside her school with whom to collaborate and together they came up with the set of solutions shown if Figure 3.8. In reviewing the solutions, she indicated that one of the solution paths suggested by a colleague (the ratio table in Solution D) helped explain why the standard algorithm (keep-change-flip) works. Mrs. Saroney explained that this connection was something she had not fully understood before.

Figure 3.8 • Solutions to the Pizza Party task generated by Mrs. Saroney and her colleagues

A. Visual—Double Number Line

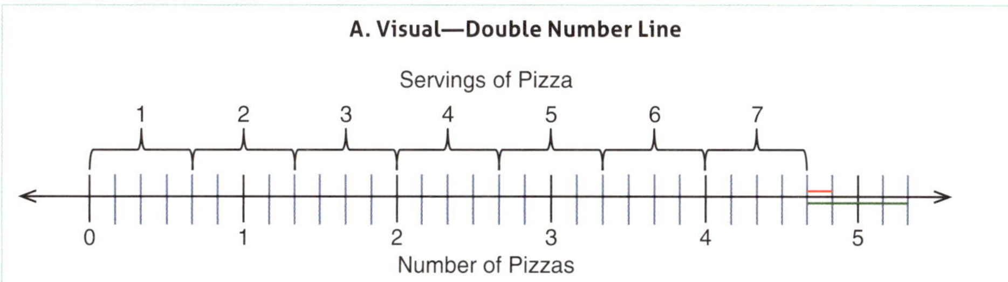

The green line is the amount it takes to make a serving and the red line is the amount left. So there are 7 full servings and $\frac{1}{4}$ of another serving.

B. Visual—Tape Diagram

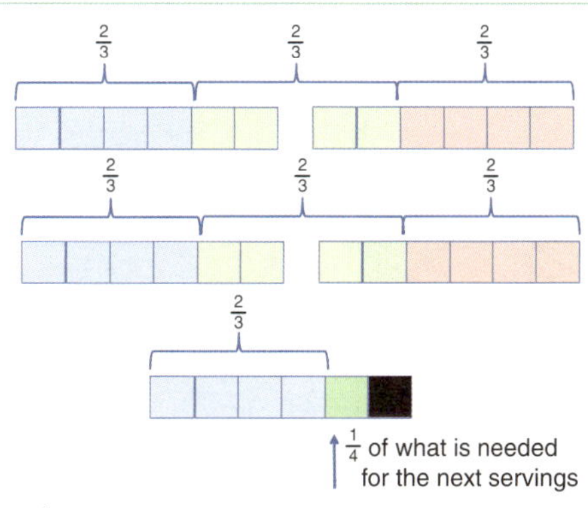

$7\frac{1}{4}$ servings

C. Numeric—Ratio Table (Pizza per Serving)

Number of Servings	1	2	3	4	5	6	7
Amount of Pizza	$\frac{2}{3}$	$1\frac{1}{3}$	2	$2\frac{2}{3}$	$3\frac{1}{3}$	4	$4\frac{2}{3}$

7 servings requires $4\frac{2}{3}$ pizzas. But you have $4\frac{5}{6}$ pizzas. So you have $\frac{1}{6}$ of a pizza left over, which is $\frac{1}{4}$ of a serving. So you have $7\frac{1}{4}$ servings.

D. Numeric—Ratio Table (Servings per Pizza)

Number of Pizzas	1	2	3	4	$4\frac{5}{6}$
Number of Servings	$1\frac{1}{2}$	3	$4\frac{1}{2}$	$6\frac{1}{2}$	$7\frac{1}{4}$

1 pizza gives you $1\frac{1}{2}$ servings, and 2 pizzas give you 3 servings, which is twice as many. So there is a pattern—you multiply the amount of pizza you have by the number of servings per pizza. This would be $4\frac{5}{6}\times1\frac{1}{2}$ or $\frac{29}{6}\times\frac{3}{2}$.
This is the traditional algorithm for dividing fractions—keep, change, flip.

(Continued)

Figure 3.8 (*Continued*)

E. Numeric – Repeated Addition and Repeated Subtraction

$\frac{2}{3}+\frac{2}{3}=\frac{4}{3}$ or $1\frac{1}{3}$ pizzas

$\frac{4}{3}+\frac{2}{3}=\frac{6}{3}$ or 2 pizzas

$\frac{6}{3}+\frac{2}{3}=\frac{8}{3}$ or $2\frac{2}{3}$ pizzas

$\frac{8}{3}+\frac{2}{3}=\frac{10}{3}$ or $3\frac{1}{3}$ pizzas

$\frac{10}{3}+\frac{2}{3}=\frac{12}{3}$ or 4 pizzas

$\frac{12}{3}+\frac{2}{3}=\frac{14}{3}$ or $4\frac{2}{3}$ pizzas

You keep adding $\frac{2}{3}$ until you use up the pizza. Since there was $4\frac{5}{6}$ pizza, you cannot get another serving once you get to $4\frac{2}{3}$ pizzas. At that point, you have added $\frac{2}{3}$ seven times. You have $\frac{1}{6}$ of the pizza that you have not used. This is $\frac{1}{4}$ of a serving.

$4\frac{5}{6}=\frac{29}{6}$

$\frac{2}{3}=\frac{4}{6}$

$\frac{29}{6}-\frac{4}{6}=\frac{25}{6}$

$\frac{25}{6}-\frac{4}{6}=\frac{21}{6}$

$\frac{21}{6}-\frac{4}{6}=\frac{17}{6}$

$\frac{17}{6}-\frac{4}{6}=\frac{13}{6}$

$\frac{13}{6}-\frac{4}{6}=\frac{9}{6}$

$\frac{9}{6}-\frac{4}{6}=\frac{5}{6}$

$\frac{5}{6}-\frac{4}{6}=\frac{1}{6}$

You subtracted $\frac{4}{6}$ seven times. So there are 7 servings. There is $\frac{1}{6}$ of a pizza left. The $\frac{1}{6}$ of a pizza represents $\frac{1}{4}$ of a serving.

F. Physical Model—Pattern Blocks

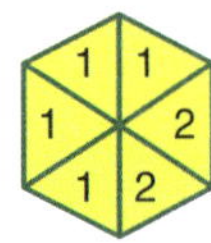

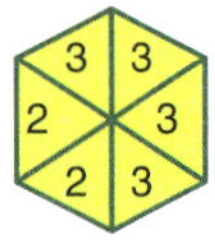

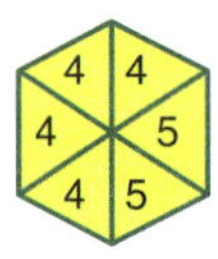

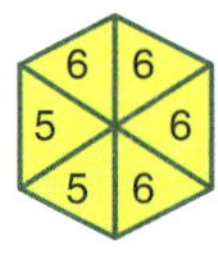

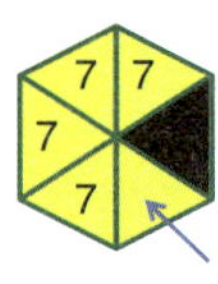

This is $\frac{1}{4}$ of a serving

Each hexagon would represent a pizza. Students might partition the hexagons into sixths using the green triangles. (Students could also partition the hexagons into thirds using the blue rhombus.) The answer is $7\frac{1}{4}$ servings.

G. Physical Model—Fraction Tiles

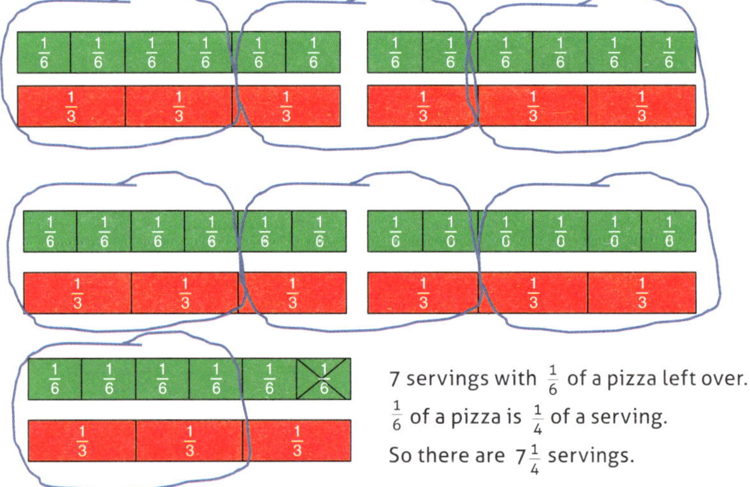

7 servings with $\frac{1}{6}$ of a pizza left over.

$\frac{1}{6}$ of a pizza is $\frac{1}{4}$ of a serving.

So there are $7\frac{1}{4}$ servings.

While Mrs. Saroney was not ready to make the connection to the algorithm in her class, and she was pretty sure students would not come up with it on their own, she explained, "So it was eye opening for me because that's one part that I struggle with as well. It's probably not going to come up today in our lesson, but we'll see." This suggests that the collaboration not only gave her additional solutions to consider but also gave her new insight into the standard algorithm and how to make sense of it. As a sixth-grade mathematics teacher who was not secondary certified, planning in collaboration with colleagues provided her an opportunity to explore the mathematics more deeply.

So what can you do to anticipate multiple possible solution paths? A first step is to consider different ways to represent the situation. The diagram shown in Figure 3.9 describes five different ways to represent a mathematical idea—visual, symbolic, verbal, contextual, or physical.

Figure 3.9 • Different ways to represent a mathematical idea

Visual
(diagrams, graphs, and pictures)

Physical
(manipulatives and models)

Symbolic
(algebraic and numeric)

Contextual

Verbal

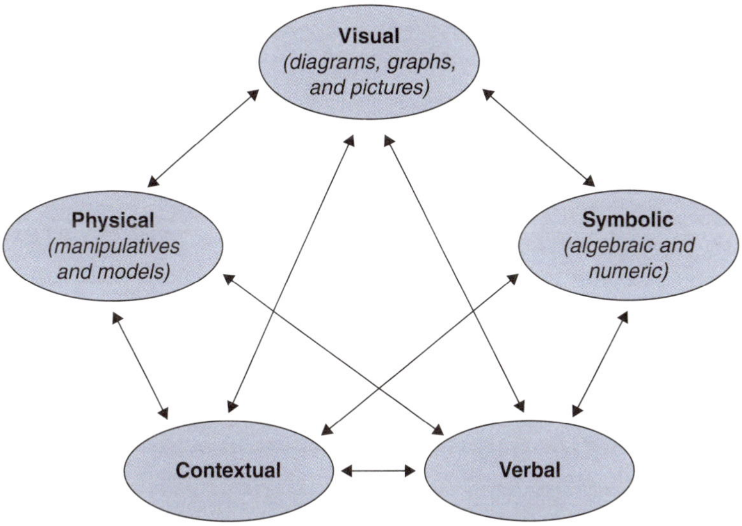

Source: Smith, Steele, Raith (2017) adapted from NCTM (2014). Reprinted with permission.

In order to illustrate how this diagram might be helpful in anticipating solution strategies, let us consider the Ice Cream Favorites task shown in Figure 3.10.

Figure 3.10 • Ice Cream Favorites task

Ice Cream Favorites

Beatriz often asks her family and friends which they like better, chocolate ice cream or vanilla ice cream. Her friends prefer vanilla ice cream to chocolate ice cream by a ratio of 3:2. If 15 of Beatriz's friends prefer vanilla ice cream, how many prefer chocolate ice cream? Explain how you know.

Source: Adapted from the Institute for Learning (2015b). Lesson guides and student workbooks available at ifl.pitt.edu.

PAUSE AND CONSIDER

How could you solve the Ice Cream Favorites task shown in Figure 3.11 using each of the representations shown in Figure 3.10?

Physical:

Verbal:

Visual:

Symbolic:

Contextual:

While your first instinct in solving this problem may have been to use a symbolic/numeric approach, there are several other ways to solve the problem as shown in Figure 3.11. The point is to think through what students might do so that you are prepared to deal with a range of different strategies that are likely to appear during the lesson. This level of anticipating will also help you think about the resources that you need to make available to students so students can pursue specific pathways. For example, if you want students to be able to create physical models of the situation, you need to provide materials they could use for this purpose. If you want students to feel free to draw pictures, you should have paper and perhaps colored pencils available for them to use. (A caution here—providing colored pencils, markers, or crayons can encourage students to turn their work into an art project. Be sure to make clear your expectations in this regard!)

Figure 3.11 • Different ways of representing the relationships in the Ice Cream Favorites task

<table>
<tr><td>Visual—Picture</td><td>Symbolic—Numeric
<table><tr><th>Vanilla</th><th>Chocolate</th><th>TOTAL</th></tr><tr><td>3</td><td>2</td><td>5</td></tr><tr><td>6</td><td>4</td><td>10</td></tr><tr><td>9</td><td>6</td><td>15</td></tr></table></td></tr>
<tr><td>Symbolic—Numeric
$\frac{2}{5} = \frac{?}{15}$
5 x 3 = 15
2 x 3 = 6</td><td>Symbolic—Numeric
$\frac{2}{5}$ $\frac{4}{10}$ $\frac{6}{15}$</td></tr>
<tr><td>Verbal—Language
If it is 3 to 2, then there are 5 people and 2 like chocolate. 15 is 3 times more than 5, so the number of chocolate must be 3 times more than 2. That means 6 who like chocolate out of 15.</td><td>Physical—Manipulatives</td></tr>
</table>

Image Source: hdere/iStock.com

While you may not be able to generate an array of strategies yourself, consider ways to collaborate with others. You may be able to work with a colleague who teaches the same grade level or a different grade level, in or outside of your building. If you do not have math-teacher colleagues to help generate and discuss an expanded set of solutions to a particular task, consider one of the following options:

- Ask your friends (either face-to-face or virtually) to solve the task. Adults who are not mathematics teachers often produce solutions that approximate what students will do!
- Post a question on www.my.nctm.org or other social media outlets. This will give you access to a community of educators, many of whom will be eager to respond!
- Take photos of solutions students produce to a particular task the first time you teach it, and add to it every time you use the same task. Over time, you will have a robust collection of approaches to consider as you prepare for subsequent lessons. (This will also be a great resource to share with colleagues who are using the task for the first time.)

Being Prepared to Help Students Who Cannot Get Started

Regardless of how carefully you set up or launch the lesson, there is often a student who is unsure how to begin the task. Smith, Steele, and Raith (2017) argue,

> *when a student can't get started on a problem, it generally is not because he or she has no relevant knowledge to bring to bear on the situation. More often, the student, for some reason, is unable to connect what he or she does know with the task at hand. (p. 187)*

This could be due to a reading comprehension issue, lack of familiarity with the context of the problem, or a lack of confidence in their ability to engage with a task for which a strategy is not provided.

TEACHING TAKEAWAY

Be prepared to help students who do not know how to get started on a problem by eliciting what they understand about the task rather than by suggesting specific steps to try or by having another student show them what to do.

Common approaches to this challenge include suggesting a strategy for the student to use or pairing the student with a student who knows how to begin. While these approaches give the student something to do, they provide you with no insight regarding what the student understands about the task, do nothing to build the student's capacity to persevere in the face of struggle, and probably add to the student's perception of him- or herself as someone who cannot do mathematics. When students move forward based on someone else's thinking, it is unlikely that they will be able to retain and appropriately use a strategy they do not understand. Therefore, it is critical to have a plan in place regarding how to support students who struggle to get started.

PAUSE AND CONSIDER

What questions could you ask a student who could not begin the Buying T-Shirts task (Figure 3.6)?

Ms. Musumeci anticipated that some students in her class might have trouble getting started on the task, so she planned questions that would provide her with insight regarding what students understood about the problem context. She planned to begin by asking students, "What do you know about each T-shirt company?" She hoped to hear students mention such things as "there are two companies," "they charge different amounts," "one company has a setup fee and one does not," "one charges $15.00 per shirt and the other charges $10.00," and "the one with cheaper shirts has a setup fee." From here, she planned to ask students, "How much would one shirt cost from each company?" If the students could answer this correctly, she would then inquire about the cost of two shirts. Once the students had demonstrated a basic understanding of how the price of shirts could be determined, she planned to leave them with an advancing question, "Can you continue to find the cost for different numbers of shirts and look for a pattern?"

The goal is to be able to support students' productive struggle—finding ways to support students so that they can move forward on their own steam. Warshauer (2015) argues while telling students what to do or providing them with directed guidance helps them to move forward, it tends to lower the cognitive demand of the task and limit students' opportunities to learn.

Creating Questions That Move Students Toward the Mathematical Goal

The questions that teachers ask students during a lesson need to be driven by the mathematical goals. You need to first determine what students know in comparison to what you ultimately want them to learn and then ask questions that move them toward the goal. You will not ask all students the same set of questions because they are not all thinking about the problem in the same way, and your questions will be driven by the different solutions they have produced. As Ms. Musumeci commented:

> *I think being specific about my goals helps me to think about where I want students to go so it's always in my mind. This is what I want students to know by the time they leave this lesson, and it helps me as I'm preparing my assessing and advancing questions, to be thinking about what students might do and how do I move them toward those goals.*

In preparation for her lesson, Ms. Musumeci created a series of assessing and advancing questions that she planned to ask her students, based on the strategies she anticipated they would use (see Figure 3.7).

PAUSE AND CONSIDER

Review Strategies A and C in Figure 3.7. What questions could you plan to ask students who produced these solutions, given the lesson goals?

Two of the solutions that Ms. Musumeci anticipated students would use, and the questions she planned to ask about those solutions, are shown in Figure 3.12. The first assessing question she plans to ask each student is, "Can you tell me about your ___?" By asking this question (or some variant), the teacher is honoring student's thinking by giving the student the opportunity to explain what they have done, not assuming that she knows what the student is thinking, and laying the foundation on which to build subsequent questions. The remaining assessing questions are intended to elicit more details on what the student understands about the solution they have produced should they be needed.

Even if a student produces the table incremented by 5 (Solution A in Figure 3.7) and determines a correct and complete solution, Ms. Musumeci will be interested in what this student *understands* and would not equate answering the questions posed in the task with understanding. Toward this end, she plans to ask the student three questions, each of which corresponds to the goals she had targeted in the lesson. Specifically:

- *How did you calculate the values in the table?* By asking this question the teacher is trying to get the student to verbally articulate a process that can ultimately be used to generate an equation. She might expect the student to say something similar to "I multiplied the number of shirts by 15" and "I multiplied the number of shirts by 10 and added 50." Getting the student to be explicit about what he or she did, and perhaps even write it down, will help the student in writing an equation—a first step toward Goal 3 (connecting tables, graphs, equations, and context).

- *How did you determine that T-Shirts R Us is cheaper after 10 shirts?* and *What happens before 10 shirts? At 10 shirts?* These questions go directly to how the student is making sense of the information generated in the table. Here, the teacher is looking for the student to recognize that the point of intersection is the point after which the company that was initially cheaper becomes more expensive. This is directly related to Goal 1 (the meaning of the point of intersection) and Goal 2 (the two equations *switch positions* at the point of intersection).

Armed with answers to these questions, Ms. Musumeci is then positioned to advance the student by asking him or her to consider two additional representations—the graph and the equation—that are needed to reach Goal 3 (making connections). What is interesting is that the teacher did not plan to ask the student to produce the graph but rather what it would look like. Based on what the student described happening before, at, and after 10 shirts, this should be within reach and will provide more insight into what the student understands about plotting a set of points. Also planning to ask the student to write an equation prompts the student to reflect on how she created the values in the table and to use this description to write the equation.

Figure 3.12 • Two strategies and related questions Ms. Musumeci anticipated

STRATEGY	ASSESSING QUESTIONS	ADVANCING QUESTIONS
Table: Student creates a table with increments of 5 and notes that both companies charge the same amount for 10 shirts, that Crazy Tees is cheaper for fewer than 10 shirts, and that T-Shirts R Us will be cheaper for more than 10 shirts.	• Can you tell me about your table? • How did you calculate the values in the table? • How did you determine that T-Shirts R Us is cheaper after 10 shirts? • What happens before 10 shirts? At 10 shirts?	• What do you think the graph of these data would look like? • You indicated that you calculated the values in the table by doing ______. Can you write an equation from this description?
Graph: Student creates a table, plots points, and finds the point of intersection.	• Can you tell me about your graph? • Why did you choose to make a graph? • What information does it give you? • How can you use your graph to help you answer the questions?	• Can you explain your answer to the questions using both the table and the graph? • How does your graph connect to your table? • Can you explain what the point of intersection means in the context of the problem?

The graph (Solution C in Figure 3.7) would likewise be an accurate answer that provides valuable information. However, a student who answers this way has not yet used the information to answer the questions regarding when you would choose each company. Hence, here, the assessing questions focus on why the student chose that graph, what information it provides, and how the graph can help answer the questions. In this situation, the goals are addressed directly in the planned advancing questions. Specifically:

- *Can you explain your answer to the questions using both the table and the graph?* If the student produced both a graph and a table (although we only see the graph), the teacher could press the student to explain how he or she could make decisions about choosing a company using either representation. This begins to get at Goal 3 (making connections).
- *How does your graph connect to your table?* This is explicitly about Goal 3 and should be answerable based on the student response to the first advancing question.
- *Can you explain what the point of intersection means in the context of the problem?* This question gets directly at Goal 1 (meaning of point of intersection) and also Goal 3 (making connections).

TEACHING TAKEAWAY

Posing questions carefully crafted around your lesson's mathematical goals *and* students' work will tell you what students understand, not just how well they perform.

The bottom line is that the lesson goals need to drive the questions you ask. If your goal is for students to understand a mathematical relationship, then the questions you ask need to focus on getting students to recognize and articulate the relationship. Being satisfied with an answer such as "Crazy Tees is cheaper before 10 shirts and T-Shirts R Us is cheaper after 10" without further probing tells you nothing about what the student understands. Some students are good at finding answers but do not know why they are doing it or what it means.

It is important to note that while the teacher establishes specific learning goals for the lesson, students will be at different places in their learning based on their prior knowledge and experiences. Therefore students are asked questions that help them make progress *toward* the goals based on their current understanding. All students may not enter the whole class discussion having made the same amount of progress on the task. This is not imperative. What is important is that the conversation provides the opportunity for students to extend and solidify their own understandings. The discussion should provide an opportunity for learning, not just a chance for students to report out what they have done.

Conclusion

In this chapter, we explored the components of the practice of *anticipating* and focused on a set of challenges that teachers often face when engaging in this practice. Anticipating is critical to planning a lesson because it provides the teacher with the opportunity to think deeply about what students are likely to do and how they will respond. This in-advance-of-the-lesson thinking eliminates much of the on-the-fly decision-making that often is required in teaching. While you may not be able to anticipate everything that students will do, our experience tells us that you can anticipate much of what will happen, especially if you do not plan alone.

Mrs. Mossotti's work on anticipating provides insight into what a teacher needs to consider as he or she engages in the process. In planning her lesson, Mrs. Mossotti thought deeply about what students were likely to do when presented with the task, including identifying aspects of the task she thought would be challenging for students, and the questions that she would ask students to assess their thinking and to move them toward the goals of the lesson. In addition, she identified specific aspects of student thinking that she planned to be on the lookout for during the lesson. This level of preparation before the lesson is likely to have a positive impact on the quality of the lesson itself because she has thought deeply about the mathematics she wants students to learn, the task, and what her students are bringing to the task.

By examining the work of Ms. Musumeci around the Buying T-Shirts task, we saw that, while there are challenges associated with anticipating, collaborating with colleagues can go a long way in addressing the challenges. Ms. Musumeci work also makes clear how important it is to never lose sight of the lesson goals—they should serve as a resource throughout the lesson and a way of evaluating students' learning.

Anticipating Student Responses—Summary

Video Clip 3.1

To hear and see more about anticipating student thinking and using the monitoring tool to plan your responses, watch Video Clip 3.1

Videos may also be accessed at
resources.corwin.com/5practices-middleschool

We now invite you to apply what you have learned from your work in this chapter to your own teaching practice by engaging in the Connecting to Your Classroom activity. We encourage you to find one or more colleagues with whom to collaborate on this activity. As one teacher commented, "A best practice for anticipating strategies for a specific task is to sit with a team of teachers to identify all of the possible inroads, rather than completing this as a teacher in isolation" (Smith & Stein, 2018, p. 49).

Linking the Five Practices to Your Own Instruction

ANTICIPATING

Identify a mathematical idea that you plan to teach sometime in the next two weeks.

1. Specify a clear goal for student learning and select a high-level task that is aligned with your learning goal.
2. Anticipate—get inside the problem, plan to respond, and plan to notice. If possible, get input from colleagues either virtually or face-to-face to gain additional insights into the task, its solutions, and its challenges.
3. Create assessing and advancing questions that are driven by your goals for the lesson but build on where students are in their thinking.
4. Produce a monitoring chart you can use to record data during the lesson that includes possible solutions, assessing and advancing questions that are driven by your goals, and questions you can ask students who cannot get started.

> “I’ve learned a lot about myself as a teacher. For example, when you’re trying to move a student forward toward the goal and they’re struggling, how do you get them there without giving them the answer? Focusing on the assessing and advancing questions, figuring out what they know, and then letting them think and kind of grapple with the idea—that has really been the biggest shift in my mind.”

—MICHELLE MUSUMECI, EIGHTH-GRADE TEACHER

CHAPTER 4

Monitoring Student Work

The next practice we explore is monitoring students' work. Having carefully selected a goal and corresponding task, and anticipated the different strategies students will use, we now turn to instruction. How do you, as the teacher, keep track of what students are doing and saying, as the lesson unfolds in your classroom? Monitoring involves paying close attention to students' ideas and methods as they relate to your goals for the lesson. With many students working at the same time, this can be quite challenging. Who is using what strategy? How far did they get? Monitoring also involves asking students questions both to clarify their thinking and to move their thinking forward. Interacting with students during instruction in ways that productively move the lesson forward is complex work. The practice of monitoring is designed to help you manage this complexity by having a clear, focused lens for attending to and keeping track of students' thinking.

Smith and Stein (2018) describe monitoring in the following way:

> *Monitoring is the process of paying attention to the thinking of students during the actual lesson as they work individually or collectively on a particular task. This involves not just listening in on what students are saying and observing what they are doing, but also keeping track of the approaches that they are using, identifying*

> *those that can help advance the mathematical discussion later in the lesson, and asking questions that will help students make progress on the task. This is the time when the assessing and advancing questions that you created prior to the lesson will come in handy. These questions include those that will make students, thinking explicit, get students back on track if they are following an unproductive or inaccurate pathway, and will press students who are on the right course to think more deeply about why things work the way that they do. (p. 54)*

In this chapter, we first describe key aspects of monitoring and illustrate what this practice looks like in an authentic middle school classroom. We then discuss what aspects of monitoring are challenging for teachers and provide an opportunity for you to explore monitoring in your own teaching practice.

Part One: Unpacking the Practice: Monitoring Student Work

What is involved in monitoring students' thinking? This practice involves tracking the thinking of students in your class and asking questions to uncover what students understand (assessing questions) and to move students' thinking forward (advancing questions). Figure 4.1 highlights the key components of this practice.

Figure 4.1 • Key questions that support the practice of monitoring students' responses

WHAT IT TAKES	KEY QUESTIONS
Tracking student thinking	How will you keep track of students' responses during the lesson?
	How will you ensure that you check in with all students during the lesson?
Assessing student thinking	Are your assessing questions meeting students where they are?
	Are your assessing questions making student thinking visible?
Advancing student thinking	Are your advancing questions driven by your lesson goals?
	Are students able to pursue advancing questions on their own?
	Are your advancing questions helping students to progress?

In the next sections, we illustrate the practice of monitoring by continuing our investigation of Mrs. Mossotti's implementation of the State Fair task. As you view video clips from her class and read the descriptions of what took place, consider how Mrs. Mossotti's attention to the key questions may have shaped her teaching.

Tracking Student Thinking

Once your students begin working on the task, you will want an efficient and productive way to follow what they are doing. Who is making progress? Who has questions? Who is feeling stuck? Tracking the diversity of students' thinking during instruction is complex work. Kazemi, Gibbons, Lomax, and Franke (2016) emphasize that it is not sufficient to wait for students to complete the task to check their progress. Instead, teachers need a way to "gain insight into student thinking that [is] manageable" during "face-to-face conversations with students" during class (p. 184).

The monitoring chart you developed during the anticipating phase can be a valuable resource for tracking student thinking. As you observe and talk with your students, you can quickly note what strategy students are using and record it in the *Who and What* column of your monitoring chart. This is where listing the anticipated strategies on your monitoring chart really comes in handy! You may also want to note anything particularly interesting that a student is doing—a question or variation in a strategy or a connection between two strategies, for example. Indicating when students are using a strategy that was not anticipated is equally important, both for the day's lesson and for the future, particularly if those strategies have the potential to illuminate the mathematical goals of the lesson. There is typically little time to make elaborate comments on the monitoring chart during instruction. Still, making some notes throughout the lesson can help you stay abreast of what is happening. Many teachers chose to print their monitoring chart before the lesson and take notes by hand as the lesson progresses. Others prefer to annotate an electronic version of the monitoring chart during instruction. Either way, the monitoring chart can help you quickly reference how students are thinking about the task.

TEACHING TAKEAWAY

Taking quick notes on your monitoring chart can help you track which students use which strategies.

As you track students' responses, you want to make sure that you are circulating throughout the classroom. Some teachers opt to move in a designated pattern around the room as a way to ensure they check in with each student during the lesson. Having students work in groups can increase collaboration and make it easier to touch base with more than one student at a time (Horn, 2012). Using the monitoring chart can help you keep track of which students you have spoken with as well as how many times you have visited each group. It may be hard, at times, to pull yourself away from a group that is having a particularly interesting discussion. Or you may find yourself spending extra time with students who are having trouble getting started with the task. In either case, making a plan for how you will circulate among and keep track of students as you monitor their thinking is an important consideration. Mrs. Mossotti explained that creating the monitoring chart is an

TEACHING TAKEAWAY

Using the monitoring chart can also help you track your interaction with students, both in terms of what students are doing and with whom you have spoken.

important part of her planning, and using it during instruction is a key part of how she teaches. "As I'm walking around, I'll write down which groups do what, who struggles, and where students are thinking about it differently than everybody else." Electronic teacher dashboards can also be a resource as you monitor student thinking. For example, the Desmos platform allows teachers quick access to individual student's work on the graphing calculator and geometry tool (Danielson & Meyer, 2016). This can provide valuable information about how individual students approach the task and can help you decide who you might need to talk with as you make your way around the room.

How do you track students' ideas during instruction?

How do you circulate among your students as they are working?

What techniques might help you more effectively track student thinking in your classroom?

Assessing Student Thinking

As you monitor students' progress, you want to interact with students in ways that take them from where they are now and move them toward the lesson goals. Jacobs and Philipp (2010) highlight the importance of this goal when they explain that teaching that "builds on children's ways of thinking can lead to rich instructional environments and gains in student achievement" (p. 101).

To start, be on the lookout for those strategies that you anticipated that students might use. Once you recognize that a student is using one of the anticipated approaches, you can examine the assessing questions you designed for that approach. The assessing (and advancing) questions in the monitoring chart are not meant to be a script. Rather, they are intended as a reference for you to use to help you consider what questions you want to ask particular students. For example, when Mrs. Mossotti sees a student making a table, she does not automatically ask, "Does this mean you can only buy 1 ticket, 8 tickets, or 10 tickets?" Instead, she looks at what this particular student is doing or saying and decides what question is appropriate to ask.

When selecting an assessing question to use in class, there are two main considerations. First, aim to meet students where they are in their current thinking about the task. Ball, Lubienski, and Mewborn (2001) emphasize that "sizing up students' thinking and responding" depends on the details of what a student is doing (p. 451). Be sure to ask about the students' ideas, about what they have written or drawn. Using students' own terminology can often be helpful. Be aware that what you anticipated students might do is not always what they end up doing. Asking students specific questions about their work is an important way to uncover how they are thinking about the task and their solution. As Mrs. Mossotti explained,

> *I [anticipate] all of these very clean solution paths. They'll either make a table, or they will do the set of operations. But then, in real life, when I actually sit down and see what they're producing, the work is all over the place or it's part of this path [and] part of this path. So even though I anticipated certain solution paths, [it doesn't usually look like that].*

Assessing questions are important because they can help you uncover what students are doing, whether or not that aligns with what you anticipated.

TEACHING TAKEAWAY

Look and listen *carefully.* Modify your planned assessing questions in real time based specifically on what the students are doing and saying, rather than what you thought they would do or say.

Second, assessing questions are most useful when they make students' thinking visible in ways that can then help you move their thinking forward toward the lesson goals. You want to understand not only *what* a student did but *why*. Understanding the reasons behind a student's strategy often provides the clues you need to help the student reconsider her position or move deeper into the task.

What does this look like in practice? In Analyzing the Work of Teaching 4.1, you will explore how students in Mrs. Mossotti's class begin to make sense of the first part of the State Fair problem. We encourage you to view the clip and consider the questions posed before you read our analysis.

Analyzing the Work of Teaching 4.1

Exploring Student Problem-Solving Approaches

Video Clip 4.1

After introducing the State Fair problem, students begin to work on the task in small groups. In this video clip, you will briefly drop in on two groups of students as they explore the first question posed in the problem: *After entering the fair, you decide to buy 4 ride tickets. What will be your cost for attending the fair? How do you know?* Crispin and Nazier are in the first group, and Nietzsche, Ejub, and AJ are in the second group.

As you watch Video Clip 4.1, consider the following questions:

1. What strategies are students using? Can you identify each strategy as one listed on Mrs. Mossotti's monitoring chart? (See Figure 3.4.)
2. What does each group understand about the cost of four ride tickets?
    - For Group 1, how did Crispin decide that the total cost for four tickets would be $10.00?
    - For Group 2, what is Ejub referring to when he mentions $3.50?
3. What assessing questions would you want to ask each group of students to be sure that you understand their reasoning about the problem?

Videos may also be accessed at **resources.corwin.com/5practices-middleschool**

Exploring Student Problem-Solving Approaches—Analysis

The first part of the video clip shows Crispin and Nazier working together. Crispin reads the first question out loud, and then he proceeds to estimate the amount spent after purchasing 4 tickets by looking at the points given on the graph. He says, "When they spent $13.00 at the fair, that matched up with 10 tickets." He shows this by pointing with one hand to the 10 on the x-axis (number of tickets purchased) and with the other hand to 13 on the y-axis (amount spent at the fair). He also notes that with $13.00, they bought 8 tickets and that "there's a pattern." Crispin then moves his pencil along an imaginary line on the graph. This seems to reflect Strategy E in Mrs. Mossotti's monitoring chart (Figure 3.4) of students drawing a line through the points. Rather than use this to determine that 0 tickets costs $8.00 however, Crispin notes that 4 tickets will cost $10.00. What might we want to ask Crispin and Nazier to check so that we are understanding their approach correctly? One possible assessing question might be to ask, "How did you come up with $10.00 for 4 tickets?"

In the second group, we hear Nietzsche and Ejub counting. AJ is also in the group, remaining quiet although attentive during the exchange. Nietzsche says, "$8.00, $8.50, $1.00, $1.50, $2.00, $2.50." Then Ejub says, "This is what I did. If it was 50 for everyone, 50¢, I was just doing 50, 100, 150, 200, 250, 300, 350." This is followed by Nietzsche commenting that "The difference between *this* and *that* is $3.50, so they must have spent $3.50 on tickets. Now we know how much the entry fee is." One possible explanation of these comments is that Ejub has noticed a pattern that for every 1 ticket increase, the total cost goes up by 50¢ and that Nietzsche recognized that the difference in price between purchasing 1 ticket at $8.50 and 8 tickets at $12.00 is $3.50. Still, there is much that remains unclear. Does Ejub believe that the total cost for attending the fair is 50¢ a ticket? Why does Nietzsche start counting at $8.00 and then shift to $1.00? This can be a great deal to process in the moments of instruction. Effective assessing questions help students articulate their thinking and give you insight into how they are making sense of the task. What might we want to ask Nietzsche and Ejub to help them reveal their ideas to us? Potential assessing questions for Ejub include, "Can you tell me why you are counting by 50?" "What do you mean when you said '50¢ for everyone?'" Assessing questions for Nietzsche might include, "You said 'the difference between this and that is $3.50.' Can you tell me what *this* and *that* is?" "What did you mean when you said, 'They spent $3.50 on tickets?'"

In Analyzing the Work of Teaching 4.2, you will investigate what Mrs. Mossotti does to support her students as they work on the task.

Analyzing the Work of Teaching 4.2

Assessing Student Thinking

Video Clip 4.2

As students worked on the State Fair problem, Mrs. Mossotti circulated around the room checking in with each group. In this video clip, she first talks briefly with Serenity and Adnawmy and then talks with Crispin and Nazier about the progress they are making.

As you watch Video Clip 4.2, consider the following questions:

1. What assessing questions does Mrs. Mossotti ask the students?
2. How do her assessing questions help Mrs. Mossotti make sense of how the students are thinking about the problem? How do her assessing questions help Mrs. Mossotti diagnose challenges the students are facing?

Videos may also be accessed at **resources.corwin.com/5practices-middleschool**

Assessing Student Thinking—Analysis

As Mrs. Mossotti approaches Serenity and Adnawmy, she notices that they have not gotten started. She uses a series of assessing questions to try to figure out what they are finding challenging. When Serenity comments, "It's hard," Mrs. Mossotti asks, "What do you mean?" offering Serenity an opportunity to say more about what is hard. In responding, Serenity states, "I don't know how much one ticket is." Mrs. Mossotti has now gone from knowing nothing about why the students have not been able to get started to knowing something important about a challenge Serenity is having interpreting the graph. Mrs. Mossotti's next assessing question involves directing Serenity to the point (1, 8.50) on the graph and asking, "This one is not the cost for one ticket then?" In doing so, Mrs. Mossotti makes an effort to unpack further how Serenity understands the graph. When

Serenity continues to be confused, Mrs. Mossotti draws on the assessing question she had prepared in case students had trouble getting started. "Give me an estimation for these four ride tickets?" Again, Mrs. Mossotti's goal here is to explore how Serenity understands the graph.

As Mrs. Mossotti talks with Crispin and Nazier, she asks several assessing questions to better understand their thinking. First, looking at the points they have drawn on the graph, she asks, "How do you know that these [points] go here?" and follows up with, "What's the pattern that you're noticing?" Crispin explains that they are noticing a pattern with even numbers of tickets—"That it skips two boxes and goes down." Mrs. Mossotti next turns to Nazier and asks, "Where are other points [on the graph] based on this pattern that Crispin's noticing?" After Nazier indicates one point on the graph, Mrs. Mossotti further assesses their understanding by asking about the total cost for an odd number of tickets. "How would you know where the points are for, like 7 or for 3?" Throughout this discussion, Mrs. Mossotti's questions aim to uncover the students' thinking—she is not asking them to think differently, rather her goal is to better understand how they have approached the problem. Having assessed their understanding, Mrs. Mossotti notes in her monitoring chart that "Crispin and Nazier see a pattern of even ticket amounts increasing by $1.00."

It is worth noting that in her conversation with students, Mrs. Mossotti does not always use the assessing questions she had prepared in advance word-for-word, and in addition, she also uses several assessing questions that she had not prepared in advance. This is to be expected! Developing assessing questions prior to instruction helped Mrs. Mossotti get her head around how she might draw out students' thinking in specific cases. In the moment, however, as she interacts with students, she also develops new questions based on what students are doing and saying.

Advancing Student Thinking

Once you have an idea of how students are thinking about the problem, the next step is to advance their thinking. For some students this might involve helping them reconsider what the task is asking them to do. For others students, it might mean encouraging them to consider a special case or pressing them to be able to explain why an approach was successful. Once again, your monitoring chart can be a resource as you decide how to help move students' thinking forward, as you select from or adapt the assessing questions you anticipated earlier.

As you choose an advancing question to use, you want to make sure that the question is driven by your goals for the lesson, and not just a way to help students produce an accurate solution. For example, for the State Fair task, Mrs. Mossotti's goal is not simply for students to identify that the total cost for 4 tickets is \$10.00; her goal is for them to do so in a way that relates to exploring the meaning of the y-intercept in context. Similarly, Ms. Musumeci explained that moving away from questions that focus on the answers to questions that focus on her goals "has really been the biggest shift in my mind" as she has become comfortable using the five practices in her teaching. As you select advancing questions, you will want to keep your goals for the lesson clearly in mind.

Another important feature of advancing questions is that they usually cannot be answered immediately. Mrs. Mossotti explained, "I think if they can answer it very quickly, it probably was not an advancing question." Instead, an effective advancing question should prompt students to think, explore, or reconsider ideas about the task. Mrs. Mossotti continued,

> *I'm hoping that after I pose the question, they have to stop and think about it, or do a little bit of work, or have a little conference with the other students they're working with where I can go in, monitor what the other groups are doing, and then come back to them.*

TEACHING TAKEAWAY

You can often gauge the effectiveness of advancing questions by noticing whether students immediately begin to explore it!

This ability for students to pursue an advancing question is key. Thus, as you pose advancing questions, you will want to gauge students' initial reaction. Do they begin working? Can you see them thinking, mulling something over? Do they ask each other questions? Mrs. Saroney suggested that when "they kind of stop and think, there's kids that ... you can see the wheels turning in their head and they might go and try something. That's when I know that they were ready for that [advancing question]."

Of course, what is most essential is that your advancing questions prompt students to move forward in their thinking. After you ask an advancing question, you will want to give students time to work but will also want to check back in with the group to see how they have progressed. Ms. Musumeci explained that in her experience,

> *I think you need to leave the students to think for a while and then go back and see what they've come up with. If they're still stuck, maybe that wasn't the right advancing question, and you need to try another one. And if they have moved forward, then possibly, you can move them forward even further, or you could ask more assessing questions to see what their thinking is at this point.*

While advancing questions are designed to help students make progress, it is important that you take time during the lesson to check whether or not they have successfully done so.

What does this look like in practice? In Analyzing the Work of Teaching 4.3, you will explore how Mrs. Mossotti's use of advancing questions helps students make progress on the State Fair problem. We encourage you to view the clip and consider the questions posed before you read the analysis.

Analyzing the Work of Teaching 4.3

Advancing Student Thinking

Video Clip 4.3

Now you will investigate Daejhor, Razaria, and Mya's work on the State Fair task.

First, take a look at Daejhor's initial written work. What can you infer about how he might be thinking about the total cost for 4 tickets?

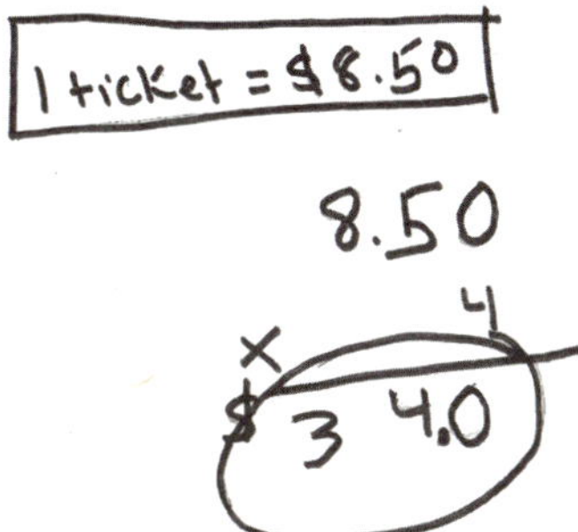

Next, watch Video Clip 4.3 in which Mrs. Mossotti visits Daejhor, Razaria, and Mya's group.

As you watch the clip, consider the following questions:

1. What advancing questions does Mrs. Mossotti ask the students? What goals were the advancing questions targeting?
2. Is there evidence that the advancing questions can or cannot be pursued by the students?

Videos may also be accessed at **resources.corwin.com/5practices-middleschool**

Advancing Student Thinking—Analysis

Daejhor's written work indicates that the cost for 1 ticket is $8.50 along with the problem "8.50 × 4 = 34.0." This may be evidence that Daejhor believes the cost of 4 tickets can be determined by multiplying the cost of 1 ticket by 4.

As Mrs. Mossotti approaches Daejhor, Razaria, and Mya, the students state, "We are kind of confused." Mrs. Mossotti begins by assessing their understanding. Daejhor explains that they know that the total cost for 1 ticket is $8.50, and if they "add all that up" the cost for 4 tickets is $34.00. Mrs. Mossotti then asks them to compare where $34.00 would be on the graph and where they estimate the total cost of 4 tickets would be, given the other points on the graph. At this time, she seems to be continuing to assess their understanding of the situation, trying to understand what it is that they are confused about. When she asks Daejhor, "What is your brain thinking?" he responds with, "I'm thinking this is wrong." Mrs. Mossotti is then ready to try to advance the students' thinking and she asks, "Why is this [34] so much higher than this 10 you're thinking over here when you are looking at this graph? I want you guys to figure that out."

As Mrs. Mossotti leaves the group, there is some evidence that they are able to start exploring the question on their own. We see the students grab their pencils, look at the graph, and Daejhor begins to restate the dilemma that "for 1 ticket apparently the cost is $8.50. …"

While not shown on the video clip, after Mrs. Mossotti left the group, Daejhor, Razaria, and Mya continued to discuss the cost for 4 tickets and ultimately concluded that the total cost for 4 tickets is $10.00. Daejhor later explains,

> *At first. … I had looked at the price of just 1 ticket, and then we times that by 4 [and] got. … $34.00, which was a lot of money, and it wasn't even on the graph. What I did was I took my ruler, I drew a line, and I made sure I landed [on] the points.*

Jennifer Mossotti's Attention to Key Questions: Monitoring

Once students begin working on a task, it is essential that the teacher carefully monitor their progress. To do this, Mrs. Mossotti tracks her students' thinking by paying close attention to what her students do and say. Because she has already listed the strategies she anticipated students will use on her monitoring chart, she can quickly note who is doing what as she circulates throughout the classroom. Using assessing and advancing questions allows Mrs. Mossotti to draw out and make sense of students' ideas, as well as to try to move students' thinking forward.

We now take a look at key challenges teachers face as they monitor students' progress during instruction.

Part Two: Challenges Teachers Face: Monitoring Student Work

Although you can prepare for monitoring prior to the lesson by setting goals, selecting a high-level task, and anticipating what students will do and how you will respond, as we discussed in Part One, monitoring occurs *during* instruction. Collecting as much information as you can about what students are doing and thinking—and providing them support to help them make progress—arms you with data that will be vital to making decisions regarding the whole class discussion. Monitoring, however, is not without its challenges. In this section, we focus on three specific challenges associated with this practice, shown in Figure 4.2, that we have identified from our work with teachers.

Figure 4.2 • Challenges associated with monitoring

CHALLENGE	DESCRIPTION
Trying to understand what students are thinking	Students do not always articulate their thinking clearly. It can be quite demanding for teachers, in the moment, to figure out what a student means or is trying to say. This requires teachers to listen carefully to what students are saying and to ask questions that help them better explain what they are thinking.
Keeping track of group progress—which groups you visited and what you left them to work on	As teachers are running from group to group, providing support, they need to be able to keep track of what each group is doing and what they left students to work on. Also, it is important for a teacher to return to a group to determine whether the advancing question given to them helped them make progress.
Involving all members of a group	All individuals in the group need to be challenged to answer assessing and advancing questions. For individuals to benefit from the thinking of their peers, they need to be held accountable for listening to and adding on, repeating and summarizing what others are saying.

Trying to Understand What Students Are Thinking

Students are not always very articulate when they are asked to explain their thinking. They often use nonacademic language to describe things (e.g., use *head start* to refer to a y-intercept that is not 0), make vague references (e.g., "I took *that* and divided by *this*."), and have difficulty providing a concise description of what they have done. In addition, students may come up with ways of solving problems (both correct and incorrect) that you had not anticipated. And even when you think that you know exactly what a student is thinking because their work resembles what *you* did, you could be dead wrong!

Trying to understand what students are thinking can be challenging work for a teacher, yet it is critical for teachers to make an effort to do so. If students have arrived at a correct solution, you will want to know how they got there so you can determine whether the process they used makes sense, always works, and how (or if) it might connect to more standard approaches. If students have arrived at an incorrect solution, you want to know what led to the result so that you can provide an opportunity for students to consider some aspect of the task they may have not attended to. It would be easier for the teacher to just tell students that they are wrong and provide them with a new pathway to pursue or ask students to use a more standard or recognizable approach, but such *help* is short term. It may allow students to get a correct answer to the problem at hand using a standard method, but since the students are moving forward based on the thinking of the teacher rather than his own thinking, it is not clear whether the student will have access to the strategy the next time he is presented with a similar problem. Telling students what to do or how does not help build their capacity to figure things out on their own or their identities as capable mathematics doers.

Assessing questions help make student thinking visible. Once student thinking is clear, then the teacher is in the position to help move the thinking forward. According to Smith, Steele, and Raith (2017),

> *Questions are the primary tool that teachers have to help them determine what students know and understand about mathematics. Specifically, purposeful questions should reveal students' current understandings; encourage students to explain, elaborate, or clarify their thinking; and make mathematics more visible and accessible for student examination and discussion (p. 77)*

In Analyzing the Work of Teaching 4.4, you will have the opportunity to make sense of the thinking of students in Ms. Musumeci's class. (Recall that Ms. Musumeci's eighth-grade algebra students were working on the Buying T-Shirts task [see Figure 3.6].)

Analyzing the Work of Teaching 4.4

Determining What Students Are Thinking—Part One

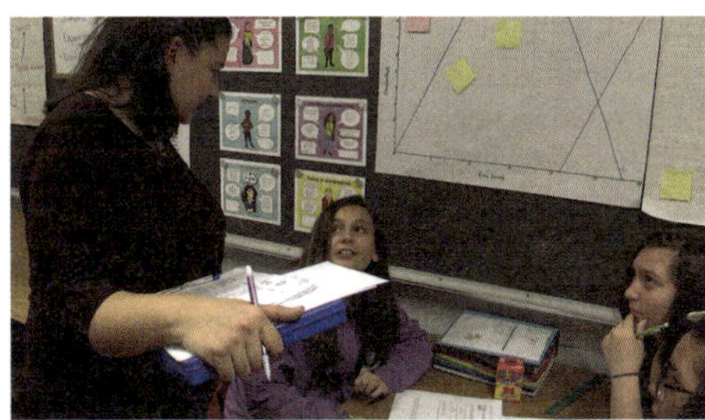

Video Clip 4.4

In Video Clip 4.4, you will visit the small group that includes Mellina, Eva, and Chelsea. They produced the table shown below, which served as the basis for their conversation with Ms. Musumeci. Before watching the video clip, consider: Why do you think students might have noted the fact that *60* appears in each column?

CT	TRU
0	50
15	60 ←
30	70
45	80
→ 60	90
75	100

As you watch the video clip, consider the following questions:

1. What are the students thinking?
2. What seems to be the source of the group's confusion?
3. What questions might you ask the students to clarify what they are thinking?

Videos may also be accessed at **resources.corwin.com/5practices-middleschool**

Determining What Students Are Thinking, Part One—Analysis

Mellina states that the two companies are going to intersect at 4 shirts. She states that 15 (the cost for one shirt at Crazy Tees) times 4 (number of shirts) is 60. She also seems to notice that 60 is also a cost of shirts at T-Shirts R Us. Mellina *may* be thinking that because the two companies have the same cost that it must be the point of intersection.

Before the teacher can even formulate a question, Mellina seems to doubt herself, recognizing that the T-Shirts R Us price of $60.00 is for only 1 shirt. While Mellina seems to be questioning her original hypothesis, Eva declares, "They're still meeting at 60." The exchange concludes with Mellina now stating, "We don't know where they are going to meet."

What the students in this group have not yet realized is that at the point of intersection the price must be the same *for the same number of shirts* at each company. There are several questions that you might decide to ask the group to clarify aspects of the explanation and help them realize they need to consider both cost and number of T-shirts:

- Mellina said, "They're going to meet." What is the *they're* she is referring to? What does it mean that they will meet? What will this meeting look like? (Purpose: To surface the idea that there are two unique nonparallel linear equations that will intersect at some point.)
- Mellina first said that they would meet at 4, then she changed her mind. Why do you think she changed her mind? (Purpose: To get the group to articulate the fact that Mellina saw that the two companies shared a cost of $60.00 but then realized that this was the cost of 4 shirts at one company and 1 shirt at the other company. The cost was the same, but the number of shirts was not.)
- So now Mellina is not sure where they are going to meet, and Eva thinks they are going to meet at 60. How can you determine exactly where they will meet in a way that will convince everyone in the room you are right? (Purpose: Press students to come up with a mathematically convincing argument.)
- So you are saying 4 shirts cost $60.00 here, but only 1 shirt costs $60.00 here. So when you put it on the graph, are they going to meet? (The question that Ms. Musumeci actually asks.)

There is no *right* set of questions that you should ask the group to better understand their thinking and to get them to reconsider where the two lines will meet and why. The key is to make sure that it is clear what students are thinking and then provide a challenge that will cause them to reflect on and move beyond their current thinking.

While not shown on the video clip, Mellina, Chelsea, and Eva ultimately determined that 10 shirts would cost $150.00 at both companies, and this would be the point of intersection. During the whole class discussion, Mellina explained her initial thinking:

> *I just thought that when they were both at 60, that's when they would meet, but then, like I realized that it's not the same number of shirts, so they have to meet at the same amount of shirts and the same cost. And that's not what I did at first.*

Analyzing the Work of Teaching 4.5

Determining What Students Are Thinking—Part Two

Video Clip 4.5

In Video Clip 4.5, you will visit the small group that includes D'Angelo and Eusebi. Students in the group had produced a table, shown below, which served as the basis for their conversation with Ms. Musumeci. Before watching the video clip, consider: What might students have done to get $150.00 as the price for both 10 and 15 shirts?

T-SHIRTS R US	
# OF SHIRTS	**PRICE**
10	150
15	150
20	200
25	250
30	300

As you watch the video clip, consider the following questions:

1. How are students calculating the cost for the T-shirts?
2. How are the students interpreting the $50.00 setup fee?
3. What does the teacher do to understand students' thinking?

Videos may also be accessed at **resources.corwin.com/5practices-middleschool**

Determining What Students Are Thinking, Part Two—Analysis

Instead of calculating the cost of orders of different numbers of shirts (i.e., this is what it would cost if we order 10 shirts, 15 shirts, etc.), students in the group appear to be thinking that you place a first order of 10 shirts for which you have to pay the setup fee of $50.00. Then, since you have already paid an initial setup fee of $50.00 for the first order, when you order additional shirts (15, 20, 25 etc.), you do not pay the setup fee again. As D'Angelo explained, "You had to add the plus 50 to your first order. . . ." Hence, students see the $50.00 as only applying to their first order of 10 shirts. For all remaining orders (values in their table), they simply multiplied the number of shirts in the order by $10.00, the cost per shirt.

Ms. Musumeci did not initially understand why the group had $150.00 for both 10 shirts and 15 shirts. Her questions made clear that this was not a calculation error—students were able to calculate the cost of 10 and 15 shirts with the setup fee, but she did not at first understand that they were seeing the context differently. At the same time, the students in the group did not understand why what they had done was not clear to the teacher. As a result of both parties persisting—the teacher in questioning and the students in explaining—the teacher finally states, "Okay. I see what you are saying now. Alright, we already paid the fee for 10." With that now established, the teacher was able to directly address the confusion by saying, "But I want you to tell me how much … like if each one of those was your first order."

The exchange between Ms. Musumeci and her students is a good example of the need to persist in understanding student thinking. The students were not incorrect in their calculation, just in their interpretation of the situation. Once the teacher understood how the group was thinking about the problem, she was able to help them make progress on the task. The students were ultimately able to produce a table that contained the correct values.

Keeping Track of Group Progress

When you have students working in groups, it is important to keep track of which groups you have visited, what they are doing, and what you have left them to work on. Without a method of tracking this information, it is easy to forget to return to a group or to miss a group completely. To address this challenge, some teachers move around the room in a defined pattern so they know where they have been and where they need to go next. Ms. Musumeci did this—she started with the group closest to the door and moved counterclockwise on her initial pass around the room. Some teachers put a small colored dot on the table with each visit to a group so that they can easily tell which groups they have visited and how many times they had been there. Alternatively, you could give each group a number tent, list the group numbers on a Post-it note, and place a check next to the group number on the Post-it each time you visit the group.

While the *Who and What* column of the monitoring chart can be used to record what a group is doing, it is also important to keep track of the advancing question you encouraged the group to pursue when you left them. Asking advancing questions is critical in moving students forward, but you need to make sure that the question you asked is having the desired effect. You could track this by highlighting the question on your monitoring chart—if it is one you anticipated—and indicate the group number to whom you asked the question next to it. Alternatively, you could jot the question on the Post-it next to the group number if you used the Post-it approach. Elizabeth Brovey, a former middle school teacher and current coach, indicates that she takes notes but also holds the group responsible for telling her what they were asked to do. As she described:

> *I have to keep track of what I told them to work on, so I try to take notes. But the other thing I do is when I come back I make them say, "What was it I was asking you to work on?... I told you guys, what did I ask you to do before I left?" And they have to tell me. So that's not just about them. That's about me too. 'Cause I also have to honor the frame that I've given them. [Conversation with Elizabeth Brovey, September 11, 2015]*

In Analyzing the Work of Teaching 4.6 and 4.7, you will return to Mrs. Mossotti's class where students are working on the State Fair task. You will consider what Mrs. Mossotti did to advance students' learning and the extent to which she had evidence, when she visited the group a second time, that students were making progress.

Analyzing the Work of Teaching 4.6

Following Up With Students—Part One

Video Clip 4.6

CONTINUED

CONTINUED FROM PREVIOUS

When Mrs. Mossotti first visited Serenity and Adnawmy (see Analyzing the Work of Teaching 4.2), they were confused about how to begin the task. After a brief conversation, the teacher challenged them to estimate the cost of 4 tickets. In Video Clip 4.6, she returns to the pair to see what progress they have made.

The work shown below was on Serenity's paper—Adnawmy had a similar set of computations. Before watching the video clip, consider: What do the students appear to be thinking?

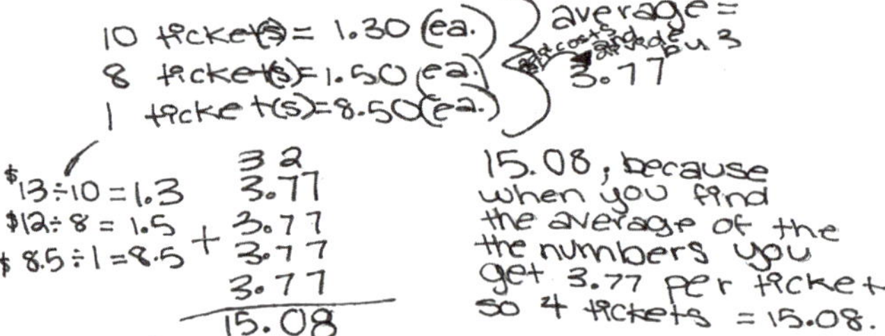

As you watch Video Clip 4.6, consider the following questions:

1. Did the advancing question students were left with help them move forward?
2. What does the teacher do to push their thinking further?

Videos may also be accessed at **resources.corwin.com/5practices-middleschool**

Following Up with Students, Part One—Analysis

At the end of her first visit to Serenity and Adnawmy (Video Clip 4.2), Mrs. Mossotti asked them to come up with an estimate of the cost of 4 tickets. Rather than produce an estimate, the students determined that the cost of 4 tickets would be $15.08. So the students actually went from making no progress on the task to coming up with a price for 4 tickets. While the answer was not correct, Serenity and Adnawmy took the charge seriously and produced work that would provide a window into their thinking that could be further explored. Mrs. Mossotti purposefully returned to the group to check on their progress.

The teacher began her interaction with the group by getting them to explain the calculations they had done: "What's all this math right here?" Once Mrs. Mossotti understood that the students used the three points on the graph—(1, 8.50), (8, 12), and (10, 13)—to find the cost per ticket for each of these amounts ($8.50, $1.50, and $1.30 respectively), she asked Serenity to consider whether it makes sense for tickets to cost different prices. This leads Serenity to state, "No. It said every ride ticket is the same price." Mrs. Mossotti then challenges Serenity—"Is that what you got?" Serenity indicates that it not what she got and goes on to explain that she found the average of these three amounts was $3.77. The teacher leaves Serenity to prove that $3.77 works—that is, if each ticket costs $3.77 that this will give you the values on the graph for 1, 8, and 10 tickets.

In her return visit to Serenity and Adnawmy, Mrs. Mossotti began by asking questions to assess what the students had done. While she had anticipated that students might come up with three different unit rates (see a portion of her monitoring chart in Figure 4.3), she had not anticipated that they would average the three unit rates and then use the average to determine the cost of 4 tickets.

Figure 4.3 • Strategy, Assessing, and Advancing questions from Mrs. Mossotti's monitoring chart

SOLUTION STRATEGY	ASSESSING QUESTIONS	ADVANCING QUESTIONS
Solution B. Student divides the total spent by the ticket quantity for each point on the graph and comes up with three different "unit rates." $\frac{8.50}{1} = 8.50$ $\frac{12}{8} = 1.5$ $\frac{13}{10} = 1.3$	• So sometimes tickets have different prices? How do I get to buy the cheap ticket ... something seems funny here? • What do each of these numbers mean? • 8.5 what? For what?	• Why is 1 ticket so expensive but 12 tickets so cheap, for each ticket? Are they having a special sale that I do not know about? • Is there a way to use the values from each point to find out a single ticket price?

The questions she asked were similar to those that appeared in the monitoring chart as she tried to understand where Serenity was in her thinking. Her advancing question went beyond what she had anticipated as she challenged Serenity to consider the mismatch between the cost per ticket she found ($3.77) and the cost associated with the points on the graph. She hoped that Serenity would conclude that multiplying the number of tickets (1, 8, and 10) by $3.77 would not produce the points shown on the graph. Upon leaving the group, Mrs. Mossotti made the following note on her monitoring chart: "Take average of 3 rates to get $3.77/ticket." [See Mrs. Mossotti's completed monitoring chart in Appendix C.]

Please review Analyzing the Work of Teaching 4.7 (at the top of the next page) before moving on to the Analysis section below.

Following Up with Students, Part Two—Analysis

During her first visit to Nietzsche, Ejub, and AJ, Mrs. Mossotti learns that they have determined that the entry fee is $8.00, the cost per ticket is 50¢, and the cost of one ticket is $8.50. However, the students were having trouble articulating exactly how they know this is true. The teacher

Analyzing the Work of Teaching 4.7

Following Up With Students—Part Two

Video Clip 4.7

Mrs. Mossotti visits Nietzsche, Ejub, and AJ on two separate occasions while they are working on the State Fair task.

As you watch Video Clip 4.7, consider the following questions:

1. What does Mrs. Mossotti learn about her students' understanding during her first visit to the group?
2. What question does the teacher leave students to pursue?
3. When the teacher checks in with the group later (her second visit), what progress have students made? What does she leave them to work on?

Videos may also be accessed at **resources.corwin.com/5practices-middleschool**

challenged them to figure out whether 8 tickets for \$12.00 and 10 tickets for \$13.00 (the other two points on the graph) fit if the cost of entry is \$8.00 and the cost of each ticket is 50¢. While a teacher might be pleased with the fact that they have the right answer, Mrs. Mossotti wanted them to be able to explain mathematically why this must be the case.

When Mrs. Mossotti returns to check in on the group, she finds them doing exactly what she suggested. Nietzsche shows that you can get from \$8.00 to the point (8, \$12.00) by increasing by 50¢ for each additional ticket. This led them to conclude that it was \$4.00 (the total of the 8 times they added 50¢) for 8 tickets. Mrs. Mossotti leaves the group to determine whether the pattern will hold for the remaining point on the graph (10, \$13.00).

Mrs. Mossotti's interactions with Nietzsche, Ejub, and AJ highlight several aspects of the ideas that we have highlighted in this chapter. First, she uses assessing questions to make students' thinking visible so that she can then move it in a productive direction. Second, she poses an advancing question to the group that is intended to push their thinking toward a more mathematically sound explanation. Finally, she returns to the group to see if they have been able to make progress on the question that was posed.

While the students were correct in stating that the entry fee was $8.00, and the cost per ticket was 50¢, by continuing to press for a mathematical explanation, she sent the message that the answer was not sufficient—they needed to be able to *prove* it. By returning to the group, she was able to see that students had engaged with the question she left them to pursue and were making progress. Although they had not completely answered her question yet, they were clearly working on it. It is interesting to note that Mrs. Mossotti never let up on her expectation of what they needed to do or her belief that they would be able to do it. When Mrs. Mossotti left the group, she made the following note on her monitoring chart: "Starts at $8.00 on graph and then continues to count by 50¢ to get total price for the 3 points given."

Involving All Members of a Group

The purpose of having students work in groups is so they can serve as resources for each other as they engage in solving challenging problems (Horn, 2012). But getting students to actually work together requires more than just telling them to do so. The teacher needs to set clear expectations regarding group work and to reinforce these expectations through her interactions with small groups. For example, if one student in the group has a question, the teacher might indicate that she will only answer a question if no one in the group can so that students see members of the group as a first source of support. When the teacher begins a discussion with one member of a group, she needs to bring in other group members to make sure they are following the discussion. There is limited value in having student desks pushed together if they are not benefitting from what their peers have to contribute. One of the teachers with whom we have worked describes how she stays with a group to ensure that all of the group members are invested in the work of the group:

> *I do decide to stay when I recognize that the students aren't in that place of being able to work with each other. So I stay if one or more of the students in a group are working in isolation … I consciously pull students in who may not be explicitly letting me know that they're part of the conversation. They may be listening … I can't assume. They may be where we're at when we're talking. But until I get evidence from them, I can't be sure of that. So, I stay until I make sure each person has demonstrated to me they have a vested interest in pursuing whatever aspect of the learning goal they happen to be working on at that time. (Conversation with Elizabeth Brovey, September 11, 2015). [See Smith, Steele, and Raith (2017), Chapter 8, for an example of Elizabeth Brovey applying these principles in her interaction with a small group.]*

While involving all members of a group in a discussion is important, it is extremely difficult for several reasons. First, it takes time. The more time you spend with one group, the less time there is to visit other groups. Second, it is challenging enough for the teacher to understand some explanations without making sure that everyone else in the group understands it too. Hence, it may not be realistic to make sure that every student speaks every time you interact with a single group. What is important is that you set norms for work that make clear what your expectations are and that you make an effort to ensure that members of the group are at a minimum paying attention to the discussion.

In Analyzing the Work of Teaching 4.8, you will drop in on Mr. Quinn's seventh-grade class as they work on the Buying Batteries task shown in Figure 4.4. As a result of engaging in this lesson, Mr. Quinn wants his students to understand that in a proportional relationship one quantity is a constant multiplier of another—specifically that $y = kx$ where k is the constant of proportionality. Mr. Quinn consistently tells his students that when they work in groups, they needed to work together. He stresses that every member of the group needs to be able to explain what the group is doing and thinking. As you explore the vignette, which depicts his interactions with one group, you will consider how he operationalizes his commitment to holding students accountable to working together.

Figure 4.4 • Buying Batteries task

Buying Batteries

The table below shows the price for buying AAA batteries at a nearby pharmacy. Use the table to answer the questions below.

Number of batteries	6	12	18	30
Price (in dollars)	3	6	9	15

Is the relationship between price and number of batteries a proportional relationship? Explain your reasoning.

Source: Adapted from the Institute for Learning (2015a). Lesson guides and student workbooks available at ifl.pitt.edu.

Analyzing the Work of Teaching 4.8

Holding All Students Accountable

In the Buying Batteries vignette, you will see Mr. Quinn's interactions with one small group in his class that consists of Sophia, Camila, and Destiny.

As you read the vignette, consider the following questions:

1. What aspects of monitoring do you see Mr. Quinn engage in as he interacts with Sophia, Camila, and Destiny?
2. What does Mr. Quinn do to ensure that all three students are involved in making progress on the task?

Buying Batteries Vignette

Mr. Q: So tell me what your group came up with.
Sophia: We said that it is proportional.
Mr. Q: What is proportional?
Sophia: The relationship between the price and the number of batteries.
Mr. Q: Why do you think it is proportional?
Sophia: It goes up in a pattern.
Mr. Q: Do you agree with her? *(Looking at Destiny and Camila who are both nodding their heads.)*
Mr. Q: Destiny, what is the pattern that Sophia is referring to?
Destiny: You just keep adding the same amount on to batteries and price.
Mr. Q: What do you mean that you keep "adding the same amount"?
Destiny: You always add 6 to the batteries and 3 to the price (pointing to her paper that shows the addition)

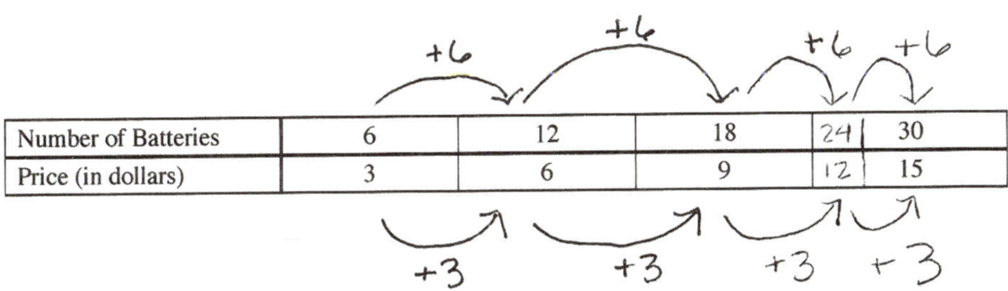

Number of Batteries	6	12	18	24	30
Price (in dollars)	3	6	9	12	15

Mr. Q: What about the last column? How does it fit the pattern? Camila?
Camila: See. They skipped 24 batteries for $12.00 that would come after 18 batteries for $9.00, so we just filled that in. Then 30 batteries for $15.00 would come next. So it still works.
Mr. Q: Can you just fill in numbers like that? Sophia?

Sophia? I think so—it still fits the pattern. They just left one out of the table.
Mr. Q: Suppose I had 50 batteries for $25.00. Is this relationship the same as the one in your table? I want the three of you to talk about it and I will check back in with you in a few minutes.

(Mr. Q makes note of the question he posed and leaves students to pursue it while he talks with other groups. He returns to check their progress.)

Mr. Q: So what did you decide? Destiny?
Destiny: We decided that 50 batteries for $25.00 doesn't fit the pattern because you could never get to 50 and 25 by adding 6 to the number of batteries and 3 to the cost.
Mr. Q: How did you determine that it didn't fit the pattern? Sophia?
Sophia: We just extended the table. We got 48 for $24.00 and then 54 for $27.00. So 50 for $25.00 will never fit.
Mr. Q: Okay. You have identified a pattern of repeatedly adding 6 to the number of batteries and adding $3.00 to the cost. Now, I want you to see if you can find a relationship between the number of batteries and the cost. I will be back.

(Mr. Q makes note of what he asked students to work on then proceeds to talk with other groups before returning to check their progress.)

Mr. Q: So what did you find? Camila?
Camila: Well, we think that the cost is $\frac{1}{2}$ the number of batteries.
Sophia: Or the batteries are 2 times the cost.
Mr. Q: Can you show me what you mean using the table?
SS: *(Sophia and Camila each repeat their explanation, while pointing to columns in the table that show the relationship.)*
Mr. Q: So now you have identified another pattern—one that connects the batteries and the cost. This is an important relationship. I want you to write a ratio that represents the number of batteries to the cost and then see if the ratio describes all the entries in your table. I may not have time to check in with you again, but I expect you to keep working on this.

(Mr. Q makes note of the final challenge posed to the group. He did not have time to return the group, but he felt that they had made sufficient progress to benefit from the whole group discussion.)

Holding All Students Accountable—Analysis

Mr. Quinn's three interactions with Sophia, Camila, and Destiny highlight many of the aspects of monitoring that we have discussed in this chapter. He begins each visit to the group by offering an open invitation to students to describe their work (Line 1: Tell me what you came up with; Line 29: What did you decide?; Line 44: What did you find?). Following the students' explanation, he asks a series of assessing questions (Lines 3, 5, 9,

11, 16, 20, 33, 47) that are directly connected to the explanations given by students and are intended to make students' thinking clearer and public. For example, when Sophia states that "*it* is proportional," Mr. Quinn asks two questions: "*What* is proportional" (Line 3)? and "Why do you think it is proportional" (Line 5)?

As a result of the assessing questions Mr. Quinn asked during his first visit to the group, he realized that while students had identified a pattern—that you keep adding 6 to the number of batteries and 3 to the cost—they did not recognize the relationship between the batteries and the cost. Since it is the constant ratio between batteries and cost that make this a proportional relationship, he asks an advancing question (Lines 22–24) intended to focus students on this relationship. Since students continued to focus on the pattern of addition (Lines 34–36), Mr. Quinn's subsequent advancing questions focused on explicitly looking for a relationship between batteries and cost (Lines 36–39) and writing a ratio that describes the relationship between batteries and cost that holds true for all the entries in the table (Lines 50–54).

In this short vignette, we see Mr. Quinn keeping track of the questions he leaves students to work on in his absence (Lines 26–27 41–42, and 56–58) so he will know what he needs to follow up on when he returns to the group. While the first advancing question did not show much progress toward the goal of the lesson, students' response to the question made clear that they needed a more explicit directive to focus their attention away from the pattern of addition. The second advancing question was successful in moving students forward and evidenced by their identification of two relationships—that the cost was $\frac{1}{2}$ the number of batteries and that the number of batteries was 2 times the cost (Lines 45–46).

Perhaps what is most striking in Mr. Quinn's interactions with the group is the way in which he holds Sophia, Camila, and Destiny accountable for participating in the discussion. Mr. Quinn has stressed the need for students to work together and has made it clear that every member of the group needs to be able to explain what the group is doing and thinking. There are several instances of this in the vignette. While Sophia is the first to indicate that there is a pattern in the table of values, Mr. Quinn turns to Camila and Destiny to see if they agree. When they nod their agreement, Mr. Quinn directs the next questions about the pattern to Destiny (Line 9) and Camila (Line 16). At the end of the first visit, Mr. Quinn makes it clear, "I want the three of you to talk about it" (Line 23). When he makes subsequent return visits to the group, he asks Destiny (Line 29) and later Camila (Line 44) to explain what the group decided in his absence. The key to holding students accountable for working together is setting clear expectations regarding what you expect and then reinforcing these expectations through your actions and interactions.

Conclusion

In this chapter, we explored the practice of monitoring. This is perhaps one of the more challenging practices because the actual practice of monitoring takes place during instruction as the lesson is unfolding in real time. There is a lot to attend to as students work individually and in small groups, and it can be overwhelming. Our experience suggests that careful attention to anticipating prior to the lesson, including the preparation of a monitoring chart, can help make monitoring more manageable.

This was evident in the work of Mrs. Mossotti. As a result of the care she took in planning the lesson (as described in Chapters 2 and 3), she entered the class with clarity about what she wanted students to learn and how she would support them in reaching the goals she set. She asked assessing questions that made students' thinking clear and public, asked advancing questions to move students forward, and checked on their progress. She made notes as she interacted with groups so that she would be able to make purposeful decisions about who and what to highlight during the whole group discussion that would follow. (You can see Mrs. Mossotti's annotated monitoring chart in Appendix C.) Mrs. Mossotti's work during the monitoring phase makes salient that assessing and advancing questions occur in cycles—you assess, then you advance, you return, and you assess again, then you advance again. The intent is that each time you return to a group, you move them further toward the goal. While one visit to some groups may be sufficient, other groups may require multiple visits.

TEACHING TAKEAWAY

Assessing and advancing questions occur in cycles.

As you will note on Mrs. Mossotti's monitoring chart, she managed to capture a great deal of what was going on while students worked on the task. Did she record everything that happened when she interacted with students as they worked on the task? No. She was able to capture sufficient detail about what students were doing to give her a good sense of what they understood and what they were struggling with. While we discussed in this chapter what would be ideal to try to capture on the monitoring chart, the reality is that you may not get every single thing. The point is to do the best you can to get an accurate picture of the ideas students have generated that will help you in achieving the goals for the lesson.

In our analysis of Ms. Musumeci's and Mr. Quinn's interactions with small groups, we saw the importance of asking questions that help clarify what students are thinking. You cannot move students forward if you do not know where they are to start with. It is critical to use questions to make student thinking visible. Although sometimes this can be straightforward as we saw with Mr. Quinn's questions to Sophia, other times this can require perseverance as we saw in Ms. Musumeci's interactions with D'Angelo and Eusebi.

Because monitoring generally involves interaction with small groups of students, it is critical to consider how you can help build students' capacity to work together. Mr. Quinn's interactions with Sophia, Camila, and Destiny provide some insights on how to hold students accountable for working together, but getting students to work together productively will not happen overnight. This will require time, patience, and persistence on your part!

Your ability to effectively monitor will improve over time as you continue to do it, reflect on what went well and what did not, make midcourse corrections, and do it again. The key is to keep at it, even if the first few times are not as successful as you would like.

Monitoring Student Work—Summary

Video Clip 4.8

To hear and see more about monitoring student work using the monitoring tool, watch Video Clip 4.8

Videos may also be accessed at **resources.corwin.com/5practices-middleschool**

In the next chapter, we explore the next two practices: *selecting* and *sequencing*. There, we will return to Mrs. Mossotti's lesson and consider what it takes to engage in these practices and the challenges it presents.

Linking the Five Practices to Your Own Instruction

MONITORING

It is now time to teach the lesson you planned in Chapters 2 and 3! (Or if you prefer, select another lesson. Just make sure that you have engaged in Practice 0 and have anticipated student responses and questions before you begin.) We encourage you to video record the lesson so that you can reflect back on what occurred during the lesson.

1. Before teaching the lesson, consider how you are going to make sure you visit every group and remember the questions you leave groups to pursue. Also, consider whether there are any specific instructions you want to give students regarding your expectations for how you expect them to work in their groups.
2. As you teach the lesson, use your monitoring chart to keep track of the strategies students are using. Be sure you are checking in with every group and returning to groups to see if they are making good progress.
3. Following the lesson, use these questions to guide reflection on your monitoring:
    - Did you interact with each group in the class? If not, what could you do differently to ensure that you have a chance to check in with all of your students? Did you return to groups when you said you would to check on their progress?
    - To what extent did students use the strategies you had anticipated? What was unexpected?
    - To what extent were the assessing questions you anticipated in planning useful in your interactions with students? Did they help you make students' thinking clear and public?
    - To what extent were the advancing questions you anticipated in planning useful in your interactions with students? Did they help students make progress on the task?
    - To what extent were you able to involve all members of a group in the conversation? What might you do differently in the future to hear the voices of more students?
4. What did you learn about students' understanding of mathematics as a result of teaching the lesson?
5. What lessons have you learned about monitoring that will help you in planning and enacting the next lesson you teach?

> “As I walk around and make notes about what students are doing, I’m trying to figure out what order I want them to come up. So I’m looking for students and solution paths to select that will build a math story around the problem so that we can, by the end, hopefully, understand the goals that we’re trying to reach.”
>
> —MICHELLE MUSUMECI, EIGHTH-GRADE TEACHER

CHAPTER 5

Selecting and Sequencing Student Solutions

Once students have had the opportunity to explore the task individually or in small groups, and you as the teacher have monitored their discussions, the next step is to bring the class together for a whole-group discussion of the key mathematical ideas of the lesson. To help ensure that the discussion is meaningful for all students, you will want to engage in the next two practices, selecting and sequencing student solutions.

Selecting and sequencing builds on the careful monitoring you did as students worked on the task. These practices involve choosing which solutions will be shared with the class, who will share those solutions, and the order in which the solutions will be shared. Selecting particular solutions to highlight provides you with an opportunity to help students move beyond the specific strategies they used to consider other approaches. In addition, being intentional about the order in which the solutions are presented provides an opportunity to build strategically on what students have done.

Smith and Stein (2018) describe selecting and sequencing in the following way:

> *Selecting is the process of determining which ideas* (what) *and students* (who) *the teacher will focus on during the discussion.*

> *This is a crucial decision, since it determines what ideas students will have the opportunity to grapple with and ultimately to learn. Selecting can be thought of as the act of purposefully determining what mathematics students will have access to—beyond what they were able to consider individually or in small groups—in building their mathematical understanding.* (pp. 63–64)
>
> *Sequencing is the process of determining the order in which the students will present their solutions. The key is to order the work in such a way as to make the mathematics accessible to all students and to build a mathematically coherent story line.* (p. 64)

In this chapter, we first unpack selecting and sequencing into their key components and illustrate what these practices look like in an authentic middle school classroom. Next, we explore what we have learned is challenging for teachers about selecting and sequencing and provide an opportunity for you to explore these practices in your own teaching.

Part One: Unpacking the Practice: Selecting and Sequencing Student Solutions

Selecting and sequencing involve identifying the student work you wish to highlight, purposefully selecting individual presenters, and establishing a coherent storyline for sequencing students' presentations. Here we explore each of these components by looking inside Mrs. Mossotti's classroom. Figure 5.1 highlights the key components of these practices.

Figure 5.1 • Key questions that support the process of selecting and sequencing student solutions

WHAT IT TAKES	KEY QUESTIONS
Identifying student work to highlight	Which student solution strategies would help you accomplish your mathematical goals for the lesson?
	What challenges did students face in solving the task? Were there any common challenges?
Purposefully selecting individual presenters	Which students do you want to involve in presenting their work?
	How might selecting particular students promote equitable access to mathematics learning in your classroom?
Establishing coherent storyline	How can you order the student work such that there is a coherent storyline related to the mathematical learning goal?

Identifying Student Work to Highlight

The first step in selecting and sequencing is to identify the student work that you want to highlight for the class. As you monitored students' progress, you will likely have noticed a range of solutions that students produced and will have noted them on your monitoring chart. Remember that you intentionally chose a task that invited multiple approaches!

Having access to different solution strategies during the discussion has the potential to help students deepen their understanding of the mathematics involved in the task (Zbiek & Shimizu, 2005). To realize this, you want to identify those solution paths that put the key mathematical ideas in the spotlight and will therefore help you to achieve your lesson goals. As you review students' work on the task, look for similarities and differences among the paths students took to solve the task, while keeping in mind the mathematical features of students' solutions that are important for the class to consider.

You will also want to consider the challenges that students faced as they solved the task. Were there any common challenges that you want to highlight? Often, we shy away from discussing incorrect solutions with students when in fact there can be important benefits to discussing errors and false starts (Santagata & Bray, 2016; Warshauer, 2015). As Kazemi and Hintz (2014) explain,

> *How we respond to errors and partially developed ideas sends important messages about taking risks. It is not easy for students to express their ideas if there is a high burden to be correct and understand everything the first time around. (p. 5)*

As you consider which solution strategies to focus on with the whole class, keep in mind the potential value in discussing some of the difficulties that students may have encountered.

As she reviewed her monitoring chart, Mrs. Mossotti could see that her students had solved the State Fair task in a number of different ways, as shown in Figure 5.2. To determine the cost of 4 tickets, some students reasoned that one ticket costs \$8.50, so 4 tickets would cost \$34.00 (Solution I). Other students connected the three given points in a line and estimated that 4 tickets cost \$10.00 and 0 tickets cost \$8.00 (Solution II). Several students plotted points on the graph to represent the cost of different numbers of tickets and decided that for every 1 additional ticket, the cost goes up 50¢ (Solution III). A few students used the cost for 8 and 10 tickets to determine that the price per ticket is 50¢ (Solution IV). Less common was to use the three given points to find an average per ticket rate (Solution V). Even though Mrs. Mossotti expected students to create a table to examine the cost per ticket, she did not observe students using this approach.

Figure 5.2 • Solutions Mrs. Mossotti noted on her monitoring chart

Solution I. Price per ticket is $8.50

"1 ticket costs $8.50. To find the cost of 4 tickets you multiply 8.50 by 4 which is $34.00."

Solution II. Draw a line to identify the cost of 4 tickets and/or the cost of 0 tickets

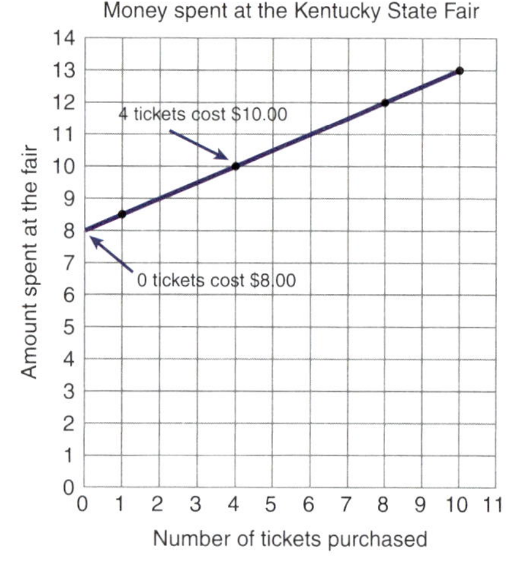

Solution III. Use increasing values on graph to determine price per ticket is 50¢

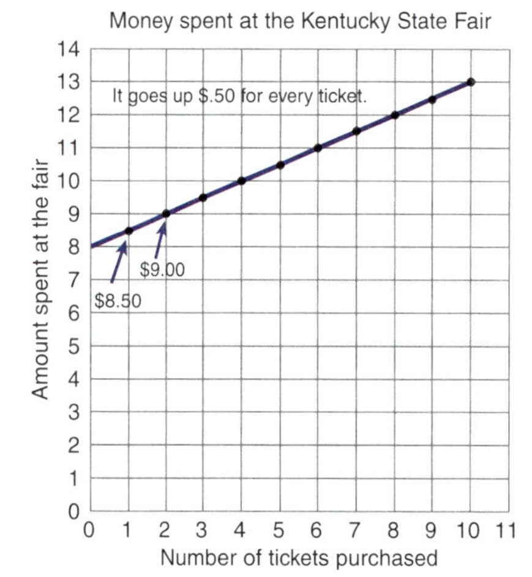

Solution IV. Use (8, 12) and (10, 13) to determine price per ticket is 50¢

8 tickets cost $12.00

10 tickets cost $13.00

"9 tickets is in the middle of 8 and 10 so the cost must be $12.50. That means each ticket is 50¢."

Solution V. Average ticket price is $3.77

1 ticket costs $8.50

8 tickets cost $12.00 so $1.50 each

10 tickets cost $13.00 so $1.30 each

"1 ticket can cost $8.50, $1.50 or $1.30 so the average ticket price is $3.77."

In Analyzing the Work of Teaching 5.1, you will analyze the approaches taken by Mrs. Mossotti's students in solving the problem and consider which strategies would be most useful in addressing the mathematical goals she had for the lesson.

Analyzing the Work of Teaching 5.1

Selecting Student Solutions

Consider the solutions shown in Figure 5.2 in light of Mrs. Mossotti's goals for the lesson.

Goal 1: The rate of change can be seen as the ratio of the change in the y-variable compared to the change in the x-variable, as the rate expressed with the words "for each, per, for every" in a verbal description, or as the coefficient of x in the equation $y = mx + b$.

Goal 2: Some functions do not *start* at 0. That is, the point (0, 0) is not a solution for all linear functions.

Goal 3: The y-intercept can be understood as the initial value of a linear function in a real-world context.

- Which solutions do you think Mrs. Mossotti might want to select to address her goals for the lesson?
- Solutions I and V are incorrect. What might be the benefit of sharing an incorrect solution?

Selecting Student Solutions—Analysis

The student solutions Mrs. Mossotti observed in her class address the lesson goals in several different ways.

Goal 1: The rate of change can be seen as the ratio of the change in the y-variable compared to the change in the x-variable, as the rate expressed with the words "for each, per, for every" in a verbal description, or as the coefficient of x in the equation $y = mx + b$.

One of Mrs. Mossotti's main goals for the State Fair task was for students to explore rate of change as the price per ticket. Both Solutions III and IV address this goal and highlight that the price per ticket is 50¢. Solution III represents the rate of change as a graphical relationship between the increase in the number of tickets and the increase in the total cost. Using the graph, students can observe this relationship among many different pairs of points.

Solution IV represents this relationship numerically using a single pair of points (8, 12) and (10, 13). Mrs. Mossotti saw this as a valuable approach and an important starting place in generalizing the rate of change. "If they can understand the difference in cost for 2 tickets, they can start to work from here."

Goal 2: Some functions do not "start" at 0. That is, the point (0, 0) is not a solution for all linear functions.

Goal 3: The y-intercept can be understood as the initial value of a linear function in a real-world context.

Only Solution II directly addresses Goals 2 and 3. As students extend the line to the y-axis, the point (0, 8) becomes an important feature of the graph. Interpreting the meaning of this point can help students recognize that 0 tickets cost $8.00 and that the $8.00 represents an entry fee to the park.

Both Solutions I and V show incorrect thinking on the part of students. In particular, both solutions start with the notion that the cost of 1 ticket is \$8.50 and do not take an entrance fee into account. Solution V goes further in this direction, taking each point as representing a unique ticket rate and then finding the average of these rates. Discussing these solutions with the class has several potential benefits. Among them, investigating the idea that 4 tickets costs \$34.00 can be a valuable jumping-off point for making sense of the graph. As students explained to Mrs. Mossotti during the monitoring phase, "Looking at the graph … the answer can't be 34." Why is that? What can we learn from the graph? What is the price of 1 ticket? Similarly, exploring Solution V with the class can provide an opportunity to test one's solution. If each ticket costs \$3.77, how much would 8 tickets cost? 10 tickets? How can we reconcile that information with the information on the graph?

In addition, discussing incorrect thinking, can—as mentioned earlier—illustrate for students that the classroom is a place where all mathematical ideas are respected and where errors are a time for reflection and discussion.

After reviewing the solution strategies in light of her lesson goals, Mrs. Mossotti decided that she wanted to highlight Solutions II and III. She had noted on her monitoring chart that "many kids draw a line to find cost of 4 tickets," so she thought using the graphical representation would be a good way to connect with what many of her students had done. In addition, Solution III would allow her to address Goal 1, the relationship between the number of tickets and the total cost, specifically that each ticket cost 50¢. Solution II would be a way to explore Goals 2 and 3 and the meaning of the y-intercept in the context of the task. Mrs. Mossotti also decided that she wanted to review Solution I with the class, since starting with the idea that one ticket cost \$8.50 was an approach that many students used initially.

Mrs. Mossotti could have made other choices. For example, she might have decided to use Solution IV to investigate the cost per ticket. Because Solution IV involves exploring the relationship between the number of tickets and the total cost with two specific points, this could have been a good choice especially if students had struggled to determine the rate of change. Similarly, she could have chosen to highlight Solution V with the class. Doing so would have had the result of addressing the idea that the cost of 1 ticket is \$8.50 along with the idea of specific rates deriving from the points (8, 12) and (10, 13). The point is, there is not just one *right way* to select the set of solutions that are shared during the whole class discussion. The key is ensuring that the selected solutions will make it possible for you to surface the mathematical ideas that are central to the lesson.

TEACHING TAKEAWAY

There is not one way to select or sequence the set of solutions to be shared. The choice should first be driven by your mathematical goals.

Purposefully Selecting Individual Presenters

Once you identify the solutions that you want to highlight, you will need to purposefully select students to present those solutions to the class. But how should you decide? One factor, of course, is which students produced the solutions that you want to share with the class. Having students present their own solutions can validate the importance of different kinds of mathematical thinking and help the class recognize their peers as valuable intellectual resources for learning mathematics (Aguirre, Mayfield-Ingram & Martin, 2013; Jilk, 2016). In addition, because it is students' own work, they can authentically answer questions about the reasoning behind their representations and solution strategies (Imm, Stylianou, & Chae, 2008). Although you may find it more efficient and less messy to share a student's work yourself, so doing robs the student of the opportunity to be seen as an author of mathematical ideas, contributing both to a student's authority and identity. [See Aguirre, Mayfield-Ingram & Martin, 2013 for a set of equity-based teaching practices that are intended to strengthen mathematics learning and the development of positive mathematics identities.]

TEACHING TAKEAWAY

Be sure to allow students to share their own work so that they are seen as the author of their mathematical ideas and can answer questions about their reasoning.

Being purposeful about the students you select can also promote equitable access to mathematics learning in your classroom. Classroom discourse in the United States is often stratified with certain students contributing more frequently than others (Hung, 2015). In addition, students from diverse racial backgrounds are often considered not as good at mathematics as their White and Asian peers (Louie, 2017; Shah, 2017). Particularly troubling is recent research that shows that racial stereotyping among peers concerning who is good at mathematics gets stronger in the middle school years (Nasir, McKinney de Royston, O'Connor, & Wischnia, 2017).

TEACHING TAKEAWAY

Your choice of who will present can send strong messages about what and who you value. Do not miss these important opportunities to promote equity.

Your choice of which students will present their solutions sends an important message about who and what is valued mathematically in your classroom. You will want to pay attention to who has recently had an opportunity to share their work with the class, and who has not; who might be comfortable sharing an incorrect or unusual solution, and who might benefit from sharing a solution that was used by many students in the class.

To be clear, decisions about what solutions to select and who to select as presenters are often closely related. Here, we have suggested that you first select the solutions you want students to share in class and then choose who should present those solutions. In practice, these decisions often happen in an integrated way. You may recognize that a particular student is more engaged than typical and decide to have him or her present his or her solution. Or you may recognize a solution as novel and interesting but realize the student who created it presented recently and decide to forgo that solution for a different one.

In talking about how she selects presenters, Mrs. Mossotti explained that she makes a conscious effort to vary which students present in class. In addition, she often tells students in advance that she plans to have them present, "I'll give them a little tap on the shoulder and say, 'Do you mind saying this in front of the room?'" Mrs. Saroney described a similar process:

> *As I walk around and make notes about what students are doing, I'll be trying to figure out who I want to come up. And I tend to let students know so they can be prepared to talk about that particular piece of their work. Also if a student's nervous, it helps that they're not put on the spot all of a sudden.*

Mrs. Mossotti also explained that while she often asks students to present individually, she also finds it productive to ask students who have worked together to present together. Mrs. Mossotti has found, particularly at the beginning of the year, that it can build students' confidence if they have "somebody who thought about it the same way up there" with them. In addition, Mrs. Mossotti stated that she routinely looks to highlight "somebody who thinks about it differently than everybody else. I like to put a spotlight on that student so that the rest of the kids can get access to different kinds of thinking." Clearly, there is much to keep in mind as you coordinate what ideas you want students to share in class and which students you want to present those ideas!

A final consideration is the process through which students share their work. If a document camera is available in your classroom, students can share their own written work for the rest of the class to see. If not, you might ask students to recreate their solution on the board, or if there is time, you might ask them to prepare a poster to present to the class. In cases where students are completing their work electronically, you may be able to project the work directly for the class to view. A new feature on the Desmos platform called Snapshots allows teachers to capture images of students' work for later sharing with the class. (Snapshots is also a useful tool for selecting and sequencing student work! See http://blog.mrmeyer.com/2018/orchestrate-more-productive-mathematics-discussions-with-desmos-snapshots/for further discussion of this feature.) As advances in technology continue to take hold, we may see more technologically based solutions for easy sharing of student work.

For the State Fair task, Mrs. Mossotti decided to have Daejhor, Razaria, and Mya, who worked together in class, present Solutions I and II. These students initially thought the cost per ticket was \$8.50 (Solution I) but after examining the graph revised their thinking (Solution II). Mrs. Mossotti

PAUSE AND CONSIDER

How do you make decisions about which students should present in class? How do your decisions promote or constrain an equitable learning environment?

noted this shift on her monitoring chart, writing their names down next to $\frac{8.50}{1} = \$8.50$ and then noting that they "came back with actual cost for 4 tix." Mrs. Mossotti thought that having the same group present both solutions would highlight for the class that it is okay to revise one's thinking.

Mrs. Mossotti also decided that she would have Crispin and Nazier present Solution III. She wanted to make sure that the class had a chance to discuss the 50¢ rate per ticket as that was essential to her lesson goals. While she had several names listed on her monitoring chart next to this strategy, she noted on her monitoring chart that Crispin and Nazier "pull out even and odd concept." This referred to the boys having commented that, "between even values of tickets the difference is a $1.00" and "between even and odd numbers of tickets the difference is 50¢." This was a case where Mrs. Mossotti thought it would be interesting for the class to see their unique way of thinking about the rate of change.

Establishing a Coherent Storyline

The final step in selecting and sequencing is to decide on the order in which students will present their solutions. Being intentional about the order provides you with an important opportunity to build a coherent storyline around the goals of the lesson. Just as the materials in a curriculum unit are carefully sequenced to build on each other in ways that support students' learning, you will want to be strategic in how you sequence students' presentations. Ms. Musumeci explained it in the following way: "I'm trying to build almost like a story about this problem that moves us toward the goal so that we can make connections along the way."

There are a number of issues you may want to consider in thinking about how to effectively create a story that brings students together and

PAUSE AND CONSIDER

What factors do you think may be important to consider when deciding how to sequence students' presentations of solution strategies in class?

highlights the lesson goals. To build conceptual coherence, you might find it beneficial to move from the most concrete strategies to more abstract approaches. This could involve starting with solutions that involve specific cases and then presenting ones that offer generalized solutions. Related, some teachers find it productive to move from less sophisticated representations to more sophisticated representations, for example, from a table to a graph to an equation.

Attending to the social organization of the classroom can also be an important consideration in thinking about how to sequence the class discussion (Horn, 2012). You may, for instance, choose to first share a solution strategy that many students used so that students will initially see work similar to their own being presented (Aguirre et al., 2017). Once students' own strategies are validated, they may be more interested in hearing about strategies that differ from their own. You will also want to think carefully about when and how to address incorrect strategies (this is explored further in Part Two of this chapter).

Whatever criteria you choose to use, it is important that you vary your approach over time. Students can become accustomed to routines, even when they are not made explicit. If students have a sense, for example, that you typically introduce the simplest strategies first, they may feel disappointed if they are asked to be the first presenter. Mixing up the criteria you use to sequence class discussions may also help to increase opportunities for all students to participate.

In thinking about how to organize the discussion of the State Fair task, Mrs. Mossotti decided to start with Daejhor, Razaria, and Mya and have them first explain why, initially, they thought that the cost of 4 tickets was $34.00 (Figure 5.3, Solution I). Many students in the class had used this approach, and Mrs. Mossotti thought it was a good place to begin the discussion. Next, she planned to have Daejhor, Razaria, and Mya explain their solution (Figure 5.3, Solution II). She expected them to show how they extended a line through the given points and how this revealed that the cost of 4 tickets is $10.00 and that 0 tickets cost $8.00. Mrs. Mossotti wanted to have this strategy shared next because she thought it was a natural evolution in the problem-solving process for this task—on first glance, it may appear that 1 ticket costs $8.50, but looking more closely at the graph, you see that the situation is more complicated. As Mrs. Mossotti explained,

> *The idea was to pull out how they knew $34.00 was not an accurate answer, that $8.50 times 4 is way off the graph, so it's probably not the correct answer. And then to show that just by looking at the graph and seeing that it's around the $9.00, $10.00 mark, and then, further doing work through the use of drawing a line, anchored them into a more precise answer.*

Figure 5.3 • Daejhor's written work

Solution I. Price per ticket is $8.50	Solution II. Draw a line to identify the cost of 4 tickets and/or the cost of 0 tickets
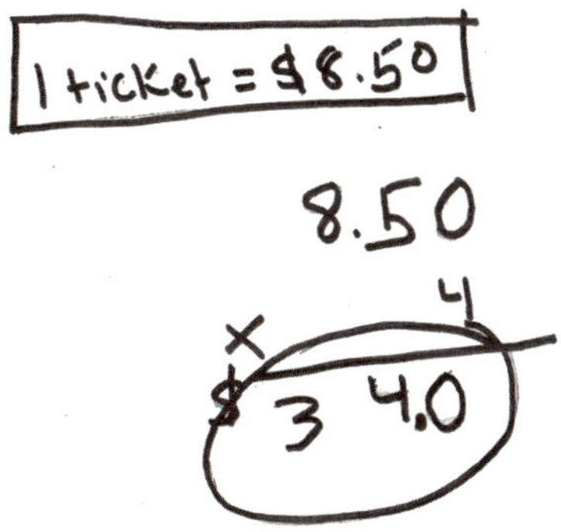 1 ticket = $8.50 8.50 × 4 $34.0	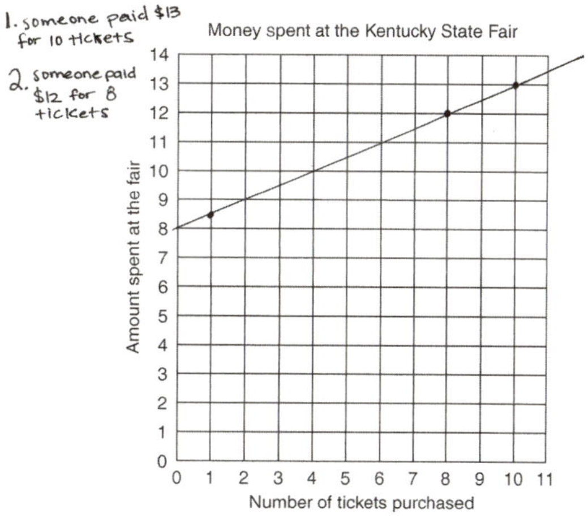 1. someone paid $13 for 10 tickets 2. someone paid $12 for 8 tickets Money spent at the Kentucky State Fair Amount spent at the fair: 0 1 2 3 4 5 6 7 8 9 10 11 12 13 14 Number of tickets purchased: 0 1 2 3 4 5 6 7 8 9 10 11

Finally, Mrs. Mossotti planned to have Crispin and Nazier describe how they discovered that each ticket costs 50¢. In particular, she hoped they would point out their method for finding the rate of change between even numbers of tickets (highlighted in pink in Figure 5.4). In the storyline for the State Fair task, Mrs. Mossotti considered identifying the rate of change as the climax, and so she chose to leave this for the end of the discussion. Crispin and Nazier's strategy was unique because it incorporated aspects of Solution III (using the cost of 8 tickets and 10 tickets to determine that 2 tickets cost $1.00) and Solution IV (connecting the points on the graph and seeing that the line rises half a unit on the *y*-axis for every 1 unit on the *x*-axis). As a result, it was likely to be a solution that other students would understand.

Figure 5.4 • Crispin's written work

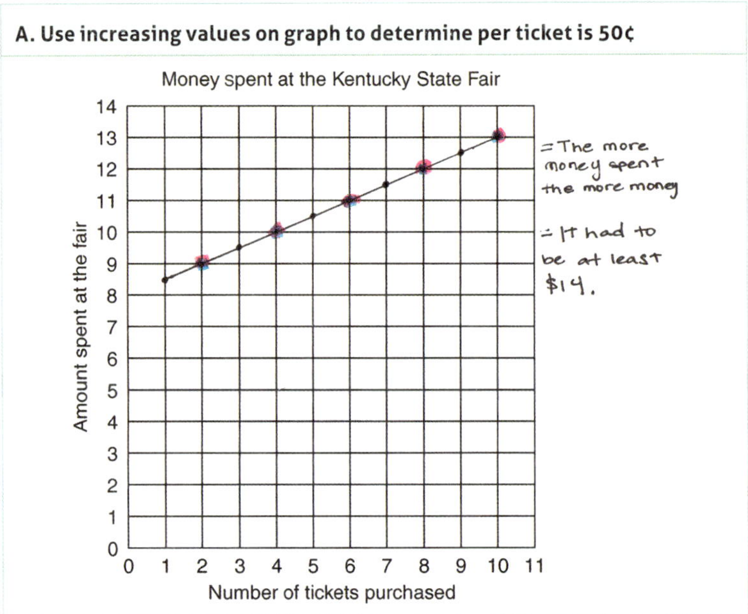

Jennifer Mossotti's Attention to Key Questions: Selecting and Sequencing

As Mrs. Mossotti prepared for her class to discuss the strategies students used to solve the State Fair task, she focused on the key questions. Using her monitoring chart, she reviewed students' solutions with the lesson goals in mind. What solutions would highlight the goal for students to understand rate of change? What solutions would highlight the meaning of the *y*-intercept for students? These questions were critical for Mrs. Mossotti as she thought about which solutions she wanted to call attention to during the class discussion. In addition, she reviewed the challenges students faced as they worked on the task and considered whether it would be valuable to discuss those with the class as well.

Mrs. Mossotti also gave careful attention to *who* would share these solutions with the class. She considered a number of factors including who had recently presented, whether to have students present individually or in groups, and the kinds of supports she might want to offer students as they present. She kept in mind that her selection of presenters matters and could play a role in promoting an equitable learning environment for students in her class.

Finally, in deciding how to sequence the presentations, Mrs. Mossotti attempted to create a coherent structure that would allow the learning goals to become visible for all students, even those who had not used those particular solution strategies. We now take a look at some of the challenges teachers face as they select and sequence students' solutions.

Part Two: Challenges Teacher Face: Selecting and Sequencing Student Solutions

You must purposefully select and sequence the solutions that will be shared to ensure that the goals of the lesson are met and that class time is used efficiently and effectively. Selecting and sequencing can be particularly challenging because, although you can give some consideration to what you would ideally like to share as you plan the lesson, the actual decisions about *what* is shared, *who* is going to share it, and *how* the solutions will be ordered is done during the lesson. In this section, we focus on four specific challenges associated with this practice, shown in Figure 5.5, that we have identified from our work with teachers.

Figure 5.5 • Challenges associated with selecting and sequencing

CHALLENGE	DESCRIPTION
Selecting only solutions that are most relevant to learning goals	Teachers need to select a limited number of solutions that will help achieve the mathematical goals of the lesson. Sharing solutions that are not directly relevant can take a discussion off track, and sharing too many solutions (even if they are relevant) can lead to student disengagement.
Expanding beyond the usual student presenters	Teachers often select students who are articulate and on whom they can count for a coherent explanation. Teachers need to look for opportunities to position each and every student as a presenter and help students develop their ability to explain their thinking.
Deciding what work to share when the majority of students were not able to solve the task and your initial goal no longer seems obtainable	Teachers may on occasion find that the task was too challenging for most students and that they were not able to engage as intended. This situation requires the teacher to modify her initial plan and determine how to focus the discussion so students can make progress.
Moving forward when a key strategy is not produced by students	In planning the lesson, a teacher may determine that a particular strategy is critical to accomplishing the lesson goals. If the success of a lesson hinges on the availability of a particular strategy, then the teacher needs to be prepared to introduce the strategy through some means.

(Continued)

Figure 5.5 (*Continued*)

CHALLENGE	DESCRIPTION
Determining how to sequence errors, misconceptions, and/or incomplete solutions	Teachers often choose not to share work that is not complete and correct for fear that students will remember incorrect methods. Sharing solutions that highlight key misconceptions in a domain can provide all students with an opportunity to analyze why a particular approach does not work. Sharing incomplete or partial solutions can provide all students with the opportunity to consider how such work can be connected to more robust solutions.

Selecting Only Solutions Relevant to Learning Goals

You may be tempted to have every group publicly share their work on a task to motivate students to produce a complete product, give all students an opportunity to share their thinking, or to acknowledge students' effort. While this strategy is well intended, it often results in long, drawn-out discussions where similar solutions are repeated, mathematical ideas get lost, and students begin to disengage. Limiting the number of solutions that are shared to those that will help you explicitly address the mathematics you are targeting in the lesson will allow you to make the best use of your instructional time and keep the class focused and engaged.

Consider, for example, Ms. Musumeci's lesson on the Buying T-Shirts task (see Figure 3.6). As we discussed in Chapter 3, as a result of engaging in the lesson, Ms. Musumeci wanted her students to understand that:

1. there is a point of intersection between two (unique nonparallel) linear equations that represents where the two equations have the same x- and y-values; this point is the solution to the system since it satisfies both equations;
2. the two equations *switch positions* at the point of intersection and the one that was on *top* before the point of intersection is on the *bottom* after the point of intersection because the equation with the smaller rate of change will ultimately be the equation closer to the x-axis regardless of the value of the y-intercept; and
3. tables, graphs, equations, and context can be connected by identifying the slope and y-intercept in each representational form.

Of the six groups in the class, five groups produced a table (most of whom increased the number of T-shirts by 1 or 5), four groups produced an equation in addition to a table, and two groups produced a correct graph. The remaining group produced two different graphs—one that did not show the point of intersection because of the scale used and one that had the point of intersection at the wrong place due to an error in using the slope to locate the points on the graph. Ms. Musumeci selected two of the six groups to present—one that produced a table and an equation and one that produced a graph in addition to a table and an equation.

The group that she selected to go first (Rylee, Khylie, and Alexis) produced the tables shown in Figure 5.6. Ms. Musumeci selected this group to present "because some students in the class had done tables in increments of 5, starting at 0, 5, or 10. I wanted to make sure that students understand that there are other points or other values in between those." For example, one of the groups that incremented by 5's in their table found the point of intersection (10, 150) and knew that Crazy Tees was cheaper for 5 shirts and more expensive for 10 shirts. But they could

Figure 5.6 • Tables and equations produced by Rylee, Khylie, and Alexis

T-Shirts R Us   y=10x+50

(x) Number of T-Shirts	(y) Cost
0	50
1	60
2	70
3	80
4	90
5	100
6	110
20	250

7:120
8=130
9=140
10=150
11=160
12=170
13=180
14=190
15=200
16=210
17=220 18=230 19=240

Crazy Tees   y=15x

(x) Number of T-Shirts	(y) Cost
0	0
1	15
2	30
3	45
4	60
5	75
6	90
20	300

7=105
8=120
9=135
10=150
11=165
12=180
13=195
14=210
15=225
16=240
17=255
18=270
19=285

not describe what happened in between 5 shirts and 10 shirts until they added values 6 to 9 to their table. Ms. Musumeci went on to explain that the first group "had a nice, clear idea of showing both ways. Here's our table where we skipped (the table with values 1 to 6 and 20 on the right side of Figure 5.6), and then here's our table where we went back and found the values in between (the table with values 7 to 19 on the left side of Figure 5.6)."

Figure 5.7 • Spencer's equation, table, and graph

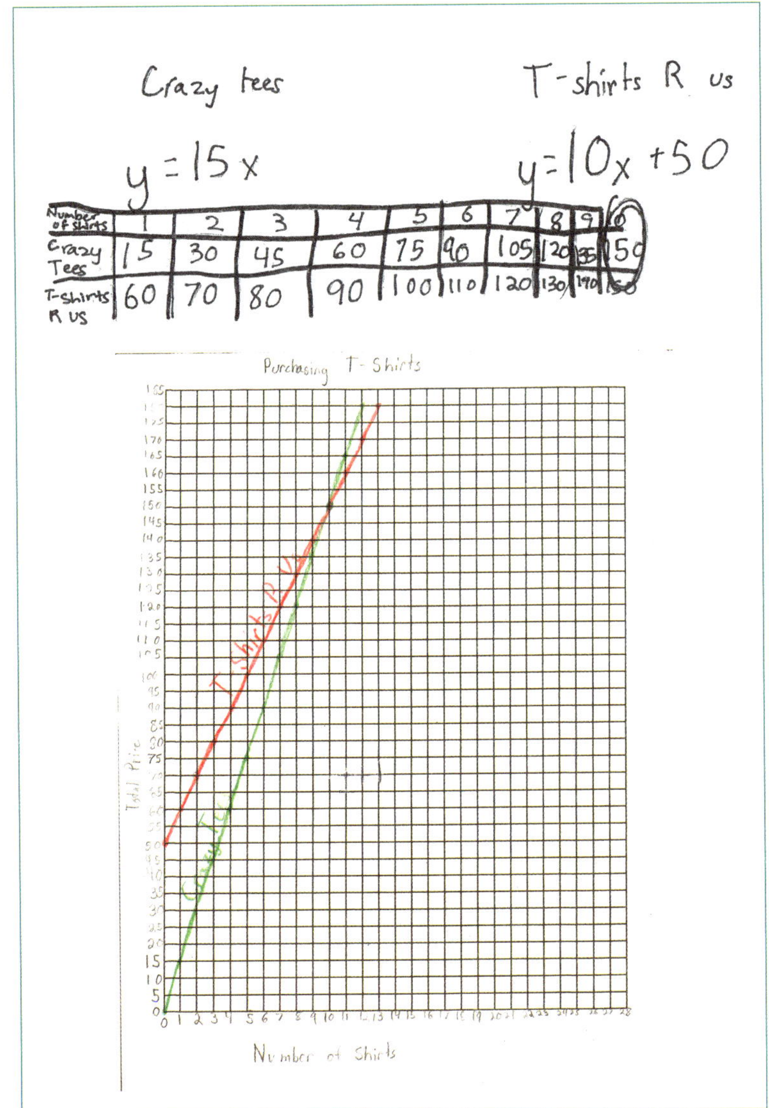

Next, the teacher selected Spencer to present his equation and graph, shown in Figure 5.7. Ms. Musumeci explained:

> *I selected the next presenter because he had a graph that he had produced relatively quickly but was accurate. He and his group members were able to explain how the graph related to the table and what happened before the intersection point and after the intersection point. So, I wanted the students to see a nice, clear graph. Also, he had color-coded it and labeled his lines, and that helped him to be able to point out and explain what happened before and after the intersection point. Then I also wanted him to explain how that related to his tables since he had done both, to kind of take it from the table to the graph.*

Why would you select only two groups to present? As it turns out, Ms. Musumeci was running out of time and probably felt that she had to limit the number of presenters to finish the discussion before class concluded. However, we would argue that even if time had not been an issue, given the task and the work that students had produced, sharing only two solutions made sense since these two solutions made salient the three key ideas she had targeted for the lesson (as indicated in her goal statement). Specifically, the point of intersection (Goal 1) was clear in the tables (Presenters 1 and 2) and in the graph (Presenter 2). The graph produced by Spencer made clear what happened before and after the point of intersection, and Ms. Musumeci's conversation with Spencer and his group convinced her that he could explain this to the class (Goal 2). Finally, the two presentations featured all three of the target representations—both solutions had tables and equations, and the second solution had a graph—which would make it possible for students to make connections between representations and the given context of the task (goal 3). Hence, the two solutions provided sufficient fodder for a rich whole class discussion.

So what do you do if there are *lots* of different solutions? How do you limit what is discussed? To answer this question, we consider the lesson taught by Maura Ingram in her seventh-grade class. Her students were working on a unit on linear functions and had previously used tables, graphs, and equations to describe linear relationships. In the current lesson, Mrs. Ingram wanted her students to understand how tables, graphs, and equations can be used to find the point of intersection of two linear functions and how the three representations could be related to each other. She had selected Henri and Emile's Race, shown in Figure 5.8, because it could be solved using all three representations, as well as a guess and check strategy, and it aligned with her lesson goals. Students, working in groups of three or four, produced the strategies shown in Figure 5.9. In Analyzing the Work of Teaching 5.2, you will consider how Mrs. Ingram could select and sequence students' solutions to accomplish her goals for the lesson.

Figure 5.8 • Henri and Emile's Race task

Henri and Emile's Race

Henri challenges Emile to a walking race. Henri's walking rate is 1 meter per second, and Emile's walking rate is 2.5 meters per second. Because Emile's walking rate is faster, Emile gives Henri a 45-meter head start. Emile knows his brother would enjoy winning the race, but he does not want to make the race so short that it is obvious his brother will win.

A. How long should the race be so that Henri will win in a close race?

B. Describe your strategy for finding your answer to Question A. Give evidence to support your answer.

Source: Lappan, Phillips, Fey, & Friel (2014)

Analyzing the Work of Teaching 5.2

Selecting Solutions That Highlight Key Ideas

Review the student solutions to Henri and Emile's Race shown in Figure 5.9. Keeping Maura Ingram's goals for the lesson in mind (elaborated below), determine:

1. which solutions she should select for the whole class discussion;
2. what each solution will contribute to the discussion; and
3. how you would sequence them to ensure that all students have access to the discussion.

Specifically, Mrs. Ingram wanted students to understand that:

- tables, graphs, and equations can be used to find the point of intersection of two linear functions—the equation can be used to generate the ordered pairs in the table, the ordered pairs in the table can be plotted on a coordinate grid, and the point where the two lines meet on the graph is the entry in the table where the x and y values for both functions is the same.
- the three representations can be related to each other—the coefficient of the x term in the equation is the slope of the line; the slope or rate of change is the difference between two consecutive y-values in the table when x is incremented by 1; and the slope or rate of change is the steepness of the line when graphed (the ratio of the change in y compared to the change in x).

Figure 5.9 • Solutions produced by students in Maura Ingram's class

Solution A

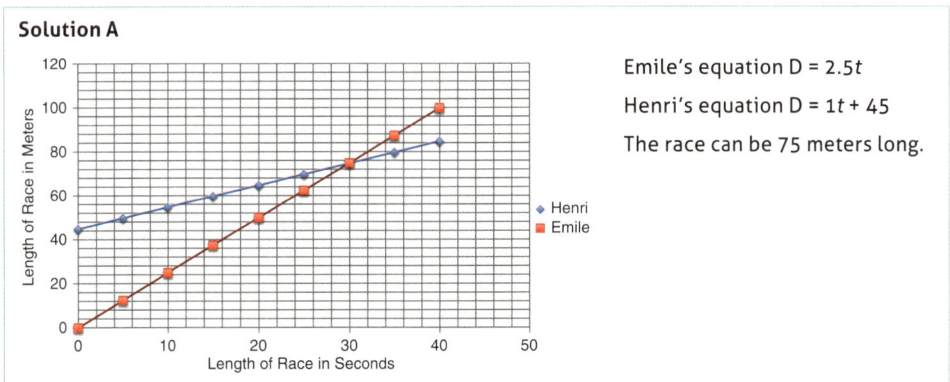

Emile's equation D = 2.5t

Henri's equation D = 1t + 45

The race can be 75 meters long.

Solution B

We estimated 70 meters. We decided that was the right answer because 70 ÷ 2.5 (Emile's rate) is 28. So it takes Emile 28 seconds to go 70 meters. But if the race is 70 meters, Henri only really needs to go 25 meters because he had the head start of 45 meters (70 – 45 = 25). So at 70 meters, we figured out that Henri would win, and it would be a close race. Henri 25 seconds and Emile 28 seconds.

Solution C

With a 74-meter distance, it takes Emile 29.6 seconds because 74 ÷ 2.5 = 29.6.

It would take Henri 74 seconds to go 74 meters, but he had a 45-meter head start, so it will only take him 29 seconds to get to 74 meters because 74 – 45 = 29. So Henri will win by .6 seconds.

Solution D

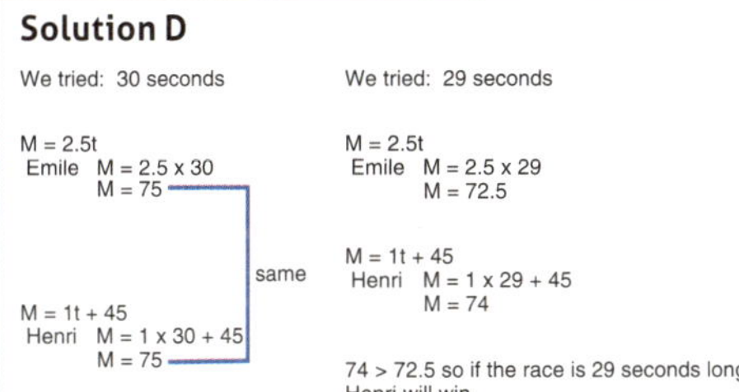

Solution E

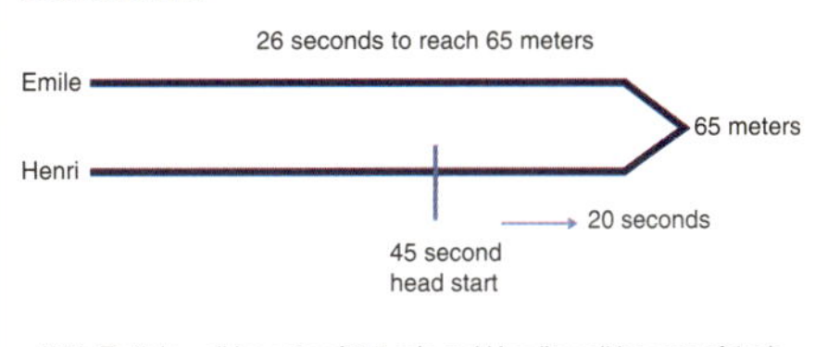

With Emile's walking rate of 2.5 m/s and Henri's walking rate of 1m/s, we decided that the race would be 65 meters. Our goal was for Henri to win the race. Henri will win the race by 6 seconds.

Solution F

Time E = D ÷ 2.5 Time H = D – 45

Meters	68	69	70	71	72	73	74	75
Emile	27.2	27.6	28	28.4	28.8	29.2	29.6	30
Henri	23	24	25	26	27	28	29	30

Solution G

Seconds	0	10	20	30	40	50	60	70	80
Henri distance	45	55	65	75	85	95	105	115	125
Emile distance	0	25	50	75	100	125	150	175	200

At 30 seconds, they have both run 75 meters. So if Henri is going to win the race, it has to be less than 75 meters.

(Continued)

Figure 5.9 (*Continued*)

Solution H

Time	Emile's Distance	Henri's Distance
0	0	45
1	2.5	46
2	5	47
3	7.5	48
4	10	49
5	12.5	50
6	15	51
7	17.5	52
8	20	53
9	22.5	54
10	25	55
11	27.5	56
12	30	57
13	32.5	58
14	35	59
15	37.5	60

Time	Emile's Distance	Henri's Distance
16	40	61
17	42.5	62
18	45	63
19	47.5	64
20	50	65
21	52.5	66
22	55	67
23	57.5	68
24	60	69
25	62.5	70
26	65	71
27	67.5	72
28	70	73
29	72.5	74
30	75	75

Emile's D = $2.5t$

Henri's D = $1t + 45$

If the race is 75 meters,
they will tie, so it needs to be shorter.

Selecting Solutions That Highlight Key Ideas—Analysis

There are a number of different ways that Maura Ingram could select and sequence her students' solutions. The challenge for her is deciding which subset of the eight unique solutions will help her accomplish her lesson goals, allow all students access to the discussion, and keep students interested and attentive. A review of the solutions indicates that four groups had equations (Solutions A, D, F, and H), three groups had tables (Solutions F, G, and H), and three groups used guess and check (Solutions B, C, D, and E). In addition, some students fixed the number of seconds and then determined the distance that could be covered (Solutions A, D, G, H), while other students fixed the distance and then determine the number of seconds it would take to cover the distance (Solutions B, C, E, F).

Since Mrs. Ingram wanted her students to understand how tables, graphs, and equations can be used to find the point of intersection of two linear functions and how the three representations could be related to each other, it would make sense for her to select solutions that used some or all of these three representations. Although the guess and check solutions all show a valid length and time for the race, they do not show the point of intersection. Therefore, Mrs. Ingram may want to avoid these solutions, since they will take time to discuss and are not likely to contribute directly to her lesson goals.

One possible sequence would be Solutions G, A, and F in this order. Solution G is a well-organized table that makes the point of intersection clear, and all students in the class should be able to understand. Solution A is a graph that shows the point of intersection. The points in the table (Solution G) for 0, 10, 20, 30, and 40 seconds can be seen in the graph, and the equation provided in Solution A can be used to generate both the points in the table and on the graph. While Solutions A and G would be sufficient to accomplish the lesson goals, including Solution F provides an opportunity to make additional connections. Specifically, Solution F also uses an equation but unlike the equations in A, D, and H that are of the form $D = R \times T$, this equation calculates time rather than distance ($T = \frac{D}{R}$). Including this solution would provide an opportunity to discuss the relationship between the two equations and to show that Solutions B and C (70 meters and 74 meters respectively) are values that appear in the table in Solution F. Hence, Solution F is a more systematic way of doing exactly what students who produced solutions B, C, and E did. Comparing tables G and H could also highlight the fact that in creating Table F, students needed to select a distance as a starting point, while in creating G students could simply start at 0 seconds.

Our point here is not that you should only select two or three solutions to share as we have illustrated in the two examples discussed in this section, but rather that the number of solutions to be shared should be driven by your lesson goals and the time you have available for the discussion. Using this rule of thumb, not all students will be able to share each day. This should not be a concern as long as over time each and every student has the opportunity to share their work and their thinking, as we will discuss in the next section.

Expanding Beyond the Usual Presenters

While selecting solutions to be presented should be done based on the mathematical potential of the solution, a secondary consideration needs to be who will do the presenting. Over time all students need the opportunity to present in front of the class. This is an issue of equity! It is also important for the development of identity and being seen by one's peers as competent. While it is tempting to call on students who you know you can count on to give a coherent and articulate explanation, students do not improve their skills at presenting and explaining simply by listening to others do it. Further, always calling on the same students sends a clear message regarding who the teacher thinks is capable.

PAUSE AND CONSIDER

Reflect on your practice of identifying presenters. Do you tend to call on the same students repeatedly? What could you do to provide more students the opportunity to improve their ability to explain their thinking and to be seen by the class as mathematically capable?

For example, consider the Painting the Gym Green task shown in Figure 5.10. During the discussion of this task, you decide that you want to have a student share the scale factor solution shown in Figure 5.11. Several different groups have produced this solution. Which student do you select to present? We would argue that you should select the student who has not had an opportunity recently to present his or her work during a whole class discussion. You can prepare for this by reviewing monitoring charts from previous discussions (focusing on who/what and order columns) and making a short list on a Post-it note of students who have not recently been featured prominently in a discussion. This will help you in making decisions about which students to select when there are options. Of course, if none of the students on your list have produced the solution you want to feature, you should select someone else and continue to look for opportunities to involve the students on your list in some way.

Figure 5.10 • Painting the Gym Green task

Painting the Gym Green

It takes 3 gallons of blue paint and 2 gallons of yellow paint to make the shade of green paint that will be used to paint the school gym. If you have 12 gallons of blue paint, how many gallons of yellow paint will you need to get the right shade of green paint?

Image Source: chekat/iStock.com

Figure 5.11 • Scale factor solution to the Paint the Gym Green task

If you have 12 blue, then that is 4 times the amount of blue paint you need to get the right shade of green. So you will need 4 times the amount of yellow paint too.

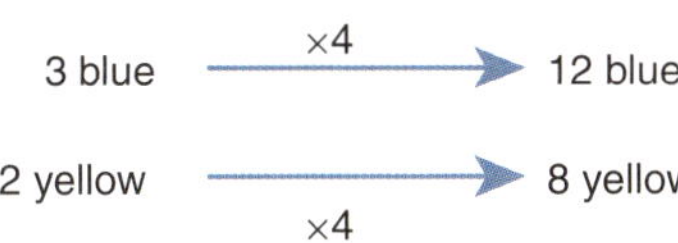

Once you have identified a student to present, you should let the students know that you want him or her to share his or her solution. This will give the student a chance to practice his or her explanation in the safety of his or her group before giving it in front of the whole class. While this is particularly important for English Language Learners students, it can help all students feel more confident about standing up in front of the class. In addition, a student may feel more comfortable presenting if he or she can do so with a partner. However, in this situation you need to make sure that the partner is not the one doing all the explaining!

So what do you do if there are some students who you want to involve in the discussion, but who have not produced the solutions you initially targeted? Consider, for example, what occurred in Mr. Rodriguez's eighth-grade class. He wanted students to understand that there were different but equivalent ways of writing an explicit rule to represent

Figure 5.12 • The Upside Down T task

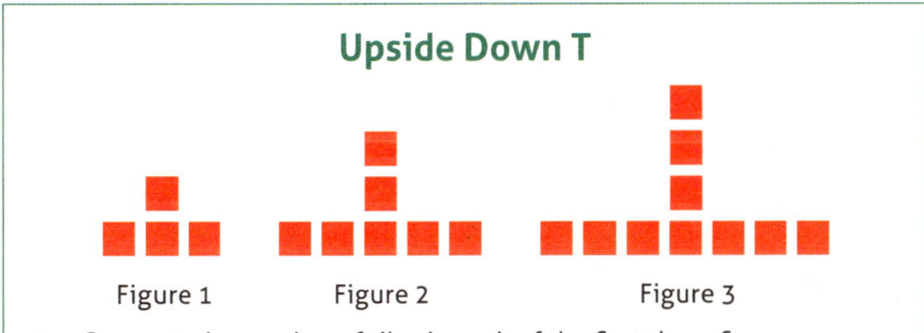

1. Compute the number of tiles in each of the first three figures.
2. Draw the fourth figure and compute the number of tiles in the figure.
3. Determine the number of tiles in the 25th figure without constructing it.
4. Write a rule that could be used to compute the number of tiles in any figure in the pattern and explain why it works.
5. Determine which figure has 109 tiles.

the relationship between two variables. He gave his students the Upside Down T task shown in Figure 5.12 because he felt it would be accessible to all students and was aligned with his lesson goal.

As he monitored students' work on the task, Mr. Rodriguez noticed that students found three different explicit rules, each of which could be related to the physical arrangement of tiles as shown in Figure 5.13, and Claire, one of the students in the class, found a fourth way of thinking about the figure but did not express it algebraically (see Figure 5.14). He also observed that a few students (Xavier, Alicia, and Tanya) had recognized that 3 blocks were added to each subsequent figure (on the end of each *arm*), but they could only tell the total number of blocks in a figure if they knew the number of blocks in the previous figure. Students using this approach had made a table that made it possible to answer the first three questions, but they were stuck on Question 4.

Figure 5.13 • Solutions produced by students in Mr. Rodriguez's class to the Upside Down T task as illustrated with Figure 3 in the sequence

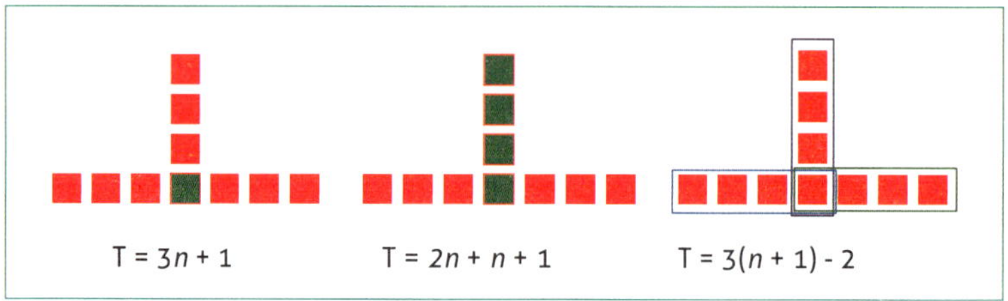

Figure 5.14 • Claire's non-algebraic solution to the Upside Down T task

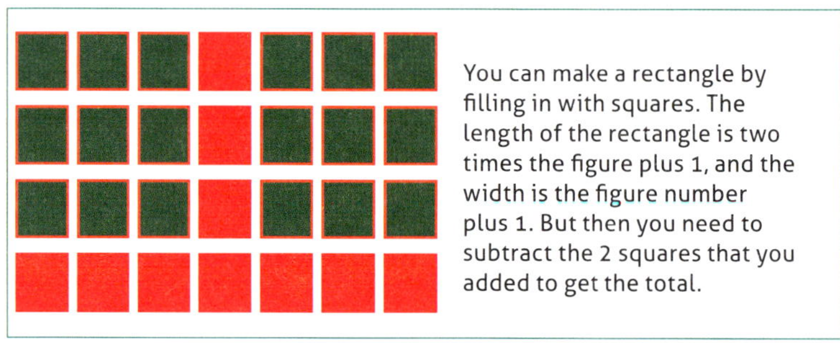

Mr. Rodriguez decided to begin the discussion by having Xavier present the recursive solution of +3. He did this for several reasons. First, he decided it was a valid solution for the class to consider since the +3 pattern could be easily seen, and it would allow all students access to the discussion. Second, it allowed him to include Xavier, who was not a frequent presenter. Finally, since the +3 that students saw being added each time was related to $3n$ in $T = 3n + 1$, he would be able to help students make the connection between repeatedly adding 3 and counting the number of 3s that are being added ($3n$) and making a connection between recursion and the explicit rule.

Mr. Rodriguez then decided to have selected students present the equations $T = 3n + 1$ and $T = 3(n + 1) - 2$ and to conclude the series of presentations with Claire's strategy. He decided to have Claire share her strategy because it was unique—no one else in the class had thought about the figures in this way—and although Claire struggled at times with the formalisms of algebra, she always had interesting ways of thinking, and he wanted the entire class to be aware of this. In addition, Mr. Rodriguez planned to engage the entire class in writing an equation that represented Claire's strategy and in relating the equation to the other two equations that had been discussed. In so doing, Mr. Rodriguez extended students' learning by pressing them to think beyond the work they had produced individually and collectively and grapple with a new idea.

PAUSE AND CONSIDER

Would you have asked Xavier and/or Claire to present their work on the Upside Down T task if they were your students? Why or why not? In what ways might their solutions enrich the discussion for all students in the class?

The point here is that each and every student needs the opportunity to participate in whole class discussions in substantive ways so that students can be seen by others as mathematically capable and can see themselves as doers of mathematics. As we saw in the case of Mr. Rodriguez, this could be sharing a solution that is not quite complete but has the potential to engage the entire class in making sense of someone else's thinking and in making important connections. Jansen, Cooper, Vascellaro, and Wandless (2016) describe a strategy for engaging more students in discussion call *rough-draft talk*. At the heart of this strategy is creating a culture of risk taking and inviting students to share initial ideas—rough-draft presentations—before returning to their groups to revise their thinking toward final-draft solutions. Rough-talk presentations serve to get a range of ideas on the table to stimulate thinking and reduce the threat of being wrong. According to Jansen and her colleagues (2016),

> *If rough-draft talk is valued, brainstormed ideas are welcomed. More students are likely to take risks rather than freeze during challenging tasks. Valuing a wider range of contributions invites greater involvement, in contrast to the same students who participate frequently or not at all. (p. 304)*

Deciding What Work to Share When the Majority of Students Were Not Able to Solve the Task and Your Initial Goal No Longer Seems Obtainable

Your lessons may not always go as planned, despite your best efforts. This may result from the task being too challenging for students, students lacking essential prior knowledge, or because students have pursued solution paths that were not productive. In such cases, continuing with your lesson as planned may ensure that you *cover* the material, but if students are struggling with aspects of the task, it is not clear that they will learn what was intended if you simply forge ahead. At times such as this, you need to readjust your lesson goals to meet students where they are.

This was the situation that Mrs. Saroney faced in her lesson on the Pizza Party task (see Figure 2.6). Although students had prior experience dividing proper fractions with common denominators and drawing models, this task represented the first time students were dividing a mixed number by a proper fraction. As we discussed in Chapter 2, Mrs. Saroney's goals for the lesson were as follows:

1. When you scale a fraction up or down, you have not changed the amount it represents ($\frac{2}{3} = \frac{4}{6}$); equivalent fractions represent the same area and name the same position on a number line. [Since the mixed number and the fraction in the task did not have the same denominator, students would need to be able to rewrite $\frac{2}{3}$ as $\frac{4}{6}$ and know that they were equivalent.]
2. When you are dividing by a fraction, the remainder is expressed as a fraction of the divisor. [The $\frac{1}{6}$ of a pizza left over after making 7 servings needs to be interpreted as $\frac{1}{4}$ of a serving.]
3. When you find "how many ___ are in____?" you are doing division. That is, in $a \div b$ you are trying to find how many times b is contained in a. [This is what division actually means whether you are working with fractions or whole numbers.]

When Mrs. Saroney reviewed the solutions that she and her colleagues generated (see Figure 3.8), she indicated that she thought that her students would most likely use visual or physical models (Solutions A, B, and F in Figure 3.8), repeated addition (Solution E in Figure 3.8), or common denominator (not listed in the table). She predicted that her students would struggle with naming the $\frac{1}{6}$ of a pizza remaining as $\frac{1}{4}$ of a serving.

The majority of students in Mrs. Saroney's class recognized the situation represented in the problem as division but struggled renaming $4\frac{5}{6}$ as $\frac{29}{6}$ or drawing a model to represent $4\frac{5}{6}$ pizzas. As a result, students were not able to make sufficient progress on the task. Although a few groups tried the strategies of repeated addition and repeated subtraction (strategies that did not require a visual or physical model), they were not able to successfully complete the task. As a result, rather than pursuing her original Goal 3, Mrs. Saroney decided to focus the discussion on what $4\frac{5}{6}$ means, how it relates to $\frac{29}{6}$, and why $\frac{2}{3}$ is equivalent to $\frac{4}{6}$. In Analyzing the Work of Teaching 5.3, you will review the work of two students in Mrs. Saroney's class and consider how this work could help her meet her revised lesson goals.

Analyzing the Work of Teaching 5.3

Selecting and Sequencing Solutions to Meet a Revised Goal

Only two students in Mrs. Saroney's class (Deangelo and Tayzir) had correct solutions to the Pizza Party task as shown below.

$\frac{2}{3}\times\frac{2}{2}=\frac{4}{6}$ $4\frac{5}{6}=\frac{29}{6}$ $\frac{29}{6}\div\frac{4}{6}=7\frac{1}{4}$

Deangelo's Solution

Tayzir's Solution

1. Analyze each solution. How could Mrs. Saroney use each solution to help students understand what $4\frac{5}{6}$ means, how it relates to $\frac{29}{6}$, and why $\frac{2}{3}$ is equivalent to $\frac{4}{6}$?
2. Which solution would you use to begin the discussion? Why?

Selecting and Sequencing Solutions to Meet a Revised Goal—Analysis

Mrs. Saroney did not have a lot of options in terms of solutions to select for discussion since only Tayzir and Deangelo produced correct solutions to the task. While other students had identified viable strategies (repeated addition and repeated subtraction), they had trouble successfully implementing them. In addition, neither strategy, even if implemented correctly, had the potential to address the issues with which many students struggled.

While both Tayzir and Deangelo had correctly identified the answer as $7\frac{1}{4}$ servings, the answer and how it was labeled was no longer the key point Mrs. Saroney needed to make. So how could these two solutions be used to help clarify the issues with which students struggled? Tayzir's model clearly shows $4\frac{5}{6}$. He drew 5 rectangles, each of which was subdivided into sixths, with 4 entire rectangles and $\frac{5}{6}$ of the fifth rectangle shaded. Students in the class could be asked to explain why there are 5 rectangles, why they are divided into sixths, and how many sixths there are all together.

Deangelo showed that he converted $\frac{2}{3}$ to $\frac{4}{6}$ and $4\frac{5}{6}$ to $\frac{29}{6}$ before using the common denominator algorithm. He could explain how he got $\frac{29}{6}$ $(4 \times 6 + 5)$ and then have students relate this to Tayzir's model (each of 4 rectangles has $\frac{6}{6}$, which gives you 24 sixths, plus the $\frac{5}{6}$ in the fifth rectangle gives you $\frac{29}{6}$). Students could also be asked to explain why $\frac{2}{3}$ and $\frac{4}{6}$ are equivalent and how you can see this equivalence in Tayzir's model. Finally, students could relate the $29 \div 4$ in Deangelo's solution to what Tayzir did in his model. Sharing Tayzir's solution first would give students an opportunity to make sense of the situation by examining a concrete model. Then they could connect what Deangelo did to the model, giving more meaning to the rules he used.

If the majority of students are struggling with some aspect of the task, moving forward as planned will leave too many students behind. By determining what students are struggling with and how to help them move beyond the struggle, the class will be better positioned to make progress on the initial lesson goals. The student work selected and sequenced needs to help students gain clarity on the aspects of the task with which they struggled.

Moving Forward When a Key Strategy Is Not Produced by Students

When you engage in the practice of anticipating, you consider the correct and incorrect strategies that students are likely to use in solving a task and how you would respond to the work students produced. This is also the time when you consider which of the strategies that you anticipate students using will be most useful in accomplishing the goals for the lesson. What happens then, if during teaching, you discover that no students used a strategy that you consider essential to discuss to meet the lesson goals. What can you do?

There are several options you might consider to prepare yourself in the event that this occurs. You might pull a solution from a previous class period or highlight student work you have saved from a previous year. Another option is one that Mrs. Saroney often uses. Although Mrs. Saroney anticipated a wide range of strategies that her students might use to solve the Pizza Party task, as shown in Figure 2.6, she identified a smaller number of strategies—tape diagram, number line, repeated addition (Figure 3.8, Solutions B, A, and E respectively), and common denominator—that she felt would be critical to share during the end of the class discussion to accomplish her goals for the lesson. Mrs. Saroney did not want to leave it to chance that students will produce these during the discussion. She explains:

> *If I know it's a strategy that will help students understand, I have it written out ahead of time. Kind of like a student wrote it. That way I can just pull it out and refer to it and say oh, you know, in one of the other blocks this is what a student did, what do you think about it?*

By preparing critical solutions in advance, or having access to key solutions saved from a previous year or from a different class period, you will be prepared to introduce a solution that your students did not produce in class that day into the sequence of solutions presented. Students could be asked to consider whether the solution strategy is viable—Does it work? Will it always work? Asking students to make sense of another student's reasoning is challenging and important work and will give you additional insight into what students truly understand.

Determining How to Sequence Errors, Misconceptions, and/or Incomplete Solutions

You may be most comfortable having students share only work that is both complete and correct so that students have models of good work. Incomplete solutions, however, can provide opportunities for analysis and discussion that completed correct solutions do not. For example, sharing the recursive approach to the Upside Down T task first could provide all students with the opportunity to explore the relationship between recursive and explicit rules. Incorrect solutions, on the other hand, can provide an opportunity for students to investigate what is going on and why it does or does not make sense. Finding a correct answer is one thing, but determining why an answer is not correct requires a different level of understanding. In Mrs. Mossotti's class, for example, having students share initial incorrect solutions to the State Fair task validated that it was okay to be wrong and to change your mind, as well as the importance of working through a problem until it made sense to you and you could explain it.

In addition to the two solutions Ms. Musumeci selected for presentation during the whole class discussion around the Buying T-Shirt task (see Figure 3.6) as discussed previously, she also planned to invite Mellina to share the misconception she had. Recall from our discussion in Chapter 4 (see Analyzing Teaching and Learning 4.4) that Mellina initially thought that the point of intersection would be at 4 shirts since the cost of 4 shirts at Crazy Tees was \$60.00 and that \$60.00 was also a cost for shirts at T-Shirts R Us. By asking Mellina to share this, the teacher wanted to ensure that all students understood that at the point of intersection the x and y values in both situations (in this case the number of T-shirts and the cost) had to be the same.

In both Mrs. Mossotti's and Ms. Musumeci's classes, the students who shared incorrect answers had revised their thinking and had ultimately arrived at the correct solution. In such cases, students may be more than willing to share their incorrect solution because they have revised their thinking. If you want to share an error that the student has made but is not yet aware of, you need to ensure that the classroom culture is such that wrong answers are seen as opportunities for new learning and that the student will not be ridiculed for being wrong. Alternatively, you could introduce an incorrect solution as one you saw in another class and ask students to determine whether or not it is correct and why or why not. This way, the student who produced it does not have to own it unless he or she chooses to identify him- or herself as the author.

All incorrect solutions, however, are not worth sharing. If the errors are simply computational in nature, the result from a misunderstanding of the problem, or are made only by one or two students, you may want to address these individually rather than during the whole group discussion. When several students have made the same error, or one or more students have a major misconception, then it makes sense to share the incorrect solution. Consider for example a student who solves the Paint the Gym Green task (see Figure 5.10) by determining that if the number of gallons of blue paint increased by 9 gallons ($3 + 9 = 12$), then the number of gallons of yellow paint would also have to increase by 9 gallons ($2 + 9 = 11$). Here, the student has identified the relationship as additive rather than multiplicative. Since this is a major misconception in the domain of proportional reasoning, it is worth discussing even if it is not widely seen in the class.

You could start a discussion of the Paint the Gym Green task by indicating that you noticed that most students had arrived at one of two answers—8 gallons of yellow or 11 gallons of yellow—and ask students to decide which answer they thought was correct and why. In this way, you are not identifying a particular presenter but rather putting on the table the issue you want the class to resolve. Students could then argue for either answer and hopefully, as a class, conclude that 11 gallons was incorrect and why. Alternatively, you could include the additive solution at the end of the presentations and ask students whether this approach could also be valid.

Incorrect and incomplete work can be used to enhance a discussion and to press students to make sense of someone else's reasoning. This may not be something you need to do in every discussion, but do not avoid something just because it is wrong! Leah Alcala (not a pseudonym) developed a routine for engaging students in analyzing mistakes. She calls it "My Favorite No." At the heart of this routine is giving students a problem to work on, collecting student responses to the problem, reviewing the solutions, identifying the most interesting wrong answers, and selecting a wrong answer for the class to discuss. The incorrect response selected for discussion shows *some good mathematics* but also some error and is not linked to a particular student. The entire class is then engaged in careful analysis of what is correct, what is incorrect, and why. While Ms. Alcala uses this routine as a warm-up activity prior to the lesson for the day, it could be used as a formative assessment activity at any point in a lesson or as a more general technique for sharing incorrect solutions. [See https://www.teachingchannel.org/videos/class-warm-up-routine for more details on "My Favorite No."]

Conclusion

As we have discussed in this chapter, it is through the process of selecting and sequencing that you determine what solutions will be shared and the order in which they will be shared. This is important because the solutions that are shared publicly provide the grist for the discussion that is to follow. Hence, the identified solutions *must* have the potential to highlight the mathematical ideas that are targeted in the lesson. The sequence in which solutions are shared must provide students with access to the discussion and achieve a coherent storyline for students to follow. The first solution presented should be one that all students can make sense of regardless of what they themselves have produced, and as additional presenters share their work, there should be a clear sense of a developing story where one solution builds on the next.

The key to successful selecting and sequencing is careful consideration of what you are trying to accomplish in the lesson. The work of Mrs. Mossotti provides an illustration of a teacher who reflected on what she was trying to accomplish in light of the work students had produced and made a thoughtful determination of what she would feature during the discussion. Her work highlighted how the data she had collected as she monitored students' work on the task served as a resource for decision-making when it was time to select and sequence.

While selecting and sequencing is not without its challenges, as we discussed in Part Two of the chapter, they are challenges you can overcome. The illustrations from the classrooms of Ms. Musumeci, Mrs. Ingram, and Mr. Rodriguez provide some concrete ideas regarding how to select and sequence solutions to limit the number of solutions shared, keep the mathematical ideas central, and ensure that different voices are heard.

The situation in which Mrs. Saroney found herself is a critical one to consider. Lessons do not always go as planned, and it is important to be sure that you are teaching children, not teaching a lesson. What students do during the lesson may cause you to revise your plan. In such cases, you will need to think about how the work students produced can help you achieve your revised goals.

Selecting and Sequencing Student Solutions—Summary

Video Clip 5.1

To hear and see more about selecting and sequencing, watch Video Clip 5.1.

Videos may also be accessed at **resources.corwin.com/5practices-middleschool**

In the next chapter, we explore the practice of connecting. Here, we will return to Mrs. Mossotti's lesson and consider what it takes to engage in these practices and the challenges it presents.

Linking the Five Practices to Your Own Instruction

SELECTING AND SEQUENCING

It is now time to reflect on the lesson you taught following Chapter 4, but this time through the lens of selecting and sequencing.

1. What solutions did you select for presentation during the whole group discussion?
    - Did the selected solutions help you address the mathematical ideas that you had targeted in the lesson? Are there other solutions that might have been more useful in meeting your goal?
    - How many solutions did you have students present? Did all of these contribute to better understanding of the mathematics to be learned? Did you conclude the discussion in the allotted time?
    - Which students were selected as presenters? Did you include any students who are not frequent presenters? Could you have?
2. How did you sequence the solutions?
    - Did the series of presentations add up to something? Was the storyline coherent?
    - Did you include any incomplete or incorrect solutions? Where in the sequence did they fit?
3. Based on your reading of this chapter and a deeper understanding of the process of selecting and sequencing, would you do anything differently if you were going to teach this lesson again?
4. What lessons have you learned that you will draw on in the next lesson you plan and teach?

"As students present, I want everybody, all the students in the class, to be able to make connections that help their understanding of the goals of the lesson."

—MICHELLE MUSUMECI, EIGHTH-GRADE TEACHER

CHAPTER 6

Connecting Student Solutions

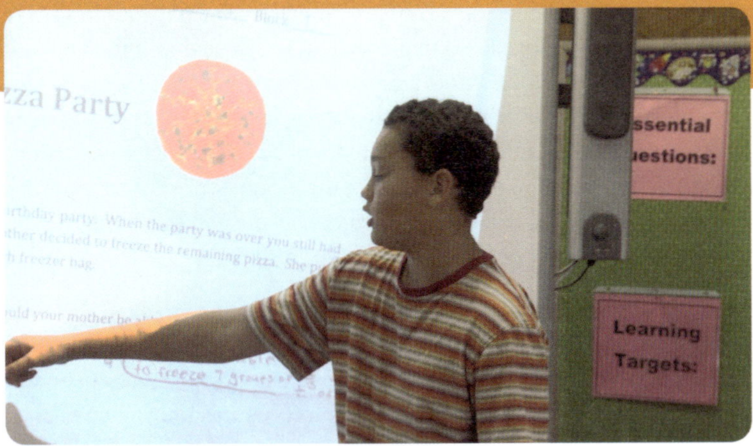

Having selected and sequenced student solutions with the goals of the lesson in mind, you are now ready to conduct a whole-class discussion and engage in the last of the five practices, connecting student solutions. While you designed the discussion so that students play a central role as they share their strategies with their peers, you also play an essential role in the discussion. For students to truly learn what is intended, you need to help students see the connections between the solutions that are shared and the goals of the lesson. To do this requires careful facilitation of the discussion on your part.

Smith and Stein (2018) describe connecting in the following way:

> *[Connecting involves asking] questions [that] must go beyond merely clarifying and probing what individual students did and how. Instead, they must focus on mathematical meaning and relationships and make links between mathematical ideas and representations (p. 70).*

Facilitating meaningful discussions involves helping students to share their thinking in a way that is understandable to others. You may need to help them recognize where to stand, how loudly to speak, and the importance of explaining both their process and their reasoning (Boaler & Humphreys, 2005; Kazemi & Hintz, 2014). Students who are not presenting may also need your help to understand their roles as they engage in active listening and prepare to ask questions of their peers (Hufferd-Ackles, Fuson & Sherin, 2015). For example, you may need to model initially how to ask a question, how to disagree, and how to share an alternate idea. Working with students to establish explicit norms for participation can help all students better understand what is expected of them during classroom discussions (Horn, 2012).

The practice of connecting goes even further. Connecting involves helping students relate strategies or ideas to one or more of the lesson goals and see the relationships between different solutions. Your task here is to consider the solution strategies you have selected and the kinds of connections that will be important for students to make. Some of this work will need to take place on the fly, during instruction, as you see how students describe their strategies, and what questions arise from peers. Still, it can be helpful to consider, before the discussion, what connections you anticipate will be critical for students to make and the questions you can ask to help students make these connections.

In this chapter, we first describe key aspects of connecting and illustrate what this practice looks like in middle school classroom. We then discuss what aspects of connecting are typically challenging for teachers and provide an opportunity for you to explore connecting in your own teaching practice.

Part One: Unpacking the Practice: Connecting Student Solutions

Connecting student solutions involves relating the ideas that students present to the class, both to the goals of the lesson and to each other. Here we explore each of these components by looking inside Mrs. Mossotti's classroom. Figure 6.1 highlights the key components of this practice.

Figure 6.1 • Key questions that support the process of connecting student solutions

WHAT IT TAKES	KEY QUESTIONS
Connecting student work to the goals of the lesson	What questions about the student work will make the mathematics being targeted in the lesson visible?
Connecting different solutions to each other	What questions will help students make connections between the different solution strategies presented?

Connecting Student Work to the Goals of the Lesson

In selecting solution strategies to have students share in class, you purposefully choose student work that contains important mathematical ideas that advance the goals of the lesson. As the discussion unfolds in your classroom, you will want to keep those ideas in mind. While it is possible that students will make these connections in their presentations, this will not always be the case. You want to be prepared to ask questions about the students' work that will make the important mathematics in the lesson visible for the class. In this way, connecting involves creating bridges from what students share to the mathematically significant ideas underlying the lesson (Leatham, Peterson, Stockero, & Van Zoest, 2015). Without seeing these connections, students may walk away from the lesson without clarity about what it was they were supposed to learn.

How can you do this? For each solution shared, you want to keep in mind the key mathematical takeaways for the class. Many times, this will have less to do with *what* a student did and more to do with *why* a student used a particular approach given the task at hand. You may need to draw out these ideas from students by asking them to share why they chose a particular solution path and to explain the reasoning that guided their work.

You will also want to highlight explicit connections between the student work and the goals of the lessons. "How does this approach help us answer the question we are working on?" "Where does this idea fit with what we are trying to figure out?" Students may be applying mathematical ideas that have important connections to the lesson goals and yet be unaware of these connections. Your objective is to help make these connections visible to the presenter and to the class. Boaler and Brodie (2004) describe the importance of using such questions because they target the key concepts in a lesson for students.

Once such ideas have been made public, it is often helpful to give everyone a chance to digest these connections. Using a *turn-and-talk* strategy (Kazemi & Hintz, 2014) can provide needed time for students to consider new information with a partner and reflect on how an idea might fit (or not) with their own approach.

What does this look like in practice? In Analyzing the Work of Teaching 6.1 and 6.2, you will have an opportunity to see how Mrs. Mossotti helps her students make connections between the solutions that are presented and her goals for the lesson. We encourage you to view the video clips and consider the questions posed before you read our analyses.

Analyzing the Work of Teaching 6.1

Connecting Student Work to the Goals of the Lesson—Part One

Video Clip 6.1

As you watch Video Clip 6.1, consider Daejhor, Razaria, and Mya's presentation of their solution and the comments from Mrs. Mossotti and the other students in the class. Recall that Mrs. Mossotti selected this group to address Goals 2 and 3 of the lesson. Here again is Daejhor's written work.

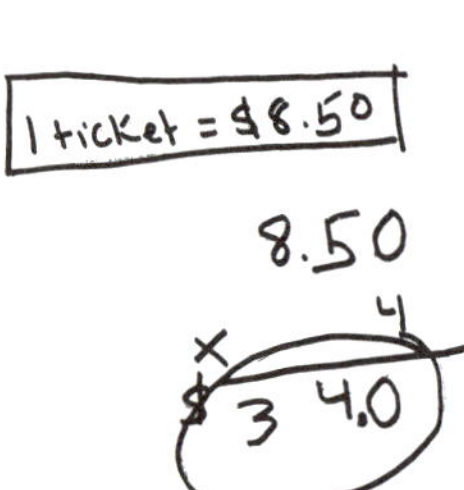

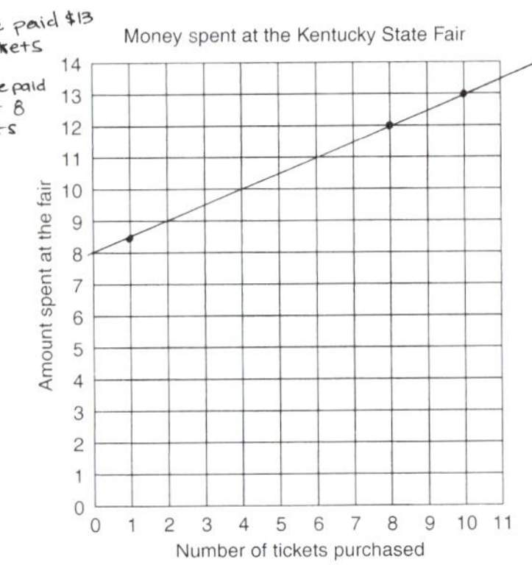

- What questions does Mrs. Mossotti ask to connect the presentation to Goals 2 and 3 of the lesson?
- How do students' responses address these goals?

Goal 2: Some functions do not *start* at 0. That is, the point (0, 0) is not a solution for all linear functions.

Goal 3: The *y*-intercept can be understood as the initial value of a linear function in a real-world context.

Videos may also be accessed at **resources.corwin.com/5practices-middleschool**

Connect Student Work to the Goals of Lesson Part One—Analysis

In this video clip, we see Daejhor and Mya explain the approaches their group used to determine the cost of 4 tickets. As Daejhor begins, it is clear that he is able to explain what they did. "[We] looked at the price of just 1 ticket, and then we timesed that by 4." He then continues, "We got . . . $34.00, which was a lot of money, and it wasn't even on the graph." What is it about this process that Mrs. Mossotti wanted to make public?

To gain insight into Mrs. Mossotti's objective, we can look closely at the questions she asks in response to Deajhor's explanation. "What did he first get?" and "Why did he change his answer and think, 'It's not 34 anymore?'"

At this point, it seems that her goal is to clarify why Daejhor, Razaria, and Mya decided that $34.00 could *not* be the cost of 4 tickets and in doing so, to focus the class's attention on the graph. The graph is, of course, key to making sense of the context of the problem. Binti responds, "He said it wasn't on the graph," and Mrs. Mossotti pursues this idea further. "What do you mean 'it wasn't on the graph?'" "What do you mean 'it's too big?'" Throughout these questions, Mrs. Mossotti explicitly works to connect the idea that the reason $34.00 is not the cost of 4 tickets is because of information that can be found on the graph. Having students understand they can estimate the cost of 4 tickets from the graph is critical to Mrs. Mossotti because the same reasoning can be applied to estimate the cost of 0 tickets, which is essential to achieving Goals 2 and 3 of the lesson. In fact, while Daejhor has mentioned drawing a line that "landed with the points," Mrs. Mossotti clarified that, "You didn't immediately draw that line, Daejhor, you estimated [first]."

In this video clip, Mrs. Mossotti does not yet achieve the lesson goal of ensuring that students understand the role of the y-intercept in the State Fair task and that the graph does not need to *start* at (0, 0). Nevertheless, she made important progress in bringing the class's attention to the graph. What happened next?

Following Mya's comments, Mrs. Mossotti decided to poll the class to see what students believed was the cost of 1 ticket. This was not something she had planned in advance. However, she was curious if students had found Daejhor and Mya's explanation for why the cost of 1 ticket could not be $8.50 compelling. She later explained,

> *When I was walking around the class, it felt like maybe 40 percent of kids were coming up with this $8.50 per ticket, and I wanted to see how many of them had revised their thinking to now think it was 50¢ per ticket.*

In class, she told the students, "I'm going to have you guys pause for a second . . . close your eyes, close them or cover them. If you think the cost of one ticket is \$3.77, raise your hand." After waiting a few seconds, she continued, "Put your hands down. If you think the cost of one ticket is 50¢, raise your hand." She again waited briefly. "If you think that the cost of one ticket is \$8.50, raise your hand. OK, put your hands down."

As she polled the class, Mrs. Mossotti noticed that most students, but not all, raised their hands in agreement that the cost of one ticket was 50¢. In addition, Mrs. Mossotti noticed that Serenity, who had previously argued that the cost of one ticket was \$3.77, raised her hand indicating that she believed the cost of one ticket was 50¢. At this point, Mrs. Mossotti decided to change her plan regarding which solution would be shared next. She saw the shift in Serenity's answer as an opportunity both to highlight another student who had revised her thinking and also as a way to further pursue the connection she wanted to make between her students' work and Goals 2 and 3. In Analyzing the Work of Teaching 6.2, you will take a look at the class discussion as it continues.

Analyzing the Work of Teaching 6.2

Connecting Student Work to the Goals of the Lesson—Part Two

Video Clip 6.2

As you watch Video Clip 6.2, consider Serenity's explanation of why she now thinks that 1 ticket costs 50¢ and Mrs. Mossotti's comments and questions. The work that Serenity produced is shown below.

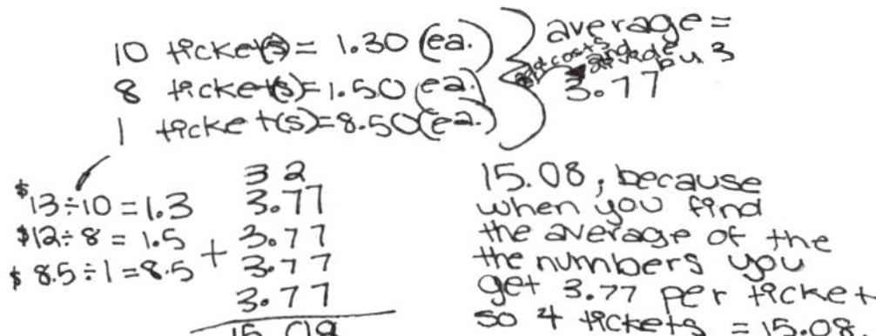

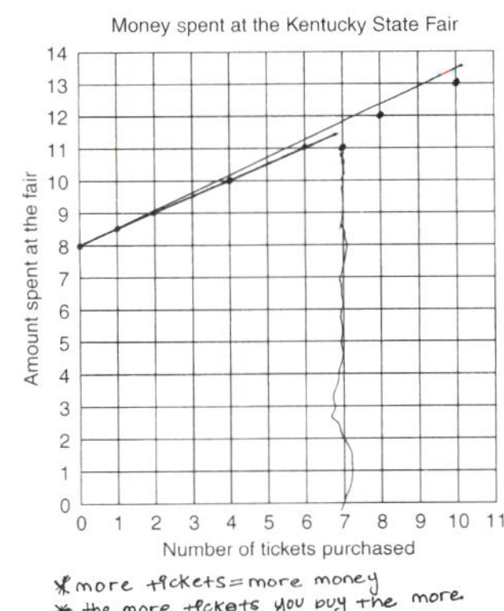

- What questions does Mrs. Mossotti ask to connect Serenity's idea to Goals 2 and 3 of the lesson?
- Following the turn and talk, in what ways does Nietzsche's response address these goals?

Goal 2: Some functions do not start at 0. That is, the point (0, 0) is not a solution for all linear functions.

Goal 3: The y-intercept can be understood as the initial value of a linear function in a real-world context.

online resources Videos may also be accessed at **resources.corwin.com/5practices-middleschool**

Connecting Student Work to the Goals of Lesson Part Two—Analysis

In this video clip, Mrs. Mossotti begins by asking Serenity to explain how she decided that each ticket would cost 50¢ because "this is not where you started." Serenity then refers to her initial answer that each ticket would cost $3.77 but (similar to Daejhor) looking at the graph it became apparent that "was too expensive."

Serenity then indicates that for 0 tickets the cost would be "right here," pointing to (0, 8). This is precisely the issue that Mrs. Mossotti had hoped to discuss with the class. However, the connection Mrs. Mossotti wanted to make was not just that the graph had a non-0 y-intercept but also the meaning of that point.

To explore this, Mrs. Mossotti asks Serenity why 0 tickets would be "right here," and Serenity explains that she made a line. Mrs. Mossotti continues to press her for further information. "You're sure it starts right here?" Eventually asking, "Why isn't 0 tickets free?" to which Serenity responds, "It's your admission."

This is an important moment in the class discussion. A key goal of the lesson is for students to understand that the cost of 0 tickets is represented by the y-intercept on the graph, the point (0, 8). To give all students in class time to consider this, Mrs. Mossotti repeats her questions for the whole class: "I'm going to pause for a second. You guys are going to turn and talk. How come 0 tickets is not free?" By providing this opportunity for students to discuss with each other, Mrs. Mossotti is hoping to raise the students' awareness of the relationship between the cost of 0 tickets ($8.00) and the value on the graph.

Following a minute for students to talk in small groups, Mrs. Mossotti brings the class together and asks Nietzsche to discuss "how come 0 tickets is not no money at all?" Nietzsche explains, "It's $8.00" and "you have to pay your entry fee to get in." Nietzsche's explanation offers a clear connection between Serenity's focus on the graph at the point (0, 8) and the goals of understanding the meaning of the y-intercept.

At this point, Mrs. Mossotti moves onto the final student presentation in the lesson. We will explore this in the next section.

Connecting Different Solutions to Each Other

In addition to connecting students' solutions to the goals of the lesson, it is important to connect students' solutions to each other. Different strategies can open up new opportunities for problem solving and increase students' learning (Schukajlow & Krug, 2014). Doing so can also help build connections for students among mathematics ideas rather than adding to a sense of mathematics as a set of disconnected facts.

You might find it important to help students investigate how various solution methods lead to the same answer, and you may help students examine whether some methods are more efficient than others. This can provide students with valuable information should they be ready to use a more sophisticated strategy in the future (Murata & Fuson, 2006). Alternatively, you might find yourself in a situation where it is necessary to investigate why different approaches lead to incorrect versus correct answers and how to explain those differences.

One important relationship among solution strategies that students should investigate concerns variations in the representations that are used. Many middle school tasks are designed so that they can be solved using multiple representations (refer back to Figure 3.9 for a discussion of different ways to represent a mathematical idea). The idea is that students should develop *representational fluency*; that is, students should have the ability to move among different representations efficiently and understand how key features in one representation appear in another representation (Suh, Johnston, Jamieson & Mills, 2008). For example, in the Buying T-Shirt task, Ms. Musumeci wanted her students to understand that tables, graphs, equations, and context can be connected by identifying the slope and y-intercept in each representational form.

Another relationship that is valuable for students to consider is the comparison between more concrete and more abstract solutions. The ability to generalize from a set of specific cases to any case is a powerful mathematical idea and one that has been shown to be appropriate for introducing in the middle school years (Yopp & Ellsworth, 2017). For example, in the Pizza Party task, Mrs. Saroney planned to have Tayzir present his tape diagram first. This concrete model made the problem context clear and would be accessible to students. Deangelo's presentation of the common denominator strategy, which would follow Tayzir's presentation, was more abstract. This more generalizable and efficient strategy could be connected to Tayzir's model.

In Analyzing the Work of Teaching 6.1 and 6.2, you began to see some of the ways that Mrs. Mossotti connected the students' solutions to each other. Daejhor, Razaria, and Mya present two solutions for the cost of 4 tickets; their initial answer of $34.00 and their revised answer of $10.00. Mrs. Mossotti presses them to explain the relationship between these answers, and specifically how using the graph helped them to see that $34.00 was incorrect. When talking with Serenity, Mrs. Mossotti draws out the connection between the graphical representation of the task and the real world context of the problem. With prompting from Mrs. Mossotti, Serenity explains the meaning of the point (0, 8) within the context of the problem: "It's your admission."

Let us now look at more of the conversation from Mrs. Mossotti's classroom and the ways that she highlights connections among the students' solutions. In Analyzing the Work of Teaching 6.3, the class hears from Crispin and Nazier as they share how they solved the State Fair task. Please review Analyzing the Work of Teaching 6.3 (at the bottom of this page) before moving on to the Analysis section below.

Connecting Different Solutions to Each Other—Analysis

In the beginning of this video clip, Mrs. Mossotti introduces Crispin and Nazier by connecting earlier comments from students to what she expects Crispin and Nazier to highlight. She reminds the class that when they first looked at the State Fair task, many students noticed that the cost "kept

Analyzing the Work of Teaching 6.3

Connecting Different Solutions to Each Other

Video Clip 6.3

As you watch Video Clip 6.3, consider Crispin and Nazier's explanation of how they discovered that each ticket cost 50¢, and listen to Mrs. Mossotti's comments and questions. The work that Crispin produced is shown at the top of the next page.

CONTINUED

CONTINUED FROM PREVIOUS

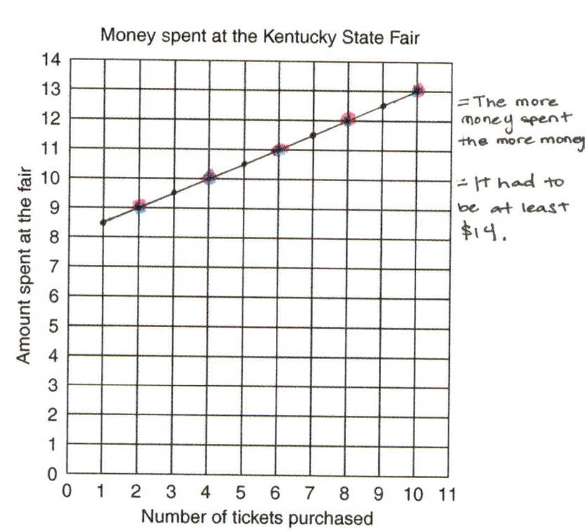

- What connections does Mrs. Mossotti encourage students to make between Crispin and Nazier's solutions and other approaches students have taken?
- How do students respond?

online resources Videos may also be accessed at **resources.corwin.com/5practices-middleschool**

going up with the more tickets that you buy," and she states that Crispin and Nazier will explain "exactly how it increases." Thus, even before Crispin and Nazier have begun to share their approach, Mrs. Mossotti has made it clear to the class that their solution builds on students' earlier ideas and is relevant for everyone.

As Crispin and Nazier share their solution, Crispin describes a pattern that he noticed among the even numbers on the graph. "They were apart by two grids gradually heading downwards." He continues by explaining that the "odd ones were in between them right in the middle." Crispin's discussion of what he noticed focuses on features of the graph, specifically the odd and even numbers on the x-axis and the corresponding changes in the position of the line. To help make this approach accessible to the rest of the class, Mrs. Mossotti encourages students to draw connections between what Crispin said and the context of the State Fair task. At one point, she approaches the graph herself and asks the class, "This even number is 10 what?" The class responds, "tickets." "This even number is eight what?" The class again responds, "8 tickets." Similarly, Mrs. Mossotti engages Kaelin in considering the relationship between the changing shape of the graph on the one hand and the idea that the distance *going up* represents a 50¢ increase on the other hand. Following Kaelin's comments, Mrs. Mossotti provides all students with an opportunity to consider this relationship as they turn and talk with a peer.

While it does not appear on the video clip, following the turn and talk, Mrs. Mossotti wraps up the discussion and tells the class, "You didn't have to think about it the way Crispin did." In doing so, Mrs. Mossotti honors the varied ways that students in her class approached the State Fair task and acknowledged that there were a number of possible strategies that could help students see that the cost of the tickets increased by 50¢ per ticket.

Jennifer Mossotti's Attention to Key Questions: Connecting

In facilitating the class discussion of the State Fair task, Mrs. Mossotti encouraged students to draw connections between the work that was being discussed and the goals that she had established for the lesson. While Mrs. Mossotti had chosen specific student solutions because they related to the lesson goals, during the discussion, Mrs. Mossotti asked a variety of questions to ensure that those connections were visible for students.

Mrs. Mossotti also made an effort to highlight for the class the ways that different solutions were related and in particular that it was important to connect features of the problem across different representations. Connecting students' solutions to the goals of the lesson and to each other is critical to fully realize the benefits of the five practices. Despite its importance, connecting is not without difficulty. In fact, many teachers tell us this is the most challenging of the practices to accomplish. We now take a look at some specific challenges teachers face as they work to connect students' solutions.

Part Two: Challenges Teachers Face: Connecting Student Responses

The whole-group discussion that takes place around the work students share is where students have the opportunity to continue to solidify their learning. It is during the discussion that you need to ensure that the key mathematical ideas that you have targeted during the lesson are made public and accessible to the students in your class. The key to a successful discussion is building on the ideas put forth by students without telling students what it is you want them to know. This is not easy. The pressures of time and accountability weigh heavily on teachers, and the temptation to summarize the lesson for students is strong. In this section, we focus on four specific challenges associated with the practice of connecting, shown in Figure 6.2, that we have identified from our work with teachers and provide some guidance on how to overcome them.

Figure 6.2 • Challenges teachers face in connecting student responses

CHALLENGE	DESCRIPTION
Keeping the entire class engaged and accountable during individual presentations	Often, the sharing of solutions turns into a *show and tell* or a dialogue between the teacher and the presenter. The rest of the class needs to be held accountable for understanding and making sense of the solutions that are presented.
Ensuring key mathematical ideas are made public and remain the focus	It is possible to have students share and discuss a lot of interesting solutions and never get to the point of the lesson. It is critical that the key mathematical ideas that are being targeted in the lesson are explicitly discussed.
Making sure that you do not take over the discussion and do the explaining	As students are presenting their solutions, the teacher needs to ask questions that engage the presenters and the rest of the class in explaining and making sense of the solutions. There is a temptation for the teacher to take over and tell the students what they need to know. When this happens, opportunities for learning are diminished. Remember whoever is doing the talking is doing the thinking!
Running out of time	Teachers may not have enough time to conduct the whole class discussion the way they had planned it. In such cases it is important to come up with a *Plan B* that provides some closure to the lesson but does not turn into telling.

Keeping the Entire Class Engaged and Accountable During Individual Presentations

It is easy for the student presentations that take place at the end of a lesson to turn into a series of show and tells, where each presenter explains what they did and the rest of the class is silent. Having some students sit passively, while other students explain, however, is not sufficient to ensure learning. The teacher needs to ensure that the entire class is engaged in and accountable for what is being presented. According to Michaels, O'Conner, Hall, and Resnick (2013):

> *When classroom talk is accountable to the learning community, students listen to one another, not just obediently keeping quiet until it is their turn to take the floor, but attending carefully so that they can use and build on one another's ideas. Students and teachers paraphrase and expand upon one another's contributions. If speakers aren't sure they understood what someone else said, they make an effort to clarify. They disagree respectfully, challenging a claim, not the person who made it. Students move the argument forward, sometimes with the teacher's help, sometimes on their own. (pp. 2–3)*

So what exactly can you do to hold students accountable? In Figure 6.3, we have identified a set of moves that teachers can make to hold students accountable for attending to the discussion.

Figure 6.3 • Talk moves intended to hold students accountable for participation in a discussion

TEACHER MOVES	PURPOSE	EXAMPLES	SOURCE
Adding on: Prompting students for further participation	To invite additional contributions to the discussion to engage more students or to gain a deeper understanding of an idea	• Would someone like to add on to what she just said? • Can you say more about how you figured that out?	Chapin, O'Connor, O'Connor, & Canavan Anderson (2009, pp. 13–16).
Reasoning: Asking students to compare their own reasoning to someone else's reasoning	To allow students to engage with and make sense of their peer's ways of thinking that may be different from their own	• Do you agree or disagree? Why? • How is what he said the same as or different from how you thought about it?	
Repeating: Having a student repeat what another student has said in her own words	To give students another version of a contribution and to ensure that students are engaged in listening to their peers	• Can someone repeat what he just said in their own words?	
Revoicing: Repeating what a student has said and then checking with the student to make sure you have accurately captured their idea	To clarify what a student has said or to amplify an important idea	• So, you are saying. . . • So, here is what I heard you say. . .	
Waiting: Giving students time to think about the question that has been posed before asking for a response	To ensure that all students have an opportunity to think about the question posed and to provide a student who has been called on time to gather his or her thoughts	• Take a minute to think about this. • I am going to wait until I see more hands. • Take your time . . . we will wait.	

(*Continued*)

Figure 6.3 • (*Continued*)

TEACHER MOVES	PURPOSE	EXAMPLES	SOURCE
Revise: Allowing students to revise their initial thinking based on new insights	To make it clear to students that changing one's mind based on new information is how learning occurs and that this is valued	• Would anyone like to revise his or her thinking? • Has anyone's thinking changed? Why?	Kazemi, & Hintz (2014, p. 21).
Turn and talk: Allowing time for students to discuss an idea that has been presented with a partner or small group	To give students time to think about a question that has been posed rather than be expected to answer immediately and to clarify and share ideas with a small number of peers before doing so publicly	• Take two minutes and turn and talk to your table group about . . .	
Challenging: Redirecting a question raised back to students or using students' contributions for further investigation	To turn the responsibility for reasoning and sensemaking back to students and develop shared understandings in the classroom	• That's a good question. What do you think about what she just said?	Michaels, O'Conner, Hall, & Resnick (2013, p. 22).
Marking: Noting a valuable contribution that was made to the discussion	To highlight a contribution that is directly relevant to what the teacher is trying to accomplish in the lesson	• Did everyone hear what she just said? She . . . • That's an important point.	
Recapping: Summarizing key points made in the discussion by several students	To make public in a concise and coherent way what can be concluded at a particular point	• So in looking across the presentations, here is what I am hearing . . . • Here is what we have discovered . . .	

Figure 6.3 • (*Continued*)

TEACHER MOVES	PURPOSE	EXAMPLES	SOURCE
Inviting: Asking a student to contribute to the discussion	To make diverse points of view available for public discussion	• ____, would you share what you and your group came up with? • ____, you have a puzzled look on your face. What are you thinking? • ____, your strategy was not the same as this one. What did you do differently?	Herbel-Eisenmann, Cirillo, Steele, Otte, & Johnson (2017, pp. liv–lvii).
Probing: Following up on what an individual student has explained or produced	To make a student's thinking process more transparent to others, to elicit additional justification for why he or she took a particular action	• Can you explain how you got...? • How do you know that? • Why does that work?	

[See Appendix D for a summary of each of the identified sources. Although we have associated particular authors with specific moves, you will find that many of the moves are addressed in each of the resources.]

In Analyzing the Work of Teaching 6.4, you will explore the opportunities afforded students to engage with the ideas presented by Tayzir and Deangelo. As we discussed in Chapter 5, Mrs. Saroney selected Tayzir and Deangelo to present their solutions to the class and sequenced them in that order.

Analyzing the Work of Teaching 6.4

Holding Students Accountable—Parts One and Two

Video Clip 6.4a

Video Clip 6.4b

In Video Clip 6.4a, Tayzir is presenting his solution (shown below on the left) with the class. In Video Clip 6.4b, Deangelo is sharing his solution (shown below on the right) with the class.

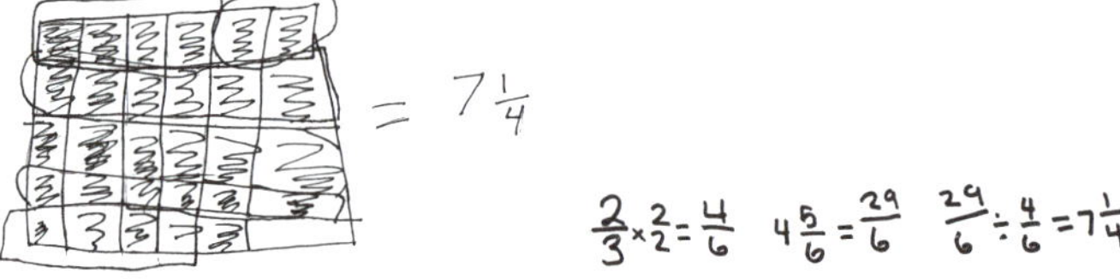

As you watch the video clips, consider the following questions:

1. What does Mrs. Saroney do to help her students make sense of what Tayzir and Deangelo were saying? What talk moves (see Figure 6.3) does she use?
2. What evidence is there that students **are** making sense of the presented ideas?

Videos may also be accessed at **resources.corwin.com/5practices-middleschool**

Holding Students Accountable—Analysis

As Tayzir and Deangelo explained their solutions, Mrs. Saroney intervened at key points to ensure that the explanations they provided were clear and students were engaged in making sense of the presented ideas. We begin our analysis by first examining Tayzir's presentation. In what follows, we indicate Mrs. Saroney's use of a specific talk move by noting the move in parentheses.

Mrs. Saroney stopped Tayzir several times during his presentation to ask him questions. For example, after he explained that he made 4 whole groups of sixths and 1 group of five-sixths, Mrs. Saroney stopped him and asked him to point to the groups that he was referring to (probing). She subsequently asked him why he had drawn $4\frac{5}{6}$ groups and why he had divided the model into sixths (probing). These questions, and others, served to improve the quality of his explanation by making his thinking transparent to the rest of the class. While Mrs. Saroney might have understood what Tayzir had done and why, she could not be sure that students would come away with a clear understanding of Tayzir's solution without having more insight into his decision-making.

While Mrs. Saroney's questions to Tayzir were intended to make his thinking clear to the class, she also did several things to make sure that students in the class understood what Tayzir had done and why. For example, after Tayzir explained why he had drawn $4\frac{5}{6}$ groups, she asked another student to repeat what Tayzir had said (repeating). She then asked students to raise their hands if they thought there were $4\frac{5}{6}$ pizzas left (reasoning). This sequence of questions allowed her to determine if students heard what Tayzir had said and whether they agreed with it. Later, when Tayzir could not explain why he divided the tape diagram into sixths beyond "because that was the denominator," Mrs. Saroney instructed the class to talk in their table groups about why Tayzir might have cut the pizzas into sixths. Rather than placing the responsibility for explaining solely on Tayzir, Mrs. Saroney used the turn-and-talk strategy we discussed earlier and asked the class to consider his reasoning, "Why might he have cut it into sixths?"

Mrs. Saroney also intervened during Deangelo's presentation. After Deangelo explained that he turned $4\frac{5}{6}$ into the improper fraction $\frac{29}{6}$, she asked the class what $\frac{29}{6}$ represented (reasoning). Then she instructed students to talk in their table groups (turn and talk) and figure out how many sixths Tayzir had in his drawing (reasoning). Her questions were intended to see if students in the class recognized that the $4\frac{5}{6}$ they had previously agreed represented leftover pizza was in fact the same as the $\frac{29}{6}$ Deangelo was talking about. She also wanted to see if they could make the explicit connection between the fraction $\frac{29}{6}$ and the number of sixths in Tayzir's tape diagram. This was a first step in helping students see the relationship between the tape diagram and the common denominator algorithm.

Now that we have examined what the teacher did, we need to consider whether the teacher's interventions served the purpose for which they were intended. That is, were students able to make sense of the ideas presented by Tayzir and Deangelo? As we noted in Chapter 5, the Pizza Party task was more difficult for students than Mrs. Saroney had anticipated. Specifically, students had trouble renaming $4\frac{5}{6}$ as $\frac{29}{6}$ or drawing a model to represent $4\frac{5}{6}$ pizzas. As a result, Mrs. Saroney decided to focus the discussion on what $4\frac{5}{6}$ means, how it relates to $\frac{29}{6}$, and why $\frac{2}{3}$ is equivalent to $\frac{4}{6}$.

By specifically targeting these ideas in the discussion through her questioning, students had the opportunity to grapple with these ideas. First, most students raised their hands to indicate that they agreed that there were $4\frac{5}{6}$ pizzas left over following Tayzir's explanation. Although Erika and her tablemates initially thought that $\frac{4}{6}$ of a pizza was lef tover, a review of the problem seemed to address this. Later, during Deangelo's presentations, Giovanni stated that $\frac{29}{6}$ also represented the amount of pizza left. Students then had the opportunity to confirm that in fact $\frac{29}{6}$ was equivalent to $4\frac{5}{6}$ by counting the number of sixths in Tayzir's diagram. Deangelo had been following the rule that if a mixed number is in the form of $a\frac{b}{c}$, then you convert to an improper fraction using this expression $\frac{(ac+b)}{c}$. While the relationship between the rule and the picture was not explicitly made, the ability to make this connection is probably within the students' reach given the work that was done.

Finally, students were given the time to investigate Tayzir's statement that $\frac{2}{3}=\frac{4}{6}$. While we did not hear the outcome of the table discussions in the portion of video reviewed, students agreed that the two fractions were equal, and Jay demonstrated that $\frac{2}{3}\times\frac{2}{2}=\frac{4}{6}$. Tayzir then went on to explain that he had circled groups of $\frac{4}{6}$ in his model. At the conclusion of Tayzir's presentation, Mrs. Saroney asked Erika what $\frac{4}{6}$ represented and why Tayzir circled it. She replied, "It represents the $\frac{2}{3}$ of a pizza that she put in the freezer bag." This is particularly noteworthy since Erika had initially thought the $\frac{4}{6}$ was the amount of leftover pizza.

In looking across the two presentations, we see the teacher using several different moves to make the ideas being presented accessible to students and to actively engage students in making sense of the solutions begin presented. In these video clips, we see a teacher asking students to provide more details about their thinking (probing), checking to see who agrees with an idea that has been put forth (reasoning), and giving students time to discuss an idea in table groups before continuing the discussion (turn and talk). In addition, we see Mrs. Saroney asking students in the class to make an explicit connection between the two solutions presented (reasoning). The critical point here is that the entire class is being held accountable for expressing their ideas clearly and for listening closely to and thinking deeply about the mathematics being discussed.

Ensuring That Key Mathematical Ideas Are Made Public and Remain the Focus

Productive discussions are ones that clearly and explicitly target the mathematical ideas that you want students to learn as a result of engaging in the lesson. Having selected students to present their solutions—even solutions of the highest quality—is not sufficient to ensure that students will learn what is intended. Students need assistance in drawing connections among methods and in tying specific solutions to disciplinary methods and concepts (Smith & Stein, 2018).

Consider, for example, a teacher who is teaching a lesson featuring the Ice Cream Favorites task discussed in Chapter 3 and shown again in Figure 6.4. Her main goal for the lesson is for students to understand that a ratio is a multiplicative comparison of two quantities (i.e., in the ratio $\frac{a}{b}$, $a = bx$). Imagine that during the lesson, students produced the solutions shown in Figure 3.11. Although all the solutions shown are correct, getting the correct answer is not equivalent to understanding the underlying idea. In fact, no combination of these solutions is going to get at the goal the teacher has for the lesson without assistance. While equivalent ratios can be found by scaling up (e.g., 3:2, 6:4, 9:6), this does not explain the relationship *between* the number of friends who prefer vanilla and the number of friends who prefer chocolate (i.e., the number of friends who prefer chocolate ice cream is 1.5 times the number of friends who prefer vanilla ice cream). Recognition of this relationship is likely to surface through teacher questioning, perhaps by suggesting that students explore the relationship between the first two columns in the table (see Figure 3.11, Symbolic-Numeric solution). The point is, that student solutions do not make the mathematics to be learned transparent. You need to identify the solutions that have the potential to address the lesson goals, and then you must ask specific questions of students that will help them make connections to the concepts you have targeted.

TEACHING TAKEAWAY

Correct solutions alone are not enough. Teachers must ask questions to help students make connections to the targeted mathematical ideas.

Figure 6.4 • Ice Cream Favorites task

Ice Cream Favorites

Beatriz often asks her family and friends which they like better, chocolate ice cream or vanilla ice cream. Her friends prefer vanilla ice cream to chocolate ice cream by a ratio of 3:2. If 15 of Beatriz's friends prefer vanilla ice cream, how many prefer chocolate ice cream? Explain how you know.

Source: Adapted from the Institute for Learning (2015b). Lesson guides and student workbooks available at ifl.pitt.edu.

What occurred in Ms. Musumeci's class provides a context for exploring this idea further. As we first discussed in Chapter 3, as a result of engaging in the Buying T-Shirts lesson, Ms. Musumeci wanted her students to understand that:

(1) there is a point of intersection between two (unique nonparallel) linear equations that represents where the two equations have the same x- and y-values; this point is the solution to the system since it satisfies both equations;

(2) the two equations *switch positions* at the point of intersection and that the one that was on *top* before the point of intersection is on the *bottom* after the point of intersection because the equation with the smaller rate of change will ultimately be the equation closer to the x-axis regardless of the value of the y-intercept; and

(3) tables, graphs, equations, and context can be connected by identifying the slope and y-intercept in each representational form.

In Analyzing the Work of Teaching 6.5, you will analyze a portion of the discussion that took place at the end of class and determine which ideas were made public and how.

Analyzing the Work of Teaching 6.5

Making Key Ideas Public—Parts One and Two

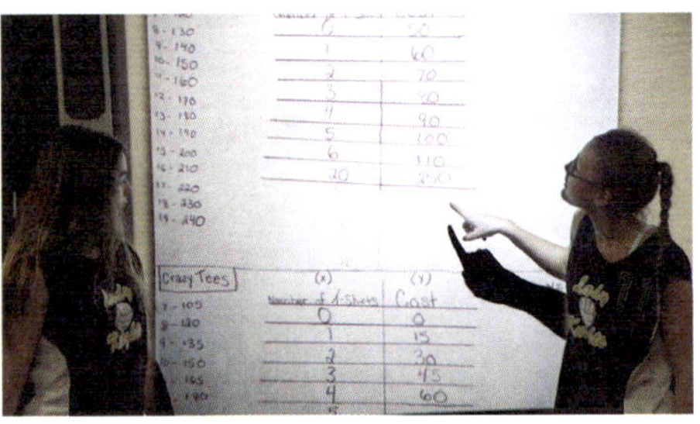

Video Clip 6.5a

Video Clip 6.5b

In Video Clip 6.5a, Alexis, Rylee, and Khylie explain their tables (shown below on the left). In Video Clip 6.5b, Spencer explains the graph he and Demarco created (shown below on the right).

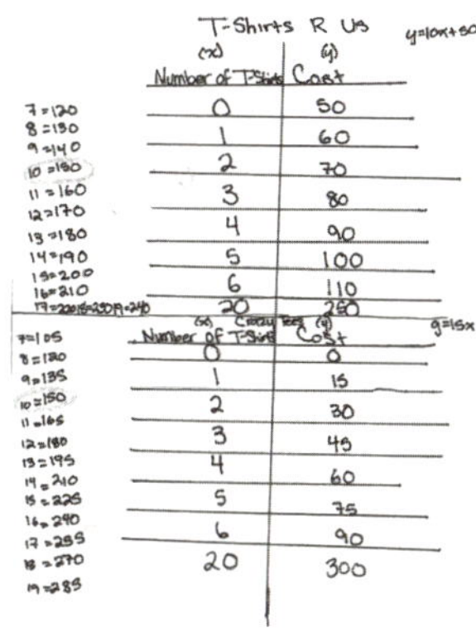
T-Shirts R Us $y=10x+50$

Number of T-Shirts (x)	Cost (y)
0	50
1	60
2	70
3	80
4	90
5	100
6	110
20	250

Crazy Tees $y=15x$

Number of T-Shirts (x)	Cost (y)
0	0
1	15
2	30
3	45
4	60
5	75
6	90
20	300

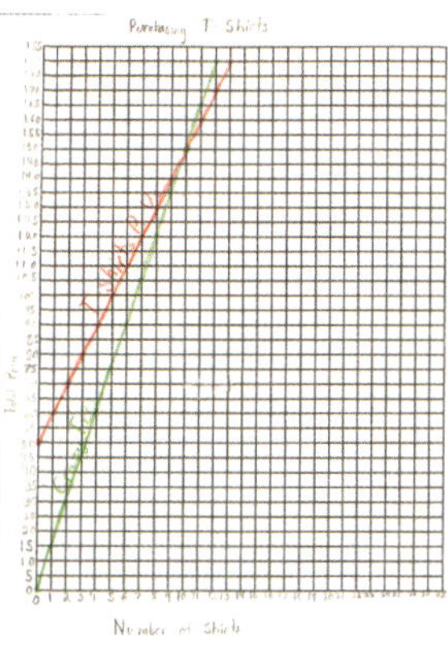

As you watch the two video clips, consider the following questions:

1. What mathematical ideas are being targeted in each of these presentations?
2. What does Ms. Musumeci do to highlight the mathematics she wants students to learn?
3. What does Ms. Musumeci do to determine if students understand the mathematical ideas she wants them to learn?

Videos may also be accessed at **resources.corwin.com/5practices-middleschool**

Making Key Ideas Public—Analysis

During the presentations given by Alexis, Rylee, Khylie, and Spencer, the students in the class, with Ms. Musumeci's guidance, began to explore the ideas that she had targeted in the lesson.

Goal 1: There is a point of intersection between two (unique nonparallel) linear equations that represents where the two equations have the same x- *and* y-*values; this point is the solution to the system since it satisfies both equations.*

Both presented solutions clearly showed the point of intersection of (10, $150.00): one in a table and one in a graph. During the first presentation, Alexis, Rylee, and Khylie indicated "they cross at 10 when they're the same amount." In the second presentation, Spencer stated, "Starting at less shirts, Crazy Tees is less until you get to 10 shirts and $150.00." He goes on to explain that after 10, T-Shirts R Us is "marginally cheaper but getting more cheaper." Following Spencer's explanation, Mark clarifies that at 10 shirts it is the same, and later Melina explains why the two companies are the same at 10 shirts for $50.00: "The extra 5 that's on Crazy Tees catches up to the 50 that's for setup. So, that's why it meets at 10 because 10 times 5 equals 50. . . ."

Although the majority of students in the class found the point of intersection during their small group work, the discussion made salient *why* the two companies had the same cost for 10 shirts. Although there was no explicit discussion regarding the fact that the value (10, $150.00) satisfied both equations, this was implicit. While there was no generalization that unique nonparallel equations always have a point of intersection, the work that was done lays the groundwork for further discussion on this point. It is likely that it will take more than one lesson to come to such a conclusion. At some point in a subsequent lesson, after students have additional experiences in finding the point of intersection, Ms. Musumeci will want to ask students how they can tell if two linear equations will have a point of intersection.

Goal 2: The two equations "switch positions" at the point of intersection, and the one that was on "top" before the point of intersection is on the "bottom" after the point of intersection because the equation with the smaller rate of change will ultimately be the equation closer to the x*-axis regardless of the value of the* y*-intercept.*

Much of the discussion was focused on the fact that the company that was cheaper changed at the point of intersection (10, $150.00). Alexis, Rylee, and Khylie indicated, "They cross at 10 when they're the same amount" and "at 11 shirts Crazy Tees starts getting more expensive." As noted in the discussion of the first goal, Spencer indicated that Crazy Tees is less expensive before the point of intersection, and T-Shirts R Us is less expensive after the point of intersection. Melina explained that Crazy Tees "gets above" T-Shirts R Us after the point of intersection because the cost for Crazy Tees is $15.00 per shirt, and T-Shirts Are Us is $10.00 per shirt. Mark explains that at 10 shirts, it is the same, but then "T-Shirts R Us is still going up by $10.00 each shirt. Crazy Tees is going up $15.00. So Crazy Tees is going to be steeper. . . ." Ms. Musumeci then begins to investigate the notion of *steepness* and how this relates to the cost of T-shirts at the end of the discussion.

Goal 3: Tables, graphs, equations, and context can be connected by identifying the slope and y*-intercept in each representational form.*

All four representations were referenced during the discussion. The task was present in a context—two companies selling T-shirts. Alexis, Rylee, and Khylie constructed and presented tables and equations. Ms. Musumeci noted that the girls also had equations on their paper, and she asked them, "So tell me how those connect to your table?" Although Alexis provided an explanation, it focused on how substituting an x value into the equation would get a y value. Later in the discussion, Ms. Musumeci asked what the numbers 10 and 15 mean in the context of the problem and what 10 and 15 mean in the context of the equation.

Although all four representations were made public during the discussion, and a few connections made, she will make explicit connections to the slope and y-intercept the next day by starting with her last question to the class: What do 10 and 15 mean in the context of the task and what do they mean in the equations? This question will set the stage for exploring slope and how it appears in each representational form.

While Ms. Musumeci did not accomplish everything she set out to do, she made considerable progress on her lesson goals. This is due in large measure to the fact that she selected students to present who had created solutions that had the potential to raise the ideas she had targeted. Both solutions showed the point of intersection and showed the costs before and after the point of intersection. As Spencer began his presentation, she reminded students that the question they were exploring was when each company would be cheaper. This served to focus students not on the point of intersection (which had already been determined) as *the* answer but on what happened before and after the point of intersection and why—one of her lesson goals. When Mark indicated that Crazy Tees was steeper than T-Shirts R Us, Ms. Musumeci repeated what Mark had said, marking this as something important. She then pursued this idea, which she ultimately wanted to relate to the rate of change or slope.

Throughout the lesson, and in the excerpts we focused on here, Ms. Musumeci asked questions to *probe* students' thinking, listened to students' responses, and asked students to *restate* what someone else had said. Rather than relying solely on the presenters to answer her questions, she *invited* other students to provide explanations or to *add on* to what had been said. This is most evident when Spencer, Mark, and Melina all provide explanations regarding why one company was cheaper before the point of intersection and one was cheaper after. Since the teacher only heard from three students on this idea, we cannot say for certain that everyone understood what was being discussed, but we do know that all students had access to the ideas and that silent students can learn as much as those who more actively participate (Inagaki, Hatano, & Morita, 1998). Asking all students to *stop and jot* would provide the teacher with insight into what each student in the class understood about the point of intersection and what occurred before and after it.

The key takeaway from the discussion in Ms. Musumeci's class is that she did not leave it to chance that the ideas she wanted students to grapple with would surface without her help or that hearing only one explanation of an idea would be sufficient to ensure that students were making sense of it. By carefully selecting the work that would be presented, and using several of the talk moves described in Figure 6.3, she was able to draw students' attention to specific aspects of the work.

Making Sure That You Do Not Take Over the Discussion and Do the Explaining

As a teacher, you know what it is you want students to learn from a lesson, and you may at times feel that the most expedient way to communicate this to students is to simply tell them what you want them to know. It is not clear, however, what students learn and retain when they simply listen to the teacher explain. Steven Reinhart (2000), an experienced middle school teacher, said it best:

> *When I was in front of the class demonstrating and explaining, I was learning a great deal, but many of my students were not! Eventually, I concluded that if my students were to ever really learn mathematics, they would have to do the explaining, and I, the listening. My definition of a good teacher has since changed from "one who explains things so well that students understand" to "one who gets students to explain things so well that they can be understood."* (p. 478)

PAUSE AND CONSIDER

Think of a time when you found yourself doing all the explaining at the end of a lesson. What do you think students learned when this occurred? How do you know? What might you have done differently that would have provided more insight into what students understood about the ideas you were targeting?

Let us return to the example from Ms. Musumeci's class that we explored in Analyzing the Work of Teaching 6.5. Instead of asking questions of students after the presentations by Alexis, Rylee, Khylie, and Spencer, she could have just summarized the key points and told students how the work was connected and why and what the big ideas were. While more efficient, it would have provided her with no idea what students were thinking or how (or if) they are making sense of the situation. Through her questioning, she learned that students could determine the point of intersection and that many understood what happened before and after that point of intersection and why.

In the case of Mrs. Saroney, she could have stuck to her original goals for the lesson and used the work of Tayzir and Deangelo to show two different ways to get the answer of $7\frac{1}{4}$ servings and explain the connections between them. This would have been much faster and less *messy* than the discussion that took place. At the end of the lesson, she explained:

> *I decided not to push on the answer because they were the only two. I felt like the rest of the students were really just struggling with . . . I don't know if I want to say making sense of the problem because I feel like they understood what the problem meant and what to do, but just that the mixed number was really throwing them off, and I just didn't feel like they were even ready to go in and answer with that or to even talk about the answer with that.*

Both Ms. Musumeci and Mrs. Saroney view classroom discussions as critical to student learning and resisted the urge to step in and take over the discussion. Reinhart (2000) echoes this sentiment:

> *Good discussions take time; at first, I was uncomfortable in taking so much time to discuss a single question or problem. The urge to simply tell my students and move on for the sake of expedience was considerable. Eventually, I began to see the value in what I now refer to as a "less is more" philosophy. I now believe that all students learn more when I pose a high-quality problem and give them the necessary time to investigate, process their thoughts, and reflect on and defend their findings. (p. 480)*

Running Out of Time

As Reinhart states in the quote above, good discussions take time. So can you facilitate a good discussion when you may only have 45 minutes for the entire class? Here are a few suggestions that might help. First, you can extend the lesson over two days. For example, Maura Ingram planned Henri and Emile's Race (see Figure 5.8) as a two-day lesson. On day one, she introduced the task and had students work in groups on the task. At the end of the first day, she collected the work. She reviewed the work prior to day two and determined which responses (see Figure 5.9) she planned to share, who would share it, and in what order it would be presented. Then on day two, she conducted the whole class discussion. This approach had several advantages. It gave her time to review the work and make thoughtful decisions regarding selecting and sequencing. It also gave her time to conduct the discussion without feeling rush. This, however, is a solution that needs to be used judiciously since every lesson cannot take two periods!

Another thing to consider is limiting the time students have to work on a task in groups. Some of the teachers with whom we have worked have set timers so that groups know exactly how much time they have and how much is remaining at any point. This will hold students accountable for moving along in their work and keep you aware of how much time has passed. You can always extend the time if students have not made sufficient progress.

It is also important to keep in mind that when monitoring student work, your goal is to help students make progress on the task, not to ensure that each and every student has a correct answer before beginning the discussion. Rather the goal is to make sure that students are positioned so that they can make sense of the discussion. As Cartier and her colleagues (Cartier, Smith, Stein, & Ross, 2013) noted:

> *the teacher's goal when intervening in a small group is not to make sure that, by the end of the work session, all students have produced a complete and correct response. Rather it is to support students' fledgling efforts to make sense of the task before them and to make sure that students are working in a productive direction. Later in the lesson, students will have the opportunity to compare their work with what other students have produced and to participate in a class-wide discussion that clarifies the thinking behind and the features of a good explanation for whatever task on which they are working. (p. 88)*

TEACHING TAKEAWAY

All students do not have to have a correct answer or need to have completed the entire task to participate in and benefit from the whole class discussion.

We saw this in Mrs. Mossotti's discussion. Serenity did not have a correct solution, but she was able to engage in and learn from the discussion that took place at the end of class. When comparing her solution to the solution presented by Crispin, she was able to refine her thinking about the cost per ticket at the fair. In addition, none of the students in Mrs. Mossotti's class had completed the task. So rather than going through all parts of the task, she focused on the first question. Once students understood what the cost of 4 tickets would be and why, they would be better positioned to complete the remaining parts of the task.

Despite your best efforts, you may still run out of time. This is what happened to Ms. Musumeci. Following the lesson, she commented:

Okay, so we did run out of time in the class discussion, and I would've loved to have 20 more minutes to continue because I felt like we were just getting to where I wanted to be at the end of class. But tomorrow I'd like to pick up where we left off with rate of change and how the equations that were written really relate to the table and the graph.

In Analyzing the Work of Teaching 6.6, you will review what occurred during the discussion of Ms. Musumeci's class, what she wanted to accomplish the next day, and propose questions she might ask to accomplish her goals.

Analyzing the Work of Teaching 6.6

Running Out of Time

Review the video clips of Ms. Musumeci's class from Analyzing the Work of Teaching 6.5, where students presented the tables and graph for the Buying T-Shirts task.

Consider: What additional questions could Ms. Musumeci ask the following day to ensure that students understand the key ideas she wanted them to learn?

Running Out of Time—Analysis

Ms. Musumeci ended the class by asking students what you call 10 and 15 in the equations. This would be a good starting point for addressing her third goal for the lesson—tables, graphs, equations, and context can be connected by identifying the slope and *y*-intercept in each representational form.

Ms. Musumeci might begin the next day by asking students how 10 and 15 (which they had established as the cost of individual T-shirts at T-Shirts R Us and Crazy Tees respectively) impact the graphs. A close inspection of the graph presented by Spencer should make clear to students that every time the number of T-shirts increased by 1, the cost increase by \$10.00 for T-Shirts R Us and \$15.00 for Crazy Tees. Students could then be asked if this was ever going to change. The teacher could then label this as *the constant rate of change* if students were not familiar with this term. The teacher might then want to connect the constant rate of change back to Mark's comment about Crazy Tees being steeper and ask how the constant rate of change impacts the steepness of the graph. The constant rate of change could then be labeled as the slope.

Ms. Musumeci could then ask how 10 and 15 appear in the table. In examining the table produced by Alexis, Rylee, and Khylie, students should note that every time the number of T-shirts increases by 1, the cost increases by 10 (for T-Shirts R Us) and 15 (for Crazy Tees). They might then examine a table where the number of T-shirts is incremented by 5, such as one produced by Myat, Albatool, Alisha, and Ayan (shown in Figure 6.5) and asked where 10 and 15 are in this table. Students should note (hopefully) that as the number of T-shirts increased by 5, the cost increased by \$75.00 for Crazy Tees and \$50.00 for T-Shirts R Us. Students might then be asked why it was not the same increase as in the first table. This could lead students to conclude that $\frac{75}{5}=15$ and $\frac{50}{5}=10$, which is exactly the same as the constant rate of change noted in the first table and on the graph. Students should then be asked to relate this to the definition of slope (the ratio of the change in y compared to the change in x).

Figure 6.5 • Table created by Myat, Albatool, Alisha, and Ayan

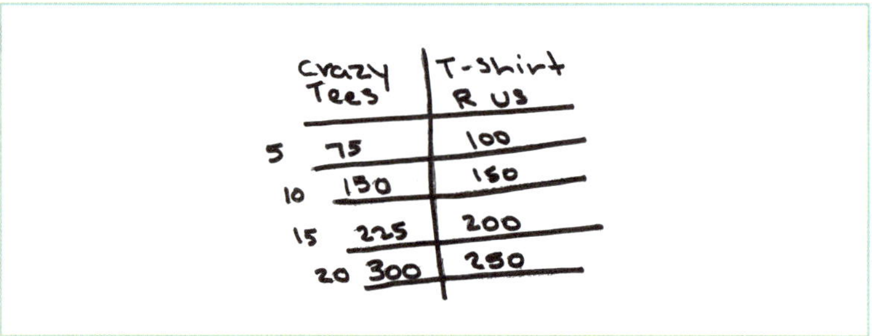

	Crazy Tees	T-Shirt R Us
5	75	100
10	150	150
15	225	200
20	300	250

Mrs. Musumeci might then ask about \$10.00 and \$15.00 in the equations. Students should recognize the coefficient of the x variable as specifying the rate of change or the slope. While this may seem like a protracted set of questions, making the connections between the context, table, graph, and equation will be extremely useful to her algebra students as they move forward. It builds their understanding of the concept and their flexibility with different representations. The discussion might conclude by asking students to consider what the \$50.00 in the equation for T-Shirts R Us means in the context of the problem, where it appears on the graph, and where it appears (or would appear) in each of the two tables.

While there are many questions that Ms. Musumeci could ask as a follow-up to the initial lesson, it is important for her to keep her eye on the goals she is trying to accomplish. This set of potential questions is directly related to her lesson goal and build directly on the work that students have already produced. So while students might not have immediate answers to the questions, working in their table groups, they should be able to work through them.

Conclusion

The practices that we have discussed in the previous chapters—setting goals, selecting tasks, anticipating, monitoring, selecting, and sequencing—are intended to prepare you to orchestrate a productive discussion. The discussion is the culmination of all your work in carefully planning the lesson and in closely attending to what students do and say as they work on a task. It is in the discussion that connections are made and the mathematical ideas that you target in the lesson are made public.

The work of students, when purposefully and carefully selected and sequenced, becomes the basis for the classroom discussion. The discussions orchestrated by Jennifer Mossotti, Michelle Musumeci, and Michelle Saroney illustrated this point. Each teacher positioned students as authors of mathematical ideas and allowed them to explain what they did and why. Through careful questioning the teachers were able to help students clarify their explanations and to engage the entire class in making sense of the presenter's work. In this way, all students were held accountable for making sense of the presenter's work and the mathematical ideas that were at the heart of the lesson.

As we noted, orchestrating a discussion can be challenging. Perhaps the biggest obstacle to overcome is yourself—resisting the temptation to tell students what you want them to know and take over the thinking. As noted in *Principles and Standards for School Mathematics* (NCTM, 2000) nearly two decades ago, "teachers must decide . . . how to support students without taking over the process of thinking for them and thus eliminating the challenge" (p. 19). The challenges we have identified highlight some of the pitfalls you may encounter as you engage students in whole class discussion. We hope that the ways in which Mrs. Saroney and Ms. Musumeci handled these challenges will help you as you continue to orchestrate discussions in your own classroom.

In the next chapter, we address questions about why you should consider using the five practices model and how you can get started in making these practices a component of your instructional toolkit.

Connecting Student Responses—Summary

Video Clip 6.6

To hear and see more about connecting student responses, watch Video Clip 6.6.

Videos may also be accessed at **resources.corwin.com/5practices-middleschool**

Linking the Five Practices to Your Own Instruction

CONNECTING

It is now time to reflect on the lesson you taught following Chapter 4, but this time through the lens of connecting student responses.

1. What connections were made between student responses and the lesson goals?
2. What connections were made between different student responses?
3. To what extent were the mathematical ideas that were targeted in the lesson made public?
4. What did you do to ensure that all students in the class were participating in and accountable for making sense of the ideas being presented?
5. Based on your reading of this chapter and a deeper understanding of the process of connecting, would you do anything differently if you were going to teach this lesson again?
6. What have you learned from this chapter that you will draw on in the next lesson you plan and teach?

“The Five Practices have taken my teaching to a whole other level. I’m putting a lot more intentionality into my planning.”

—MICHELLE SARONEY, SIXTH-GRADE TEACHER

CHAPTER 7

Looking Back and Looking Ahead

In Chapters 2–6, we explored each of the five practices for orchestrating productive mathematics discussions, identifying the components of each practice and the related challenges. The lessons taught by Jennifer Mossotti, Michelle Musumeci, and Michelle Saroney brought the five practices to life and provided a rich context for analyzing teaching and learning in real urban classrooms.

At this point, you may be feeling overwhelmed. You may be starting to wonder if you can really do this and if it is really worth the effort. If so, you are not alone. What we are asking you to do takes a considerable amount of time to *get good at*, and it may require rethinking current practices. The three Syracuse teachers had similar feelings when they started, but over the past three years they have reinvented their teaching. They offer the following advice:

> *I think a lot of teachers (myself included) felt successful after seeing kids successfully solve an equation or complete a series of steps to solve a problem. But looking back, the student success was more characteristic of compliance and understanding of the underlying concepts was actually very shallow. Building a foundation based upon a concept prior to teaching the procedure may seem daunting as everyone is rushing to "fit the curriculum in," but it will always*

save time in the long run. Even if it feels like a failure the first time, or even if it feels like it's taking a lot more time than you anticipated, that time is going to be earned back when students have that conceptual understanding. . . .

—*Jennifer Mossotti*

Don't be afraid to try! At first, I was nervous to try doing math tasks with the monitoring tool and facilitating the discussion. However, every time I did it, it got easier and more efficient. Now, I feel more comfortable and love doing the math tasks. The thinking that comes from the students during a task is so much deeper than what I was getting from them before teaching this way. I feel like by actually doing this, actually trying the lessons and practicing, you get more comfortable with it as you go.

—*Michelle Musumeci*

Try it! The students who don't really talk much in class and are not as confident with their math skills, they tend to shine. They'll do something, and you call them up to the board and . . . they flourish as math students. And on the other end of it, the higher-level students who are so used to getting the answers all the time . . . it challenges them to really look at strategies and how they're connected and how they can draw a model. Give it time and you will find your students loving math. It is not easy but the rewards are endless. You do not have to be certified in math to be successful with this.

—*Michelle Saroney*

In the remainder of this chapter, we address three questions: Why should you consider using the five practices model? How can you get started in making these practices a component of my instructional toolkit? How often should you be engaging your students in discussions around high-level tasks? Answers to these questions may relieve some of your anxiety and provide a pathway for moving forward with the five practices.

Why Use the Five Practices Model

Discussions around high-level mathematical tasks, such as those discussed in Chapters 2 to 6, are the primary means through which students develop an understanding of mathematics. Research shows that learning outcomes are the greatest when students have consistent opportunities to engage with high-level tasks (Boaler & Staples, 2008; Stein & Lane, 1996; Stigler & Hiebert, 2004). High-level tasks, however, are the most difficult to implement in ways that maintain the demands of the task (Stein, Grover, & Henningsen, 1996). When the cognitive demands of a task are not maintained during a lesson, opportunities for student's thinking and problem solving are lost, and students are often left to apply a rule or procedure with limited effort. (For example, see the

Case of Sandra Pascal in Smith, Steel, & Raith, 2017, or The Case of Fran Gorman and Kevin Cooper, Stein, Smith, Henningsen, & Silver, 2009.)

The five practices model is intended to help teachers maintain the cognitive demands of a high-level task during a lesson by focusing on thoughtful and thorough planning prior to the lesson. By limiting the number of decisions that you need to be made during the lesson, you are better prepared to support students by asking questions rather than telling them what to do. As Smith and Stein (2018) note:

> *Simply put, the five practices can equip teachers in supporting students' work on challenging tasks without lowering the demands of the task. In particular, by anticipating what students are likely to do when solving the task (including not being able to get started) and the questions that can be asked to assess and advance their understanding, the teacher is in a much better position to provide scaffolds that support students' engagement and learning without taking over the thinking for them. (p. 131)*

Each of our three featured teachers were successful in maintaining the demands of the high-level task they selected, and we would argue, this was due in large measure to their use of the five practices. Because each teacher had a clear goal of what she was trying to accomplish, selected a high-level task that was aligned with the goal, and anticipated what students would do and how she would respond, she was prepared to interact with students in ways that supported their work on the tasks, without doing too much of the thinking for them, and keep them moving toward the goal. For example, when Mrs. Mossotti interacted with Daejhor, Razaria, and Mya (Analyzing the Work of Teaching [AWT] 4.3) and with Serenity and Adnawmy (AWT 4.6) as they worked on the State Fair task, she could have told these students that their answers ($34.00 for 4 tickets and $3.77 per ticket respectively) were wrong and suggested a more productive pathway to follow. Instead, she asked questions that allowed students to rethink what they had done and to reconsider the information on the graph. In the end, when these students presented their work to the class (AWT 6.1 and 6.2), they were able to discuss their incorrect solutions and how they came to see things differently. While it may have been more expedient for Mrs. Mossotti to simply tell students what to do when they were stuck or confused, this would have taken the opportunity for thinking and learning away from the students and left them to follow a pathway based on the teacher's thinking rather than their own. Through her actions, Mrs. Mossotti was able to maintain the demands of the task and maximize students' opportunity to learn.

TEACHING TAKEAWAY

Using the five practices model helps teachers enact high-level tasks without lowering the demands of the task.

In addition to promoting learning, discussions around high-level tasks can also promote access and equity. According to the National Council of Teachers of Mathematics (2014), providing access and equity requires teaching that "ensures that all students have opportunities to engage successfully in the mathematics classroom and learn challenging mathematics" (p. 68). Using high-level tasks that have multiple entry points that allow for the use of different representations and can be solved in different ways is the first step in giving each and every student access to meaningful mathematics. According to Boaler and Staples (2008), "When there are many ways to be successful, many more students are successful" (p. 16).

Engaging students in discussions featuring their work on a high-level task is the next step in achieving access and equity. Discussions provide the opportunity to honor student thinking, position students as authors of mathematical ideas, and acknowledge contributions to understanding the task and its solution. Sorto and Bower (2017) describe the ways in which discourse can advance access and equity:

> *Productive discourse provides opportunities for students to contribute and to understand, through discussion, mathematical concepts and strategies. Students also are offered access to the problem and its understanding while being supported by fellow students. As the teacher creates an environment of safe intellectual contributions, there is a sense of high expectations and accountability for everyone in the classroom. Students' participation and reasoning is always validated to the extent that it contributes to the approach to successfully solving the problem. (p. 68)*

Take for example the discussion that took place in Mrs. Saroney's class. Only two students—Tayzir and Deangelo—had solved the task correctly. By inviting Tayzir and Deangelo to present their solutions, she was honoring their thinking and positioning them as authors of important mathematical work. Through the discussion of their solutions (AWT 6.4), all of the students in the class were offered access to two different ways of conceptualizing the situation and solving the task. Students were held accountable for making sense of the presented solutions. Mrs. Saroney asked questions to the class (e.g., Why did Tayzir cut his tape diagram into sixths? How many sixths are in Tayzir's model?) and expected students to answer these questions through conversations in their table groups. Finally, students felt safe to disagree with a majority opinion. For example, when Mrs. Saroney asked the class how many agreed that there were 4 and $\frac{5}{6}$ pizzas left, most students indicated agreement. Since Erika did not raise her hand, Mrs. Saroney asked her how much pizza she thought was left. Erika indicated that her group thought that $\frac{4}{6}$ was left. The classroom environment was such that Erika was comfortable admitting she did not understand something, and no one in the class seemed fazed by this. Hence, the discussion in Mrs. Saroney's class provided each and every student in the class with access to challenging mathematics and with the opportunity to extend their understanding of the problem.

TEACHING TAKEAWAY

Using the five practices model helps teachers provide each and every student with access to high-quality mathematics.

Discussions around high-level tasks can also support the development of students' identities as mathematical doers. Aguirre, Mayfield-Ingram, and Martin (2013) define *mathematical identities* as "the dispositions and deeply held beliefs that students develop about their ability to participate and perform effectively in mathematical contexts and to use mathematics in powerful ways across the contexts of their lives" (p. 14). Many middle school students see themselves as *not good* at math—a perspective that has long-term consequences for course taking and career options.

Michelle Saroney commented, "It makes me so sad when on the first day of school students talk about how they hate math or they don't understand why they have to learn it because they are 'never going to use it.'" All three of our featured teachers want to change their students' view of themselves as capable of doing mathematics. Michelle Musumeci states,

> *I want students to feel like they can do math no matter what their previous experience was. I truly believe all students can learn in my classroom, not just about math, but about being part of a (classroom/school) community, about teamwork, about positivity, and about perseverance.*

So how do you help students develop positive mathematical identities? Aguirre, Mayfield-Ingram, and Martin (2013) identify a set of equity-based teaching practices that help build students' positive identities. At the heart of these practices is engaging students in high cognitive demand tasks that offer multiple entry points, supporting students in justifying their solutions, promoting persistence, and positioning students as sources of expertise.

We would argue that the five practices lessons developed and enacted by Jennifer Mossotti, Michelle Musumeci, and Michelle Saroney supported students' learning of meaningful mathematics, provided access and equity for each and every student, and in so doing, help students develop identities as competent and capable of doing mathematics with effort.

TEACHING TAKEAWAY

Using the Five Practices model helps teachers develop students' positive identities.

Getting Started With the Five Practices

Whether you are a newcomer to the five practices or someone who was using them prior to reading this book, practice and reflection will help you either begin or continue your journey to orchestrating productive mathematics discussions in your classroom. The key to making progress on this challenging work is to collaborate with and learn from other teachers. Michelle Musumeci sums it all up:

> *It's important to participate in any professional development that you can, or talk with other teachers about it, because I think that really helps you reflect and see what went well, what didn't go well, and it's always a learning process.*

In the sections that follow, we provide some guidance on how to get started with or continue your work on the five practices.

Plan Lessons Collaboratively

Plan lessons with colleagues. While planning with teachers in your school or district may be optimal since you are working in the same context, given the technologies now available, your collaborators could live in another city, state, or country!

Each of three lessons that we featured in this book—Pizza Party, Buying T-Shirts, and State Fair—were planned collaboratively using the lesson planning template shown in Appendix E and the monitoring chart shown in Appendix B. Working on the lessons in collaboration with colleagues provides teachers with access to a broader set of ideas regarding what can be learned from engaging in a task, the ways in which students could respond to the task, questions that will assess and advance student learning, and the solutions that will be most useful in ensuring that the mathematical ideas that are targeted in the lesson are made public. Such detailed collaborative lesson planning shares many of the characteristics of lesson study, a professional development approach that originated in Japan (Lewis, Perry, & Hurd, 2004).

TEACHING TAKEAWAY

The lesson-planning template shifts the focus to what students are doing and how the teacher will support them.

The lesson-planning template supports the discussion by providing a set of questions that focus on key aspects of the lesson. While many lesson-planning tools focus on what the teacher is going to do during the lesson, the lesson-planning template shifts the focus to what students are going to do and how the teacher is going to support them. As Smith, Bill, and Hughes (2008) explain, "The goal is to move beyond the structural components often associated with lesson planning to a deeper consideration of how to advance students' mathematical understanding during the lesson" (p. 137).

While the five practices model addresses many of the key aspects of planning (shown in grey shading on the lesson-planning template in Appendix E), there are other aspects of planning that should also be considered, such as the prior knowledge that students will draw on in solving the task; the tools, resources, and materials that will be provided to students; how the task will be launched; what homework will be assigned that will extend the learning; and what you will take as evidence that students understand the ideas you have targeted. These additional questions help ensure that students have what they need to engage with the task and that the teacher is clear on what will count as evidence of learning.

You can find completed planning documents—lesson plans and monitoring charts—for each of the three lessons we have featured in this book at resources.corwin.com/5practices-middleschool. You and your colleagues may find it helpful to review these plans in light of what you have learned about instruction in these classrooms and consider ways in which you think the planning supported teaching and learning. [See Smith, Steele, & Raith (2017) and Smith & Stein (2018) for additional examples of lesson plans created with the lesson-planning template.]

If taking on the entire lesson-planning template initially seems overwhelming, you can begin by focusing on the subset of the practices. While the five practices when taken together are greater than the sum of their parts—there is synergy in doing all of the practices—you could begin by focusing on setting goals, selecting tasks, and anticipating responses and questions. Engaging in these three practices as a first step will prepare you to support students by giving you clarity regarding what you are trying to accomplish, a task that will give students something challenging to work on, and questions to help students make progress. Once you are comfortable with the practices that can be done in advance, you can begin to add others to your repertoire.

Observe and Debrief Lessons

Engage in observations and analysis of teaching with one or more colleagues. The point of the observation is not to see if you can find evidence that the teacher used the five practices, but it is rather to see if you can find evidence that students learned mathematics. The following questions could structure your observation and debriefing of the lesson.

- What are students doing and saying? Who are students talking with?
- Who is asking questions? What questions are being asked?
- Who is offering explanations? What counts as an explanation?
- What evidence is there of learning?

In a live observation of a five practices lesson, each observer could be given a copy of the completed monitoring tool to use to collect data on what students are doing and saying during the lesson. The annotated monitoring charts produced by observers can then be used to support an evidence-based discussion on what students were doing and saying during the lesson and the extent to which students appear to learn what was intended.

Reflect on Your Lesson

Reflect on your lesson in close proximity to the completion of your lesson. At the end of each lesson, it is important for you to ask yourself whether you accomplished what you set out to do and what you take as evidence that students learned (or are in the process of learning) what was intended. While it is easy to feel satisfied with a lesson if there were no major disruptions and students were engaged with the task, this does not necessarily imply that students learned what was intended. It is important to press yourself to find evidence to support your beliefs about what occurred. A video recording of the class discussion, student work from the lesson, your completed monitoring chart, and/or an exit ticket given at the end of class are a few sources of data that can inform your reflection of student learning.

If you cannot find evidence that students learned what was intended, you need to decide your next steps. Reflection is only worth doing if you are willing to do something different as a result of what you learned. This may mean doing something different the next day, and/or it might mean changing some aspect of your instruction.

In her reflection following the lesson, Mrs. Mossotti explained what she thought students currently understood, what aspects of the task contributed to their understanding, what surprised her, and what she planned to do next. She was able to recall many details about what had occurred, perhaps due in part to the proximity of the class and her reflection (the sooner you do this the better!), but the notes she took as students worked and her close attention to student thinking played a major role in her ability to recall what occurred during the class.

Mrs. Mossotti indicated,

> *I'm not sure that every single student came away with the understanding that I wanted them to come away with. I think they were right on the brink of it. ... I think, maybe around 75 percent of them could understand and elaborate on the cost for each ticket being 50¢.*

When asked what she would do to address the 25 percent of the students who did not yet understand, she indicated she would check to see their homework (which was to complete Questions 3–6, shown in Figure 7.1). She explained,

> *So, if they have a description (Question 4), then I'll say, "What about a hundred tickets?" Something that cannot be determined from the graph or cannot be easily counted up from, to make sure that they understand the algebraic manipulation that needs to be done with 100 to get that final amount.*

Figure 7.1 • Questions 3–6 from the State Fair task

3. After entering the fair, you decide you want to go on a lot of rides. What will be the total cost for attending the fair and then purchasing 15 ride tickets?
4. Write a description, in words or numbers and symbols, that can be used to find the total cost after entering the fair and purchasing any number of tickets.
5. How does the ticket price appear in your description or expression?
6. How does the ticket price appear in the graph?

She also indicated that she would engage students in another task that was parallel to the State Fair task. She indicated that with the parallel problem she wanted to see

> *if they're using the same lines of thinking that they used today to figure out the rate of change. And depending on where they go with*

that, we may continue with the line on the graph to illustrate the rate of change with the concept of rise and run and slope. Or I may pull it out from the table using the numerical values dependent on where I want to go from what they're understanding of the parallel question.

Through her reflection, Mrs. Mossotti was able to identify what students understood, about how many of them understood, and what she was going to do next to move the class forward. The honest appraisal of where students are in their thinking and understanding is key to ensure that each and every student learns mathematics with understanding.

Video Clubs

Start a video club at your school. Video clubs are opportunities for groups of teachers to come together to view and discuss videos of one another's teaching. These clubs could meet before or after school, during a designated shared planning period, or during a meeting of a professional learning community.

The purpose of video clubs is to help teachers learn to notice and make sense of significant events that occur in their classrooms and the classrooms of their colleagues (Sherin & Linsenmeier, 2011). Learning to notice through the use of video helps teachers learn where to focus their attention in the moment as events unfold in their classrooms. According to Sherin and Dyer (2017):

> *Working with video can help shift how teachers make sense of what they notice. The reasons underlying student thinking are often complex and not easily observable on first glance. Video provides space for teachers to consider intricacies of student thinking in ways that are not always possible during the moment of instruction. (p. 51, p. 53)*

Simply looking at any video clip, without guidance however, does not guarantee that teachers will attend to aspects of instruction that matter most. Sherin and Linsenmeier (2011) provide a set of guidelines for using video, which support the development of teachers' professional vision (i.e., the ability to make sense of significant classroom events):

- Attend to the evidence: Focus on what did take place, not on what might have been.
- Attend to the details: Focus on specific aspects of classroom events (e.g., student thinking).
- Attend to what's typical: Focus on examples of everyday practice, not on exemplars. (p. 41)

It is also critical to capture video that will provide interesting fodder for discussion. If you and your colleagues are working on the five practices, you may find it particularly helpful to focus on capturing what happens during monitoring when the teacher interacts with students as they work on a task or on students' presentations when the teacher helps students make connections between strategies and the mathematical ideas targeted in the lesson.

Sherin and Dyer (2017) provide suggestions on how to best capture video in your own classroom. These guidelines can help you consider where and when to video record so that you capture interesting interactions, where to place the video recorder, the value of annotation tools, and the lens through which your colleagues will view your video.

Using video recordings in this way can make it possible to *get inside* classrooms that would otherwise be impossible to visit, to collaborate with teachers near and far, to expand your professional networks, and to further develop your ability to notice and attend to classroom events.

Organize a Book Study

Organize a book study with colleagues either face-to-face or virtually around this book. Set up a regular meeting (weekly, biweekly, monthly) during which time you and your colleagues near or far can work through the chapters in this book together, discussing the Pause and Consider questions, the Analyzing the Work of Teaching activities, and the Linking the Five Practices to Your Own Instruction assignments. Through discussion of each chapter you can share insights and reactions, your personal experiences, and challenges, and determine next steps.

Explore Additional Resources

Explore resources outside of this book that may give you additional tools to enacting the practices. For example, in Chapter 6, we identify several resources that provide additional insights for holding students accountable during whole class discussions. In addition, throughout the book we have identified references that will provide more insight on particular topics.

What will you do to get started? Who will be your collaborators?

Frequency and Timing of Use of the Five Practices Model

Two questions you may be asking at this point are: "How often do I need to engage my students in a discussion using the five practices to support my work? Is this something I should be doing every day?" While you do not have to engage students in discussions around challenging tasks every day, we do know from research that students need regular opportunities to engage in high-level thinking and reasoning—hence, once a unit, once a month, or once a quarter is not sufficient.

We recommend that you work toward engaging students in a whole class discussion around a *doing-mathematics* task once a week. To start, it is often productive to partner with one or more colleagues (face-to-face or virtually) and collaboratively plan lessons, even taking turns leading the planning effort. By collaborating with others, you will share the responsibility for creating lesson plans and at the same time benefit from a broader set of ideas about a specific lesson. Over time, you will compile a set of lesson plans that you can continue to refine and use in subsequent years. As your library of lessons grows, you can continue to add to it, increasing the number of lessons and relatedly the frequency with which you engage students in such discussions.

In addition to frequency, it is important to decide when working on a doing-mathematics task what will be most beneficial to students. If you give such a task after you have taught a procedure that could be used to solve the task, you are likely to see many students doing what has been taught. When this occurs, there is limited opportunity for students to think and reason, and you will learn little about what students understand about mathematics. By contrast, engaging students in solving a doing-mathematics task before they have learned specific procedures, they will have the opportunity to actually learn through their engagement in the task. In the process, you will learn how students are making sense of the situation and what it is they understand.

So what happens on days when you are not engaging students in a whole class discussion around a doing-mathematics task? Students will also need time to engage in other activities such as making sense of procedures and developing procedural fluency (see Smith, Steele, & Raith, 2017, for examples of what this might look like). While such activities may not require the same level of planning or discussion, we encourage you to look for ways to elicit and support student thinking regardless of the level and kind of activity in which you engage your students.

Conclusion

Making the five practices a central component of your instructional toolkit will not happen overnight. It is a personal journey that will take time and effort. As with any journey, taking someone along with you can enhance the experience by providing a sounding board when you need one as well as having someone with whom to share the joys and tribulations.

We encourage you to keep a journal throughout your journey, documenting the challenges you have faced, how you are dealing with them, and describing your personal victories. There may be times when you want to tweet about something you have discovered, write a blog about a victory or challenge, or post a request for assistance through an established network. Extending your professional network can provide you with additional insights and support.

Keep documentation from your completed lessons! This includes lesson plans, completed monitoring charts, photos or scanned images of student work, and exit tickets. These artifacts will provide evidence to support your reflection on the lesson immediately following the lesson, but they will also be useful when you are ready to teach the lesson again. You can begin your planning of a previously taught lesson by reviewing what occurred in previous implementations of the lesson—what went well, what did not, what should change, and what should remain the same. Rather than start planning from scratch each time, you can build on your prior work and gradually improve your lessons (and your teaching) over time. Through this cycle of planning, teaching, reflecting, and revising, you will build a storehouse of good lessons to which you can continue to add.

The best advice we can give you is *do not give up*! As a teacher commented,

> *Investing time and effort into learning/implementing the five practices is far from easy and has taken me a while (and I still have a long way to go) but is well worth the investment. Using them has created "magical moments" where students are engaged and truly learning from one another, discovering mathematics, and gaining insight into the mathematical process of discovery, connections, revision, etc. It truly shifts the responsibility and workload onto the students, allowing the teacher to become a facilitator and empower students to take responsibility for their learning. In [this] day and age, the five practices become an incredibly powerful tool to push students toward problem solving and critical thinking. (Smith & Stein, 2018, p. 131)*

Resources

APPENDIX A Web-based Resources for Tasks and Lesson Plans (not a comprehensive listing)

National Council of Teachers of Mathematics:

Activities with Rigor and Coherence (ARCs): *Sequences of lessons (K–12) that address a specific mathematical topic and support the implementation of the eight effective mathematics teaching practices (NCTM, 2014) and the five practices for orchestrating productive discussions (Smith & Stein, 2018).*

http://www.nctm.org/ARCs

Illuminations: *Lessons and activities (K–12) that are aligned with NCTM's* Principles and Standards for School Mathematics *(2000) and the National Governors Association Center for Best Practices & Council of Chief State School Officers'* Common Core State Standards for School Mathematics *(2010).*

http://illuminations.nctm.org

Problems of the Week: *Tasks per grade band (K–2, 3–5, 6–8) and content strand (algebra, geometry, trigonometry, and calculus), plus solution strategies, rubrics, and teaching suggestions.*

http://www.nctm.org/Classroom-Resources/CRCC/Math-Forum-Problems-of-the-Week-Resources

Reasoning and Sensemaking Task Library: *High school tasks that engage students in reasoning and sensemaking that are linked directly to* Focus in High School: Reasoning and Sense Making *(NCTM, 2009) along with suggestions for facilitating student work on the task and insights into how students might think about the task.*

http://www.nctm.org/rsmtasks

Illustrative Mathematics Curriculum: *A Grades 6–8 problem-based curriculum that is free—you need to sign up to access the curriculum.*

https://im.openupresources.org

Inside Mathematics: *A K–12 resource for educators that includes video lessons, problems of the month, performance assessment tasks, and a range of resources.*

http://www.insidemathematics.org

Mathalicious: *Real-world lessons, aligned to* Common Core State Standards, *designed to build proficiency in mathematical practices and build conceptual understanding; some lessons are free but access to all resources requires membership and a fee.*

http://www.mathalicious.com

Mathematics Assessment Project: *Formative assessment lessons and summative assessment tasks (including scoring rubrics and student work samples) from Grades 6–12.*

http://map.mathshell.org/materials/index.php

Robert Kaplinsky's Lessons: *Lessons for K–8, Algebra 1, Algebra 2, and geometry built around visual images and general questions that are intended to engage students in further exploration.*

http://robertkaplinsky.com/lessons

Dan Meyer's Three-Act Lessons: *Lessons for Grades 6–12 that follow a particular structure—show students an image or video clip that depicts an interesting situation; engage students in asking questions about and identifying information in the image or video clip; creating models to answer the questions.*

http://blog.mrmeyer.com/2011/the-three-acts-of-a-mathematical-story

APPENDIX B Monitoring Chart

Strategy	Assessing Questions	Advancing Questions	Who and What	Order

online resources Download the Monitoring Chart from resources.corwin.com/5practices-middleschool

<table>
<tr><th>Solution Strategy</th><th>Assessing Questions</th><th>Advancing Questions</th><th>Who and What</th><th>Order</th></tr>
<tr><td>Students cannot get started.</td><td>• Where on the graph do you estimate 4 tickets would be?
• Let's role play, here's my wallet, and I'm about to enter the state fair… you tell me what happens and when I will need to pay money.</td><td>• Is there a way to determine the actual amount spent for 4 tickets besides estimating?</td><td>Adnawmy + Serenity - not sure of cost 2nd visit - take average of 3 rates to get #3.77/ticket</td><td></td></tr>
<tr><td>Solution A. Student creates a table using the information about the three points on the graph.<table><tr><th>Number of Tickets</th><th>Total Spent</th></tr><tr><td>1</td><td>$8.50</td></tr><tr><td>8</td><td>$12.00</td></tr><tr><td>10</td><td>$13.00</td></tr></table></td><td>• Does this mean you can only buy 1 ticket, 8 tickets, or 10 tickets?
• Does this mean that 1 ticket has a cost of $8.50?</td><td>• What is a way to determine values that are missing from the table?
• How much would 9 tickets cost? How do you know?
• What if I don't buy any ride tickets? Would I need to spend any money?</td><td></td><td>No one used a table!</td></tr>
<tr><td>Solution B. Student divides the total spent by the ticket quantity for each point on the graph and comes up with three different unit rates.
$\frac{8.50}{1} = 8.50$ $\frac{12}{8} = 1.5$
$\frac{13}{10} = 1.3$</td><td>• So sometimes tickets have different prices? How do I get to buy the cheap ticket… something seems funny here?
• What do each of these numbers mean?
• 8.5 what? For what?</td><td>• Why is one ticket so expensive but 12 tickets so cheap, for each ticket? Are they having a special sale that I don't know about?
• Is there a way to use the values from each point to find out a single ticket price?</td><td>Binti, Mahamed
- $8.50 for 1 so $8.50 × 4 for 4 tix
-Daejhor, Mya, Razaria
- Claire + Fadumo
2nd visit - Daejhor, Mya, Razaria - came back with actual cost for 4 tix - look at graph</td><td>Lots of kids thought 4 tix -$8.50 each so $34.00 start here!</td></tr>
</table>

Solution C. Student uses the points (8, 12) and (10, 13) to determine that 2 tickets have a cost of \$1.00.	• Do you have to buy tickets in pairs? • What if I only wanted one ticket, why doesn't it show 50¢ on the graph? • What exactly did you pay money for after buying 8 tickets?	• Knowing this, could you determine the cost after buying 5 tickets? 10 tickets? How?	*Crispin + Nazier – see pattern of even tix amounts rising by \$1.00 on graph* *use line on graph to see pattern* *-pull out even/odd concept*	*Use Crispin to describe how graph changes as more tix purchased – 2nd*
Solution D. Student connects the three points on the graph with a line and sees that at the *y*-axis the value is \$8.00 and determines that it must cost \$8.00 to enter the fair without buying any tickets. Since it costs \$8.50 for 1 ticket, this means it must cost 50¢ per ticket. Student sees that the line rises half a unit on the *y*-axis for every 1 unit on the *x*-axis.	• Why did you draw a line? • What does this point (the *y*-intercept) mean? • Talk about how the graph is changing. Describe how the cost is changing. *Many kids draw line to find cost of 4 tix*	• How could the total amount spent for any point on the line be calculated?	*Keaton, India, Pray- line and estimating points* *Kaelin, Daniel -look at line, not sure what's happening at 0 tix* *– 2nd visit – rise/run pattern* *Jazmen & Jelani connect points* *(2nd visit – Jazmen sees 50 cent pattern)*	*many kids did this*
Solution E. Student determines that total amount spent is calculated by taking \$8.00 and then repeatedly adding 50¢ depending on the number of tickets purchased.	• How did you know that we start with \$8.00? Why not start with 12 or any other number? What does starting with \$8.00 mean? *\$8.00 plus half of tix quantity to get tix cost*	• How would your expression be different if the ticket price was 75¢. How would this be reflected on the graph?	*Nietzche, Ejub, AJ (using graph)* *Starts at \$8.00 on graph and then continues to count by 50¢ to get total price for 3 points given*	
Other				

Chapin, S. H., O'Connor, C., & Anderson, N. C. (2009). ***Classroom discussions: Using math talk to help students learn*** **(2nd ed.). Sausalito, CA: Math Solutions.**

In this book, the authors described five talk moves that they have found effective in supporting students' mathematical thinking and learning: revoicing, asking students to restate someone else's reasoning, asking students to apply their own reasoning to someone else's reasoning, prompting students for further participation, and using wait time. (See Smith & Stein, 2018, for an illustration of these moves in the context of a lesson.)

Herbel-Eisenmann, B., Cirillo, M., Steele, M. D., Otten, S., & Johnson, K. R. (2017). ***Mathematics discourse in secondary classrooms: A practice-based resource for professional learning.*** **Sausalito, CA: Math Solutions.**

This resource provides a set of discourse moves and tools that provide support for teachers to begin to change discourse practices in their classrooms. The video clips and cases provide powerful images of discussion-based learning in middle and high school classrooms.

Kazemi, E., & Hintz, A. (2014). ***Intentional talk: How to structure and lead productive mathematical discussions.*** **Portsmouth, NH: Stenhouse.**

In this book, the authors provide a set of principles and a collection of tools that will help you in facilitating productive classroom discussions. The classroom vignettes provide images of productive talk in elementary classrooms.

Michaels, S., O'Conner, M. C., Hall, M. W., & Resnick, L. B. (2013). ***Accountable Talk™ sourcebook: For classroom conversations that work.*** **Pittsburgh, PA: Institute for Learning, University of Pittsburgh.**

This resource provides an overview of the three components of accountable talk—accountability to the community, accountability to rigorous thinking, and accountability to accurate knowledge—and a set of talk moves associated with each component. (Free download available at http://iflpartner.pitt.edu/index.php/educator_resources/accountable_talk)

APPENDIX E Lesson-Planning Template

Learning Goals (Residue) What understandings will students take away from this lesson?	**Evidence** What will students say, do, or produce that will provide evidence of their understandings?
Task What is the main activity that students will be working on in this lesson?	**Instructional Support—Tools, Resources, Materials** What tools or resources will be made available to give students entry to—and help them reason through—the activity?
Prior Knowledge What prior knowledge and experience will students draw on in their work on this task? **Essential Questions** What are the essential questions that I want students to be able to answer over the course of the lesson?	**Task Launch** How will you introduce and set up the task to ensure that students understand the task and can begin productive work, without diminishing the cognitive demand of the task?
Anticipated Solutions and Instructional Supports What are the various ways that students might complete the activity? Be sure to include incorrect, correct, and incomplete solutions. What questions might you ask students that will support their exploration of the activity and *bridge* between *what they did* and *what you want them to learn*? These questions should *assess* what a student currently knows and *advance* him or her toward the goals of the lesson. Be sure to consider questions that you will ask students who cannot get started as well as students who finish quickly. Use the monitoring chart to provide the details related to Anticipated Solutions and Instructional Support.	
Sharing and Discussing the Task	
Selecting and Sequencing Which solutions do you want students to share during the lesson? In what order? Why?	**Connecting Responses** What specific questions will you ask so that students— • make sense of the mathematical ideas that you want them to learn? • make connections among the different strategies/solutions that are presented?
Homework/Assessment What will you ask students to do that will allow you to determine what they learned and what they understand?	

Connections to the five practices are noted by the gray shading.

This template is taken from Smith, Steele, and Raith (2017, pp. 219–221) and was adapted from Smith, Bill, and Hughes (2008).

References

Aguirre, J., Mayfield-Ingram, K., & Martin, D. (2013). *The impact of identity in K–8 mathematics: Rethinking equity-based practices.* Reston, VA: National Council of Teachers of Mathematics.

Arbaugh, F., Smith, M. S., Boyle, J. D., Stylianides, G. J., & Steele, M. D. (2018). *We reason and we prove: Putting critical skills at the heart of your mathematics teaching.* Thousand Oaks, CA: Corwin.

Balfanz, R., & Vaughan, B. (2016). Closing the mathematics achievement gap in high-poverty middle schools: Enablers and constraints. *Journal of Education for Students Placed at Risk, 11*(2), 143–159.

Ball, D. L., Lubienski, S. T., & Mewborn, D. S. (2001). Research on teaching mathematics: The unsolved problem of teachers' mathematical knowledge. *Handbook of Research on Teaching, 4*, 433–456.

Boaler, J., & Brodie, K. (2004). The importance, nature, and impact of teacher questions. In D. E. McDougall, & J. A. Ross (Eds.), *Proceedings of the twenty-sixth annual meeting of the North American Chapter of the International Group for the Psychology of Mathematics Education*, Volume 2, (pp. 774–90). Toronto: Ontario Institute for Studies in Education at the University of Toronto.

Boaler, J., & Humphreys, C. (2005). *Connecting mathematical ideas: Middle school video cases to support teaching and learning.* Portsmouth, NH: Heinemann.

Boaler, J., & Staples, M. (2008). Creating mathematical futures through an equitable teaching approach: The case of Railside School. *Teachers College Record, 110*(3), 608–645.

Boston, Melissa D., & Wilhelm Anne Garrison. (2017). "Middle school mathematics instruction in instructionally focused urban districts." *Urban Education, 52*(7), 829–861.

Boyle, J. D., & Kaiser, S. B. (2017). Collaborative planning as a process. *Mathematics Teaching in the Middle School, 22*(7), 407–411.

Cartier, J. L., Smith, M. S., Stein, M. K., & Ross, D. K. (2013). *Practices for orchestrating productive science discussions.* Reston, VA: National Council of Teachers of Mathematics.

Chapin, S. H., O'Connor, C., O'Connor, M. C., & Anderson, N. C. (2009). *Classroom discussions: Using math talk to help students learn, Grades K–6.* Sausalito, CA: Math Solutions.

Danielson, C., & Meyer, D. (2016). Increased participation and conversation using networked devices. *Mathematics Teacher, 110*(4), 258–264.

Franke, M. L., Webb, N. M., Chan, A. G., Ing, M., Freund, D., & Battey, D. (2009). Teacher questioning to elicit students' mathematical thinking in elementary school classrooms. *Journal of Teacher Education, 60*(4), 380–392.

Herbel-Eisenmann, B., Cirillo, M., Steele, M. D., Otten, S., & Johnson, K. R. (2017). *Mathematics discourse in secondary classrooms: A practice-based resource for professional learning.* Sausalito, CA: Math Solutions.

Hiebert, J., Gallimore, R., & Stigler, J.W. (2003). The new heroes of teaching. *Education Week*, *23*(10), 42, 56.

Hiebert, J., Morris, A. K., Berk, D., & Jansen, A. (2007). Preparing teachers to learn from teaching. *Journal of Teacher Education*, *58*(1), 47–61.

Horn, I. S. (2012). *Strength in numbers: Collaborative learning in secondary mathematics.* Reston, VA: National Council of Teachers of Mathematics.

Horn, I. S. (2017). *Motivated: Designing mathematics classrooms where students want to join.* Portsmouth, NH: Heinemann.

Hufferd-Ackles, K., Fuson, K. C., & Sherin, M. G. (2015). The math-talk learning community: Looking back and looking ahead. In E. A. Silver, & P. A. Kenney (Eds.), *Lessons learned from research: Volume 1, useful and useable research related to core mathematical practices* (pp. 125–134). Reston, VA: National Council of Teachers of Mathematics.

Hung, M. (2015). Talking circles promote equitable discourse. *Mathematics Teacher*, *109*(4), 256–260.

Hunt, J., & Stein, M. K. (forthcoming). Constructing goals for student learning through conversation. *Mathematics Teaching in the Middle School.*

Imm, K. L., Stylianou, D. A., & Chae, N. (2008). Student representations at the center: Promoting classroom equity. *Mathematics Teaching in the Middle School*, *13*(8), 458–463.

Inagaki, K., Hatano, G., & Morita, E. (1998). Construction of mathematical knowledge through whole-class discussion. *Learning and Instruction*, *8*(6), 503–526.

Institute for Learning. (2015a). *Seventh grade lesson set: Proportional relationships.* Pittsburgh, PA: Institute for Learning, University of Pittsburgh.

Institute for Learning. (2015b). *Sixth grade lesson set of related lessons: Rations: A focus on part-part and part-whole relationships.* Pittsburgh, PA: Institute for Learning, University of Pittsburgh.

Jackson, K. J., Shahan, E. C., Gibbons, L. K., & Cobb, P. A. (2012). Launching complex tasks. *Mathematics Teaching in the Middle School*, *18*(1), 24–29.

Jacobs, V. R., & Philipp, R. A. (2010). Supporting children's problem solving. *Teaching Children Mathematics*, *17*(2), 98–105.

Jansen, A., Cooper, B., Vascellaro, S., & Wandless, P. (2016). Rough-draft talk in mathematics classrooms. *Mathematics Teaching in the Middle School*, *22*(5), 304–307.

Jilk, L. M. (2016). Supporting teacher noticing of students' mathematical strengths. *Mathematics Teacher Educator*, *4*(2), 188–199.

Kazemi, E., Gibbons, L. K., Lomax, K., & Franke, M. L. (2016). Listening to and learning from student thinking. *Teaching Children Mathematics*, *23*(3), 182–190.

Kazemi, E., & Hintz, A. (2014). *Intentional talk: How to structure and lead productive mathematical discussions.* Portsmouth, NH: Stenhouse.

Lambert, R., & Stylianou, D. A. (2013). Posing cognitively demanding tasks to all students. *Mathematics Teaching in the Middle School, 18*(8), 500–506.

Lampert, M., & Graziani, F. (2009). Instructional activities as a tool for teachers' and teacher educators' learning. *The Elementary School Journal, 109*(5), 491–509.

Lappan, G., Phillips, E. D., Fey, J. T., & Friel, S. N. (2014). *Moving straight ahead: Linear relationships connected mathematics 3.* Boston, MA: Pearson.

Leatham, K. R., Peterson, B. E., Stockero, S. L., & Van Zoest, L. R. (2015). Conceptualizing mathematically significant pedagogical opportunities to build on student thinking. *Journal for Research in Mathematics Education, 46*(1), 88–124.

Lewis, C., Perry, R., & Hurd, J. (2004). A deeper look at lesson study. *Educational Leadership, 61*(5), 18.

Louie, N. L. The culture of exclusion in mathematics education and its persistence in equity-oriented teaching. *Journal for Research in Mathematics Education, 48*(5), 488–519.

MARS Shell Center Team (2007–2015). *Mathematics assessment project.* Nottingham, UK: Mathematics Assessment Resource Service, University of Nottingham.

Martin, D. B., Gholson, M. L., & Leonard, J. (2010). Mathematics as gatekeeper: Power and privilege in the production of knowledge. *Journal of Urban Mathematics Education, 3*(2), 12–24.

Michaels, S., O'Conner, M. C., Hall, M. W., & Resnick, L. B. (2013). *Accountable Talk™ sourcebook: For classroom conversations that work.* Pittsburgh, PA: Institute for Learning, University of Pittsburgh.

Mills, V. L. (2014). Mathematical goals: The alpha and omega of effective practice. *NCSM Summer Newsletter, 44*(4), 2–3.

Murata, A., & Fuson, K. (2006). Teaching as assisting individual constructive paths within an interdependent class learning zone: Japanese first graders learning to add using 10. *Journal for Research in Mathematics Education, 37*(5), 421–456.

Nasir, N. S., McKinney de Royston, M., O'Connor, K., & Wischnia, S. (2017). Knowing about racial stereotypes versus believing them. *Urban Education, 52*(4), 491–524.

National Council of Teachers of Mathematics. (2000). *Principles and standards for school mathematics.* Reston, VA: National Council of Teachers of Mathematics.

National Council of Teachers of Mathematics. (2009). *Focus in high school: Reasoning and sense making.* Reston, VA: National Council of Teachers of Mathematics.

National Council of Teachers of Mathematics. (2014). *Principles to actions: Ensuring mathematical success for all.* Reston, VA: National Council of Teachers of Mathematics.

National Governors Association Center for Best Practices & Council of Chief State School Officers. (2010). *Common core state standards for mathematics.* Washington, DC: Author.

Nolan, E. C., Dixon, J. K., Roy, G. J., & Andreasen, J. (2016). *Making sense of mathematics for teaching grades 6–8.* Bloomington, IN: Solution Tree Press.

Reinhart, S. C. (2000). Never say anything a kid can say. *Mathematics Teaching in the Middle School, 5*(8), 478–483.

Santagata, R., & Bray, W. (2016). Professional development processes that promote teacher change: The case of a video-based program focused on leveraging students' mathematical errors. *Professional Development in Education, 42*(4), 547–568.

Schukajlow, S., & Krug, A. (2014). Do multiple solutions matter? Prompting multiple solutions, interest, competence, and autonomy. *Journal for Research in Mathematics Education, 45*(4), 497–533.

Senk, S. L., & Thompson, D. R. (Eds.). (2003). *Standards-based school mathematics curricula: What are they? What do students learn?* Mahwah, NJ: Lawrence Erlbaum Associates.

Shah, N. (2017). Race, ideology, and academic ability: A relational analysis of racial narratives in mathematics. *Teachers College Record, 119*(7), 1–42.

Sherin, M. G., & Dyer, E. B. (2017). Teacher self-captured video: Learning to see. *Phi Delta Kappan, 98*(7), 49–54.

Sherin, M. G., & Linsenmeier, K. A. (2011). Pause, rewind, reflect: Video clubs throw open the classroom doors. *The Learning Professional, 32*(5), 38.

Sherin, M. G., & van Es, E. A. (2009). Effects of video club participation on teachers' professional vision. *Journal of Teacher Education, 60*(1), 20–37.

Smith, M. S. (2001). *Practice-based professional development for teachers of mathematics.* Reston, VA: National Council of Teachers of Mathematics.

Smith, M., Bill, V., & Hughes, E. (2008). Thinking through a lesson protocol: A key for successfully implementing high-level tasks. *Mathematics Teaching in the Middle School, 14*(3), 132–138.

Smith, M. S., Steele, M. D., & Raith, M. L. (2017). *Taking action: Implementing effective mathematics teaching practices in grades 6–8.* Reston, VA: National Council of Teachers of Mathematics.

Smith, M. S., & Stein, M. K. (1998). Selecting and creating mathematical tasks: From research to practice. *Mathematics Teaching in the Middle School, 3*(5), 344–350.

Smith, M. S., & Stein, M. K. (2011). *Five practices for orchestrating productive mathematics discussions.* Reston, VA: National Council of Teachers of Mathematics.

Smith, M. S., & Stein, M. K. (2018). *Five practices for orchestrating productive mathematics discussions—Second edition.* Reston, VA: National Council of Teachers of Mathematics.

Sorto, M. A., & Bower, R. S. G. (2017). Quality of instruction in linguistically diverse classrooms: It matters! In A. Fernandes, S. Crespo, & M. Civil (Eds.), *Access & equity: Promoting high-quality mathematics* (pp. 27–40). Reston, VA: National Council of Teachers of Mathematics.

Stein, M. K., Grover, B. W., & Henningsen, M. (1996). Building student capacity for mathematical thinking and reasoning: An analysis of mathematical tasks used in reform classrooms. *American Educational Research Journal, 33*(2), 455–488.

Stein, M. K., & Lane, S. (1996). Instructional tasks and the development of student capacity to think and reason: An analysis of the relationship between teaching and learning in a reform mathematics project. *Educational Research and Evaluation, 2*(1), 50–80.

Stein, M. K., Smith, M. S., Henningsen, M., & Silver, E. A. (2009). *Implementing standards-based mathematics instruction: A casebook for professional development* (2nd ed.). New York, NY: Teachers College Press.

Stigler, J. W., & Hiebert, J. (2004). Improving mathematics teaching. *Educational Leadership, 61*(5), 12–17.

Suh, J. M., Johnston, C., Jamieson, S., & Mills, M. (2008). Promoting decimal number sense and representational fluency. *Mathematics Teaching in the Middle School, 14*(1), 44–50.

Warshauer, H. K. (2015). Productive struggle in middle school mathematics classrooms. *Journal of Mathematics Teacher Education, 17*(4), 375–399.

Yopp, D. A., & Ellsworth, J. L. (2017). Generalizing and skepticism: Bringing research to practice. *Mathematics Teaching in the Middle School, 22*(1), 284–292.

Zbiek, R., & Shimizu, J. (2005). Multiple solutions: More paths to an end or more opportunities to learn mathematics. *Mathematics Teacher, 99*(4), 279–287.

Index

NOTES

NOTES

NOTES

NOTES

NOTES

Empowering
STUDENTS

Other new Corwin Mathematics resources designed for middle school!

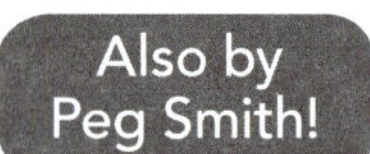

MARGARET (PEG) SMITH, MARY KAY STEIN

The same five practices teachers know and love for planning and managing powerful conversations in mathematics classrooms, updated with current research and new insights on anticipating, lesson planning, and lessons learned from teachers, coaches, and school leaders.

FRAN ARBAUGH, MARGARET (PEG) SMITH, JUSTIN BOYLE, GABRIEL J. STYLIANIDES, MICHAEL STEELE

Develop concrete instructional strategies that support your students' capacity to reason-and-prove across all mathematical content areas in 6–12 classrooms, while becoming adept at reasoning-and-proving.

JOHN HATTIE, DOUGLAS FISHER, NANCY FREY, LINDA M. GOJAK, SARA DELANO MOORE, WILLIAM MELLMAN

The what, when, and how of teaching practices that evidence shows work best for student learning in mathematics.

JOHN ALMARODE, DOUGLAS FISHER, JOSEPH ASSOF, SARA DELANO MOORE, JOHN HATTIE, NANCY FREY

Leverage the most effective teaching practices at the most effective time to meet the surface, deep, and transfer learning needs of every middle school mathematics student.

To order your copies, visit corwin.com